MATRICENTRIC NARRATIVES

Recent British Women's Fiction

in a Postmodern Mode

This book has been awarded
The Adèle Mellen Prize
for its distinguished contribution to scholarship.

Original drawings by Joseph DiBella from authors' photographs.
Clockwise from top to right: Maureen Duffy, Wendy Perriam,
Margaret Drabble, Pat Barker, Elizabeth North, Sara Maitland,
center.

MATRICENTRIC NARRATIVES

Recent British Women's Fiction

in a Postmodern Mode

Dan Dervin

Women's Studies
Volume 16

The Edwin Mellen Press
Lewiston·Queenston·Lampeter

Library of Congress Cataloging-in-Publication Data

This book has been registered with the Library of Congress.

This is volume 16 in the continuing series
Women's Studies
Volume 16   ISBN 0-7734-8644-5
WS Series ISBN 0-88946-118-X

A CIP catalog record for this book is available from the British Library.

The Edwin Mellen Press   The Edwin Mellen Press
Box 450   Box 67
Lewiston, New York   Queenston, Ontario
USA 14092-0450   CANADA L0S 1L0

The Edwin Mellen Press, Ltd.
Lampeter, Dyfed, Wales
UNITED KINGDOM SA48 7DY

Printed in the United States of America

MATRICENTRIC NARRATIVES
Recent British Women's Fiction
in a Postmodern Mode

Preface

To an anglophone woman author in the mid to late twentieth century is to be subjected to and to be the subject of a multiplicity of cultural discourses, some of which are enabling some of the time. However, to be bound by the demands of a theoretical or political discourse arguably imposes a straight-jacket on the autonomy of the literary imagination. While women authors have witnessed a proliferation of ideologies, they have also needed to interrogate, or resist or ignore them in the interests of conceiving narratives which arise from and respond to the complexities of contemporary experience, and which consequently result in a body of texts which demonstrate a diversity of narrative strategies and a plethora of textual politics. Dervin's wide-ranging study moves from the "protofeminist writings" of post World War 2, through the consciousness-raising narratives of the seventies, to the proliferation of "feminist" novels which were encouraged by the setting up of a number of women's publishing houses in the eighties and early nineties in the UK, and on to the effect of the present reabsorbtion of some of those feminist publishers back into mainstream publishing. At no point does he simplify his account in order to promote a unified interpretation of his materials; on the contrary he respects and applauds the diversity and fertility of women-authored texts, and defers to the authors' own stated sense of how they perceive their works. On the other hand, he doesn't pretend that the revolution in critical theory and in feminist theory has not taken place. His is not an attempt to deny the tremendous energy of theoretical thought in the past few decades, but rather to critically assess the extent of its relevance to both women authors and their readers.

Postmodernism has proclaimed the death of the author, but this is to deny agency to women writers, an agency which Dervin is determined to restore in them, even if this is at the expense of sacrificing his position as privileged critic. Feminist readings have liberated authors and readers alike, by permitting a shift in aesthetics and by validating previously undervalued themes and subjects; but feminism has also threatened to limit the author to the articulation of politically correct narrative discourse, and Dervin points out how many women authors have felt the need to distance themselves from that label in order to permit the messier business of creating novelistic form out of the chaos of inarticulate perception and experience to proceed according to its own less programmatic devices.

That is not to say that Dervin doesn't have a thesis; he does, but it always defers to his material, rather than make his material defer to an over-riding idea. His thesis is threefold, and hence avoids the either/or dichotomies of feminist debate. He allows biological difference back into the equation, but posits the presence of socio-cultural gender construction and the necessity of psychoanalytical dimensions if we are to have a fuller understanding of the heterogeneous and polyvocal phenomenon which is contemporary women's writing.

His guiding premise is that the concept of the matricentric can illuminate this body of writing more usefully than a more politically loaded or fashionable "porno" term might. In arriving at his premise he has committed an act of courageous empathy with contemporary women, and his use and application of the concept will be illuminating to the male reader but arguably even more facilitating to the female reader and author. In a sentence which echoes Virginia Woolf's call for a new conception of the novel which accommodated itself to the rhythms of the female body, Adrienne Rich foregrounds the real differences of female biology: "the diffuse, intense sensuality radiating out from clitoris, breast, uterus, vagina; the lunar cycles of menstruation; the gestation and fruition of life which can take place in the female body" and argues that these have far more radical implications than realized hitherto (*Of Woman Born*, 1976). Dervin does realize these implications, and adjusts his readings of individual texts and his interpretations of cultural meta-narratives to take them into account. While avoiding the trap of essentialism, Dervin acknowledges the central significance of the affect of female sexuality on the phenomenological process. At the same time he neatly side-steps the postmodernist tendency to reduce us all to a cultural script.

Dervin argues convincingly that in a variety of ways the matricentric provides a lens which allows us to focus more accurately on the actual textual strategies adopted by women authors. He defines matrix as referring to the actual womb, as indicating some of the patriarchal myths of woman, including theories of hysteria, and as also representing the female quest for selfhood conducted via the womb as origin and source. As Barthes reminds us in his delightful essay on photography (*La Chambre Claire*, 1980), the one place we know we have been (and yet do not know) is our mother's womb. Contemplating the womb urges us to confront our immanence, our desire, our identity and our death. Our original home, our ultimate felicitous space, it remains strangely unknown and unknowable in itself. For the woman author the womb is a triple matrix. It is her source to which she can only return metaphorically through death, yet it is part of her own sexualized body, potently dedicated to the potential reproduction of life, and playing its role in a complex system of hormonal balance which contributes to the formation and experience of individual identity; then again it is the site of powerful matrifocal mythopoeia, and of equally powerful misogynist myth-making too. As Dervin demonstrates it is a source and resource for contemporary women writers in English, who draw on its power through diverse narrative strategies to reflect multifariously on issues of personal and social identity. If one were engaged in feminist dialectic one might ponder why the female-authored narrative should not constitute a symbolic order, with the male a subordinate other, in which the matrix was to the womb as the phallus to the penis in a Lacanian discourse. But the point of Dervin's thesis is that it is high time to escape these gendered dichotomies, which he playfully characterizes as red and blue on the cultural spectrum, and to go instead for the richer purple: a fully articulated humanism in which neither gender is the suppressed other of a dominant discourse, yet equally a humanism in which real differences are not obliterated to produce a neutered norm.

For my part I welcome with metaphorically open arms the color purple, but would perhaps make it plural: there are many shades of purple, just as there are many ways of experiencing and articulating narratives of female identity, just as there are many ways of eloquently expressing female sexuality. Dervin's work opens up many of these, in a study which is permissive of and sympathetic to a variety of cultural positions. His refusal to simplify is an eloquent testimony to the achieved autonomy of the women authors he studies In his hands relegated cultural ciphers become speaking subjects.

Helen M. Dennis
University of Warwick
April 1997

MATRICENTRIC NARRATIVES

Foreword

Writing in the Galaxy

> I feel the point of writing for a woman is to take,
> magpie-like, anything they please from anywhere,
> and produce a subversive text out of the scraps; out
> of patriarchal or any kind of material they can get
> in their beaks.
> —Emma Tennant

This study of British women's fiction engages three discrete spheres: 1) fictional texts; 2) their authors; 3) critical and theoretical writings related to these texts. Together, these spheres produce a triangulated whole; but since each sphere assumes a distinctive integrity, their relative importance arises largely from the perspective foregrounded at any moment. Authors, for example, though nominally the sources of their work, are far from a final authority. If they were once properly constrained by the intentional fallacy, they are now more dubiously impeded by notions about their death and replacement by the new authority of intertextuality, which converge to promote (con)textual and linguistic autocracy.

This eclipse of the second sphere occurred awkwardly just as many women writers were gaining a long overdue visibility; moreover, the degree of recognition some had received was being overshadowed by ideologically-driven emphases on their silencing, their marginalizing, their victimization, their confinement to gaps in male texts, or their absorption into dominant male discourses that promised emancipation by denying difference. Thus when women writers weren't being numbered among the dead, they were being deprived of agency. In addition, to whatever degree these shadows obscured successful women writers, their texts were often re-figured by the chiaroscuro of critical discourse and made to perform according to light rays cast from a distant sphere. The proportional balance of the three spheres of text/author/theory has in recent decades shifted radically: not only has the third sphere of theory vastly increased its distance from the other two, but in the continual warp and weave of this literary cosmos, the author's sphere has virtually been eclipsed.

Not appreciating this conflicting three-sphere system—least

of all the author's death—and in pursuit of living, practicing women writers, I once devised a project to survey and interview British women authors on questions of creativity, influence, feminist allegiances, and generally on how they viewed themselves as writers.   Though conducted in passable social-science fashion, the findings were more promising than conclusive. The experience was memorable, however, because the many diverse voices came across loud and clear; and long after I had returned to America and waded into the rising tide of theory, I kept focused on the obscured sphere of authors who are women.

No doubt this enduring bias kept my interests in their fictions alive even as I was inundated by theory and eventually inflated my own raft of anti-theory (which is theory all the same). Having come to this position not only through direct encounters with the authors and their texts but from a prior appreciation of psychoanalysis's singular capacity for allowing a discourse of the most elusively subjective, I admit my approach angles from sphere to sphere to sphere.   Turning up coins of theory's realm like the female novel, feminine sensibility, a literature of their own, oppositional voices, a supposed wild zone of female space or lifestyle, gynecritics, *l'écriture feminine*, I would reach expectantly for confirmation of the emerging configurations from my research, but inevitably end disappointed. Thus I have had to mint my own *matricentric* currency for the many-sided but unifying patterns in women's fiction. Although I ask the reader's forbearance until the term can be better contextualized, *matrix*—womb, source, identity—evokes the three-fold process in which women create themselves through the *biology* that constitutes them, the *psychological* needs and relationships that energize them, and the *culture* that finally envelopes them. In exploring how women authors produce the three-fold matricentric through their texts, a more adequate discourse was clearly needed, and only then did I feel a reasonable case for a gendered differential in imaginative writing could be made.

Though contemporary British women novelists form this study's umbra, penumbras include the Canadian Margaret Atwood, a few U. S. women, and earlier British women writers. Aspiring to be representative, the present selection cannot presume to be comprehensive as no literary study could be. For the most part, the writers included are those most read and discussed in Britain, and thus deserving more attention in America. There is no attempt to include lively sub-genres like romance, mystery, and science-fiction, which are currently being subverted and so warrant separate treatment; likewise, the unfolding story of Asian, Caribbean, and African women writers. The same applies to lesbian writing, which, in expanding into erotica, feminist, and non-political directions, confounds the taxonomic enterprise. For this and other reasons, many oppose an apparent ghettoizing of literature by author's origin or sexual orientation. From various quarters, questions of inclusion are highly contested; and for whatever cultural reasons, such writers as Sara Maitland, Michele Roberts, and Wendy Perriam, who are prominent in England, were mostly unknown in the U.S. in the mid-1980s when this project began. In similar fashion, the women writers' sphere has been overshadowed by such international luminaries as Margaret Drabble, Iris Murdoch, and Doris Lessing.

As an interplanetary visitor among the three spheres, I found my sojourn on the planet of theory most curious of all. Engulfed in its tidal waves, I watched my social-science data wash away. I also noticed that most inhabitants were quite happy among themselves and that the few outer space missions to the sphere of imaginative literature (which of course skirted the dead authors' planet) would just as likely excite highly politicized debates as generate fresh information. Producing its own liveliness, theory had lit up the horizon and thrived under its reflected lights. As theory came to relish its privileged place in the postmodern era, the real action was seen to occur in the foreground of its own discourses, not in events on remote planets where living artists struggle with their creative demons.

But, confusing as all this was initially, even a casual visitor had to recognize—as the battlegrounds shifted and the combatants expended their fire-power or re-armed—that the literary terrain would never again be the same. It is from this permanently altered landscape of theory's sphere that this study begins. For good or ill, postmodernism had left its mark, and it was necessary to work through its ruins and surviving structures to establish a separate vantage point for matricentric narratives.

Introduction

A Quest For Adequate Critical Discourse, or What *Was* Postmodernism?

[He] had learned to see himself, theoretically, as a crossing place for a number of systems, all loosely connected. He had been trained to see his idea of his 'self' as an illusion, to be replaced by a discontinuous machinery and electrical message-network of various desires, ideological beliefs and responses, language-forms and hormones and pheromones.
—A. S. Byatt, *Possession*

Everything is contestable; nothing is off-limits; and no outcomes are guaranteed.
—Andrew Ross, *Universal Abandon?*

Quasi-philosophical doctrines such as poststructuralism, deconstructionism, and the critical theories such as new historicism along with linguistic, gender, and cultural studies have in recent years been filtering literary texts through a distinctive postmodern sensibility. Feminist theory, which had generated so many challenging literary studies in the 1970s, had likewise entered the postmodern millworks and turned to de/re-constructing its own discourses in such critiques as white-feminism. Concurrently, these events were either being mediated through race, class, coloniality, and locale, or being absorbed into a gender-consciousness replacing a discredited class-consciousness.[1] Patriarchy, feminism's essential other which was routinely demonized in its more militant discourses also emerged in part as a subjective construction.[2] Feminist approaches became absorbed in gender studies that were in turn reconfigured as queer studies. Consequently, many problems that formerly had circulated around the peripheries of writing and gender became centralized, while formerly stable assumptions took flight or dissolved. Humanism was dubunked; questions of aesthetics were denounced as Eurocentric or hegemonic colonizing: in time, not only Joseph Conrad but also Jane Austen came under suspicion.

These developments and other questions shaped the direction of this study. It became much more difficult to ask: if there is in fact a gender-inflected quality in women's writing, how does it arise and how is it manifested? How does a so-far hypothetical matricentric quality impact on prevailing critical and gender theories? One also needed to ask whether there is a patricentric other constituted as difference in feminist thought. How do history and cultural change interact with women's writing? Is there a feminist Monomyth of the Woman Writer? Why so much demonstrable yet unaddressed antagonism between women authors and feminist critics? Might it point to politically repellant matricentric alloys in women's fiction? What are the prospects in all this for a deeper understanding of gender's impact on creative processes? Finally, how does psychoanalysis, once implicated in gender-biases by feminists, also implicate feminist and postmodern discourses?

For starters, given the shutters closed as well as the windows opened by postmodernism, what might be the proper postmodern discourse through which the present study is to emerge? Certainly, the great energy expenditures in interpreting and theorizing would place postmodernism on the far side of modernism's heroic creativity, though as a result most literary texts lay gasping for air beneath dense thickets of rhetorical and philosophical theorizing.[3] Now, as postmodernism's new clothes are being marked-down, many *aperçus* once delivered with such panache or prestige as to pass for bona-fide theories—language speaks man, all writing is rewriting, nothing outside the text, the dead author, the male gaze—may be appreciated for the pithy aphorisms, witty axioms, and catch phrases they shrink to en route to the New Dictionary of Received Ideas. In many respects, much of this new theory, when it doesn't involve political positioning, proves to be mainly about...theory. Some favored postmodern positions—no more metanarratives, totality as terrorism, language games, pastiche/parody—are central to the *zeitgeist* but peripheral to the present study.[4] Others, like the politics of inclusion, the replacement of a subsisting *self* by a decentered *subject*, and anti-hierarchical ideals problematizing all *-isms* are more resonant. Feminism's totalizing equations (personal is political/sisterhood is global) have, for example, been interrogated and intersected by class/race/ethnic concerns.[5] But by espousing a politics of identity (e.g., postcolonials, sexual minorities, people of color) while disparaging essentialism as naive fundamentalism, postmodernist agendas also embarked on self-collision courses.[6] The tedious spread of political correctness was symptomatic of trying to have it both ways; intertextuality, for example, insulates texts from a problematized real, while a politics of subversion pitches the texts' referentiality to a presumed order of reality to be changed. Consequently, as a politics that includes plays off against a theory that excludes, elitism insulated itself against the populism it would embrace.

Another famous claim (stemming from Althusser and expanding feminism's personal-is-political) equates culture with ideology. Inevitably, this play outs as a dualistic discourse between an oppressive hegemonic ideology (High-modernism, Late-Capitalism, Patriarchy, Eurocentrism, etc.) and a more promising, subversive other (Marxism, Feminism, New Historicism, Africancentrism, New Age-ism)—all with paradigms ultimately paring down to match-ups of victims/oppressors. Preeminently, as the postmodern resolves the Age of Anxiety into the Age of the Victim, texts that articulate the voice of the marginalized, the oppressed, the subaltern, the colonized, the inner child, are reflexively privileged. Up to a point, this may be understandable and laudable; but in feminism thought, *victim* implies something more specific: one who has been raped, abused, or harassed, and any critique of feminist discourse risks activating this paradigm as victimizer (see App. A).

Thus while binary binds may be banal, even moderately true dichotomies, insofar as they lock the mind into either/or, we/them modes, are hardly better. Moreover, with cultural resistance reflexively privileged, resulting ideological positions remain uninterrogated, naive new utopias are hatched, gender-purity campaigns are periodically launched, and postmodernism's war on totality ends up ambushed on its own premises.

An inescapable ambience all the same, the postmodern can be an engaging hatchery, an energy field of conflicting sign systems, of conceptual networks, of performative gestures, as well as an overly dense thicket of theory—offering for some the prospect of playful and provisional mastery, for others a convergence of hegemonic resistance, but always with transformative potential. For the less sympathetic, postmodernism is conflated to POMO, a sign of *fin-de-siècle* decadence: as for living (*ugh!*), our texts can do *that* for us. Such critics have concluded that an earlier "resistance to theory" is replaced by a resistance to reality.[7] Inevitably, everyone is likely to approach this mobile field from different paths, and unavoidably so here. Given postmodernism's aim to span the cultural and the subjective, I will be writing against the postmodern whenever a distinctively personal, dynamic unconscious system is compromised or replaced by a purely ideological unconscious. When postmodern probes the subjective only to locate oppressed subjects, it is merely instantiating its cultural predilections, and then the more admirable postmodern insistence on writing as affirming difference and opposing totality is weakened by overreliance on highly politicized or purely rhetorical readings that muddle other genuine differences.

Thus we arrive at the crux of this inquiry: postmodernism's compelling ambience confronts us with the need for an *adequate* discourse, i.e., one that is as urgent as—it seems—impossible. In fact, most writers in the postmodern mode swear off truth, disparage criteria of correspondence given language's solipsistic liabilities, and engage in *agent provocateur* missions to dismantle oppressive 'truth'-systems and settle for a more or less politically engaged consistency against a targeted other. Given the complexity of present conflicting discourses, none of these strategies meet a test of adequacy.

Amid so many high-powered discourse-systems, the unheralded word *adequacy* will hardly raise a rumpus much less a revolution; yet any gender-deflected discourse aspiring to adequacy must respect and not conflate the three ineluctable forces that are continually constituting human lives: biology, psychology, culture. As the body has been historicized largely through a discourse of representations, biology has been tactically downgraded; yet the defining effects of human evolution in persisting sexual dimorphism and allied reproductive strategies, for example, produce their own potent discourses of difference. The fact that culture brings about a whole new edition of *homo sapiens* (summoning a second *sapiens*) wherein sex and gender get misconstrued and misrepresented need not delete—but may bracket—sociobiological excesses; nor mean that culture, like Durkheim's society, is god; nor finally that gendered bodies wither away like the state in Marxist utopias. In effect, biological realities should not be automatically disparaged as supporting a naive essentialism or an anatomy-is-destiny equation.[8] "I have come to believe," writes Adrienne Rich, "that female biology—the diffuse, intense sensuality radiating out from clitoris, breasts, uterus, vagina; the lunar cycles of menstruation; the gestation and fruition of life which can take place in the female body—has far more radical implications than we have yet come to appreciate."[9] Whether there is a site immune from cultural encroachments and so uncontaminated by their ideologies rather than a case of displaced idealization is foregrounded by such moderns as D.H. Lawrence and Norman O. Brown and revised through feminist speculations about woman's "wise wound" and a-topia writing through the body.[10]

While cultural studies would replace DNA encodings with semiotic ones, a different postmodern hand is dealt to psychoanalysis. It is accepted as a genuine system of theory, but the price of acceptance comes high: through erogenous zones, orifices, cathexes, and displaced representations, the Freudian psyche had kept the body very much in the picture, while the Lacanian psyche performs as a purely mental system of signifiers. Foresaking the clinic for the library where all the world's a text, Lacanians disparage the mundane clinician in favor of the exalted philosopher; thus their trail doubles back to Heidegger, Nietzsche, and Hegel. POMO's paving Lacan over Freud may facilitate a bridging to the high-rise metropolis of philosophical, linguistic, and cultural structures—but at a certain cost. Lacan's *aperçu* that the unconscious is structured like a language effectively renders psychoanalysis safe for academia where textual mastery is the royal road to advancement. While it's true that the unconscious is always constituted by language insofar as it enters discourse, nevertheless, narrowing the field to a Lacanian system of metaphor/metonymy relegates psychoanalysis to a branch of lit/crit, trivialized to the "level of rhetorical tropes."[11] Similarly, Lacan's distinction between the Imaginary (roughly the child's preoedipal dyad) and the Symbolic Order (the oedipal triad plus social affiliations) as a ground for constructing gender has been bracketed into nondynamic categories more suitable to a phenomenology of the self (or subject); and the spurious arguments supporting a "mirror stage" collapse the moment one tunes into the actual transactions between kids and their mom (or any other caregiver).[12] Finally, his formulation of the Law of the Father (who is always already absent but always already omnipresent through his Law) goes well beyond Freud's incest taboo and legal codes; instead of being empirically situated, it is linguistically placed in an elusive system of signifiers stemming from the phallus as determinant of sexual diference. Thus the great appeal Lacan holds for academics is not only that he conveniently mentalizes psychoanalysis or scales it to a branch of culture theory but that his unwritten but ubiquitous Law bifurcates culture into a universal impersonal oppressing agency and victimized subjects.

A pivotal moment occurred in May, 1968 when Parisian activists reshaped Lacan's reshaping of Freud from an inquiry into filial hostility to an interrogation of paternal rule, and provided a context for Juliet Mitchell to propose in *Feminism and Psychoanalysis* (1974) that despite legitimate misgivings over Freud's account of female development, feminists should not reject psychoanalysis but relegitimize it as a tool for analyzing and deconstructing patriarchal structures. The argument was irresistible, but it decisively shifted the realm and operations of psychoanalysis to political utility and cultural change; moreover, it fatally sanctioned selected Freudian/Lacanian texts to the exclusion of major advances within psychoanalysis. The result was a highly skewed discourse of women as confined-in-psychoanalysis but liberated-in-feminism that preempted working-through the conflicts within an unfolding psychoanlytic field. Not that Freud or Lacan had made things easy; but if it is one thing to problematize femininity as Freud did, it is another to impossibilize woman (as lacking separate and authentic developmental lines) as Lacanians are prone to do; and just as feminists have queried woman's exclusion from the Symbolic Order, so have others begun to miss the mother in the mirror phase.[13] Yet, for all its abridgments, the Lacanian rite-of-transition from the Imaginary (maternal dyad) to the Symbolic

Order (law of the father) can be an implicating one; and while his myth of persistent self-alienation stemming from distortions of the mirror-stage has been claimed by the Left to implicate dominant ideology, all cultural constructs are distorting mirrors for the Lacanian infant.[14]

Michel Foucault's ploy of contrasting his sexual discourse with Freud's "repressive hypothesis" also pivots on the either/or dichotomy of binary constructions. In fact, Foucault's engrossing account of the transformation of sexuality into various discourses from the Renaissance on—confessional, pedagogical, medical, psychiatric, media—far from disputing the Freudian claim that civilization thrives on repression, effectively documents the ingenious maneuvers that repression invents when direct outlets are barred—transformation, displacement, and affirmation-by-negation being but a few weapons in the arsenal of defenses. Seen more fully, the repression and the production of sexuality as discourse are two sides of the same coin.[15]   In Foucault's nonetheless useful historicizing of sexuality, some feminists have found a new way to access the rise of feminism (and of women's writing) as both "implicated in the 'technologies of sex'"...and a "form of resistance to them"; others, like Sheila Jeffreys insist that Foucault's "sexual map of the world is simply a male gay map," oblivious to women and feminism.[16] By foregrounding (male) gender in Foucault's knowledge=power formula, feminists reenforce female subjectivity as the oppression of the subject—mastery of the unconscious implies becoming conscious of being oppressed.

But even historicized, psychoanalysis is more subversive than Foucault's subversions of it and has always been the Trojan horse sneaked into utopian citadels; however, its banner does not proclaim the inevitability of patriarchy, as is sometimes held, but a more unsettling inevitability of gender as entrenched fantasy-systems mediated through narratives of repression.[17] At best, POMO's various appropriations of psychoanalysis deal a compromise that enables non-analysts to avail themselves of quasi-analytic insights by serenely discoursing on castration *sans* castration-*anxiety*; at worst, it absorbs a dynamic unconscious into a cultural unconscious-of. "Psychoanalysis is above all a drive psychology," lamented Anna Freud in 1974: "but for some reason people do not want to have that."[18]

Among them are feminist revisionists. When, for example, Chodorow's attempt to construct a theory of female development by citing psychoanalytic ideas without entering into their spirit was found to skirt drive development, her response has been to arrange psychoanalysis to her revisions. As Chodorow elides drives, so Gilligan excludes negative affects.[19] Yet current (ms)appropriations of psychoanalysis stem from genuine recognitions of Freud's *méconnaissances* of female development as well as his enduring insights into mental life, and, as long as sweet-revenge temptations to simply turn the tables and render men the second sex are surmounted, more adequate readings of Freud and women will emerge (see App. A).

With the exclusion of evolutionary perspectives, with Foucauldian historicism, and with Lacanian or other abridgments passing as new-improved or old-authentic psychoanalysis, the cultural viewpoint dominates postmodern discourse as the preferred way to real women's texts; but gains in consistency do not equal adequacy. More often, adequacy has been upstaged by agendas. Having depicted culture as an ideological sign-system, culture-theorists read the culture by reading the signs; for it follows that changing the signs changes the culture.[20] Unfortunately, what passes muster in theory has little bearing on actual human beings, who, for instance, in 1989 in Eastern Europe began engaging in extratextual behavior on a massive scale. These events have been described in the *New Left Review* as one of those spontaneous uprisings by the people—but who are the people? In POMO, there are only problematized subjects, colonized subalterns, and defined victims, not agents as persons capable of independent thought or action. Thus while academics excel in reading sign-systems, these prove an inadequate basis for a narrative of social change because they are inadequate accounts of the subject, the sign, the real, the person.[21]

Stumbling over the elusive subjectivity of the subject, the project of postmodernism thus remains unfinished: problematizing our current condition, it is itself problematic. The autonomous individual may indeed be counterfeit, but the elision of personal history only reenforces a new myth of cultural totality. Thus when the deconstructing spirit demeans quality as Eurocentric, postmodernism may clear the way for multiculturalism but also risk dilution by mixing sentimental protest with veiled utopianism (Fascism, with its own kitschy brand of folk art, also disparages quality, labeling avantgarde elitism degenerate).[22] In any case, it is probably only POMO's unacknowledged inner child that wants to believe all texts are equal—real children know better.

Such naivete sets the scene for utopianism as the last idol on the postmodern stage, yet history unpleasantly suggests that one person's utopia always excludes someone else's. Utopian discourses encode denial. The author of *Herland* was beset by "racist, anti-Semitic, and ethnocentric ideas," and the color of the yellow wallpaper in that famous story has been associated with contemporary xenophobia about the yellow peril; Margaret Sanger's admirable ideals for women embraced an antisemitic eugenics.[23] To be diversified and inclusive is to invite the world, and this world is no utopia. Yet inclusion in itself may be transformative, so POMO may reply (though no one ever says into what kind of utopia). Postmodernism rightly frowns on monocausality, but its utopian gaze with its excessive theorizing papers over its gaps and, by skewering the lack without, skips the lack within.

Whether a threefold approach can surmount these liabilities, psychoanalysis, judiciously deployed, can open breathing spaces between as well as within otherwise tightly sealed compartments of biology and culture. Regarding gender, the one contributes information about genetic endowment, hormonal cycles, reproductive strategies, and neural bases for mental/affective operations; the other envisions gender as socially produced and encoded with a deep structure of conformist messages. But this process is imposed on the subject (as the thrown-under, the subordinate, the subjected-to); and the utopian corollary that to deconstruct gender constructions will render one gender-free requires serious probing. With its instinct-vocabulary and its object-relations theories, psychoanalysis has been claimed in turn by biology and culture, but is not geared to adjunctive roles: its only genuine value arises from being taken—though not uncritically—on its own terms.

All the same, the postmodern invites psychoanalysis to sit

as one among equals: once seated, however, it need not proffer a system of ready-made interpretations but may open a uniquely implicating mode of inquiry. So doing, it may shed light on how individuals create, unconsciously as well as consciously, their own sense of gender-identity out of a mix of biological givens, developmental conflicts, and cultural codings. In postmodern terms, psychoanalysis, with its panoply of drives, impulses, wishes, fantasies, needs, desires, longings, etc., accesses subjectivity while problematizing the subject through an inherent overdeterminism (as distinct from both biological determinism and cultural construction production); above all, psychoanalysis uniquely impacts on desire by articulating internal contradiction and inevitable collapse from inherently impossible aspirations within the natal family. Without denying agency, psychoanalysis both complicates it by showing how it is mediated through conflicts and affirms it by utilizing our capacity for insight and working-through.

There being no metalanguage through which to structure gender discourse, the accepted division along the following lines must serve: *male / female*—focus a biocentric context; *boy / girl / / man / woman*—a psychological sense of gender; *masculine / feminine*--sociocultural constructions.[24] Discourses that have settled for a dialectics of (gendered) self /(oppressing) other lead inevitably to a rhetoric of resentment; a 'tri-alectics' of biology/psychology/culture on the other hand encompasses complicity and complicates without negating inequities. Simply put, cultural studies implicates *them*; psychoanalysis *us*.

If *post*modern factors in *time*, feminism, as it is transformed into discourse, has become so highly contextualized as to be virtually undefinable on all but such basic levels as: *against* the subordination of women and *for* their optimal development.[25]   Immediately thereafter, priorities of engagement, diversities of discourse, and degrees of complexity intrude, conflict, and often cancel; cultural relativism rears its hydra heads, the swords of distinction are raised, and any promise of a common discourse is sliced into numerous portions. Each of the following partial terms have stood for the whole: *agendas* set by political action groups, *theories* about the nature of women, *ideologies* of transhistorical oppression, and *myths* of matriarchal origins. A quest for adequate discourse on women would have to precede the manner in which these multiple discourses contribute to the three-fold criteria of adequacy. As it now stands, there are unassimilated and often competing discourses establishing in turn a biocentric base, a cultural-production-of-gender perspective, and various narratives of development: some psychosexual, others moral.[26]

Any given feminist source addressing woman's condition is likely to foreground one of these areas, but any given representation of *woman* may generate exclusive or overlapping views of her three-dimensional presence. For this inquiry, insofar as *cases, slogans, theories, ideology, agendas*, and *myths* impact on definitions of feminism with varying degrees of determinance, the better part of valor is to opt for the irreducible aims of the women's *cause*: against subordination; for full opportunity.[27] So doing would be beneficial in defining a no-less elusive feminist fiction.   For instance, if women's writing is distinguished biocentrally as something women do, is feminist fiction also an essentialist product—something that only feminists do?

Pondering that, one may consider feminine writing, which men as well as women perform, according to one study.[28]   Thus James allegedly owes to the literary feminine his inwardness; Musil his sense of an intuitive "other" in contrast to masculine rationality; Joyce his excess; Proust the imaginative faculty itself. Some of these apparently distinguish feminine art as "interiorization and the conscious creation of mystery."[29]   If early feminist fiction were distinguished by content, then the laurels would go to James' *The Bostonians* (1882), who was probably no feminist and definitely not female (nor male if a heterosexual marker is applied).[30]   Other hypotheses of feminist fiction as *l'écriture feminine*, an excess of *jouissance* placed beyond the Lacananian system of phallic signifiers and the law of the father, falter when tested against the lived-experiences of women writers (and fail to reach any consensus about Joyce.)[31]

Although gender is one of the least stable of categories, it is indispensable in initiating a discourse of sexual difference wheresoever it may lead.   Like other gender-based studies of literature, this one acknowledges as well as questions fixed categories of masculine/feminine (e.g., dominating vs sharing;

autonomy vs connectiveness) with their political baggage. Those which advance supposedly more sophisticated conceptions of androgynous authorship or cyborg sisterhood are even more bound for suitable mixes to a trait psychology that is likely to be less psychological than sociocultural in reifying the relative.[32]

Still, it can be conceded that on narrowly descriptive grounds, a trait approach is not only appealing but to a degree unavoidable, even if it cannot replace a psychoanalytic one. Since the point of the Henry James example was to construe the work with the person and then to assign it appropriate gender traits grouped under a supposed "feminine," the psychoanalysis of character would interrogate these traits as compromise-formations, stemming from intrapsychic conflicts which are not necessarily gender-specific. Enabling a discourse of difference by foregrounding gendered features of British women's fiction, *matricentric* may at the outset be descriptively useful in offering cultural as well as biological signifiers, though it only comes into its own when presumed traits are refracted through a psychoanalytic prism.

First, however, a purely descriptive mode allows the painting of literary texts along a color band ranging from an exclusively male grouping of blue, shading into a sexually mixed purple, then turning red as exclusively female varieties emerge. Received wisdom holds that masculine and feminine narratives culminate respectively with the hero's getting the object of his desire into bed while the heroine must get hers to the altar—stereotypically, Updike versus Austen. Indeed, it seems that in women's erotic fiction men live for love, while in men's erotic fiction women live for their lovers (no wonder popular writing gives stereotypes a bad name). But it is also the popular sub-genres with "little overlap" that affirm gender deflections: men have their true-blue war/adventure/sports tales; women their glowing red gothics/romances.[33] Counterbalancing the gender-enhancing macho strains among the blues are the feminine sensibility, lesbian, and feminist fictions shading the reds. Heightening the more literary tones are quest themes for erotic-fulfilment or self-realization, which may retain strong red or blue tinges respectively or yield to the blendings that move originally gender-bound writing toward the more heterosexually mixed area

of purple. That this effect need not be constrained by the writer's
gender is apparent in Eudora Welty's remark: "I think women tell
their kind of story to women and men tell theirs to men. But
when there's a reunion, and everybody comes together for an
occasion, then the stories are mingled."[34] More disposed to loop
gender to genre, Joyce Carol Oates construes "tragedy, the
quintessential male form," while the "trajectory of what we may
call the female vision...is toward accommodation...compromise....
The collective hunger for happy endings is predominantly
female."[35]

Still if the median purple is accessible to writers regardless
of gender, they access it from different directions: reared in blue,
one encounters purple differently from one reared in red.
Binding genre to gender are also extra-literary forces, affecting
not only to how men and women experience themselves and their
world differently but also their ongoing needs for gender
reinforcement. Females are more likely to be awakened to their
sexuality by males in men's narratives; whereas in their own tales
awakening more likely occurs through menarche, female
friendship, or sexual violation. For women, such biocentric
events as menstruation, pregnancy, and childbearing form
powerful nuclei around which coalesce experiences of relatedness,
caring, and generational continuity that also circulate through the
culture but are never circumscribed by its messages.[36] As will
be shown in the next three chapters, such biosexual awakenings
to gendered consciousness are precisely what initiate matricentric
narratives; the conflicts stemming from these awakenings form
characters, fuel plots, and figure in their resolution.

At the extreme blue/red poles, same-sex characters assume
normative proportions and are more fully drawn than their
opposite numbers, who may respectively be debased as
chicks/dames/whores and pigs/brutes/cads; but in the purple the
trick is to enliven the other sex as well as one's own and to endow
men and women alike with due quotients of humanness.
However, since the muses have never been equal-opportunity
employers, the writer's aim here is not to draw accurate portraits
according to some ideal model but to endow the characters, no
matter how terrible or awful or unfair they appear, with seething,
believable life-energy, be it the Wife of Bath, Miss Julie, or Molly
Bloom.[37] Finding herself surrounded by images of nice girls,

sex pots, and politically-correct feminists, Margaret Atwood
lamenting, "Where have all the Lady Macbeths gone?" answered:
"Gone to Ophelias."[38] Atwood's distinctive exercise of agency to
divest her writing of monochromatic predictability has been in
Cat's Eye and *The Robber Bride* to examine "women's cruelty to
women."[39] More typically, at the blue/red extremes the sexual
'other' is either depersonalized into insignificance or demonized
into monstrous malevolence, while the 'other' in the purple field
may be de-gendered for free-floating status in the human family.
The 'other' may also suggest the absence out of which more
enigmatic fictional presences are constituted.   In effect,
characterization in the blue/red areas will more likely presume
essentialist pigments or ideological broad-brushing than in the
purple where gender is constructed with an empathic eye to
dimensionality and where presumed gender traits are freely
mixed. Thus one no more expects to encounter believable women
in male war novels than believable men in feminist fiction; but in
some writers, Chekhov or Iris Murdoch, one encounters credible
and even-handed gender portrayals. When gender is caricatured,
impersonated, or subverted, usually a red or blue agenda is
driving the process (unless one attends to the strategy of Atwood's
Cat's Eye or Weldon's *Puffball*); but gender transgressions more
often than not remain color-bound, and if gender is ever to be
transcended, it will most likely occur in the purple.

If the objection is raised that power as well as gender
distinguishes reds from blues—that the sexes are not in fact
playing on a level field—this may be granted, but the corridors of
power are tilted for many entrance-ways, as evidenced
historically by class-privileges among English women writers and
recently by the protest of women of color at being shut out from
white feminist presses.[40]   More elusive power-moves—the
privileging of the victim, the inverted hierarchy of ideological
purity—can also disrupt discourse insofar as noncreative writers
situate their theoretical base solely in a normative blue or red and
promote a polarizing essentialism.

From this brief sketch, one may infer that some writers are
content to operate within their gender-specific hues; some move
around freely through the purple and back to red; while others
may have mistakenly been perceived within the purple mix but

were actually sticking to their colors. Notably, certain male authors, once perceived to have been writing about humanity at large, were more precisely writing about their normative masculine selves and their objectified desires/fears.[41]

To consider matricentric writers as women who tell their stories differently is not to opt for essentialism but to specify more acutely their homebase of red, which they may dispense in pure tints or in mixed hues as they engage blue's otherness or enter purple's wide fields. That writers need not simply replicate biocentric or inherited cultural positions may be felt by readers as a kind of indeterminant desire-in-writing which, rather than severing links with an author, presumes a desire-for-writing, mediated by personal history and imagination's priceless stock of playfulness and empathy.[42]

Soon to materialize by way of examples, the *matricentric* foregrounds creativity's gendered component as it affects woman's creative work and varieties of reader response. Stemming from *Matrix* as womb, source, and woman-centered, the definition addresses the three necessary biological, psychoanalytic, and sociocultural dimensions. The *matricentric*, then, is one way of assigning content to gender as difference in a more neutral space than those occupied by more limiting discourses of desire or oppression.

While impacting texts at various levels, psychoanalysis functions here in three main capacities: to interrogate theory, to dissolve artificial oppositions by means of an implicating discourse, and, adapting Lacan's notion of the unconscious as a "discourse of the other," to foster alterity by tuning in to the other's voices. Thus, Althusser's definition of culture: a "system of representations by which we imagine the world as it is," may be interrogated for non-ideological overdeterminisms as desire not only selects from but also shapes the range of the real.[43] Implication exposes the sources of we/them strategies as splitting and uncovers the pleasures of blaming; alterity fosters spaces for women's writing as being different from hostile as well as from ostensibly friendly theories.

The first three chapters foreground women's fiction (mostly British) since the 1950's with an eye to establishing the texts and tracing matricentric trends as they prevail, divide, and become problematized during the resurgence of feminism and the shift toward postmodernism. The method here is mostly literary-criticism—drawing inferences from representative texts; terms like *deconstruction* are not invoked to signal Derrida or more technical rhetorical analyses.[44] The next three chapters take wider and deeper tacks: Chapter Four structures the material conditions of women's writing as it has evolved through the capitalist marketplace and traces the feedback loops engendered among readers, especially in the reds of spinster fiction, that further shape the matricentric. The dual Foucault/Freud model cited above helps explain how the proliferation of women's writing also presumes the repression of their sexuality. Chapter Five interrogates feminist constructions of the Woman Writer which overshadow actual women writers and their matricentric configurations. Chapter Six clears space for assessing the matricentric shaping in women's fiction, probes psychoanalytic sources of difference, and engages questions of gender-deflected conservatism by way of further delineating matricentric modes.

Notes

1. Nupur Chaudhuri and Margaret Strobel, editors, *Western Women and Imperialism: Resistance and Complicity*; Vron Ware, *Beyond the Pale: White Women, Racism and History.*

2. See my "Making Utopia Out of Dystopia," app. C in *Enactments.*

3. On modernism's three phases—early, heroic, late—see David Harvey, *The Condition of Postmodernity.*

4. For sources, see Jean-Francois Lyotard, *The Postmodern Condition* and "Re-Writing Modernity," *SubStance* (1987), 54:3-9.

5. Elizabeth Spelman, *Inessential Woman*; Nancy Scheper-Hughes, *Death Without Weeping*; Marianne Hirsch and Evelyn Fox Keller, editors, *Conflicts in Feminism*; Susan Ostrov Weisser & Jennifer Fleischner, editors, *Feminist Nightmares: Women at Odds.*

6. Identity politics jumped through its own hoop when a person of color, Dinesh D'Souza, attacked multiculturalism (*Illiberal Education*). The various impasses in identity politics are explored in a *Village Voice* Symposium, "Identity Crisis: Queer Politics in the Age of Possibilities," conducted by Alisa Solomon (30 June 1992), 29-33; President Bush's appointment of Clarence Thomas to the U. S. Supreme Court illustrated how the game of identity politics could be cynically played by anyone for any stakes.

7. Paul De Man, *The Resistance to Theory*, discussed in David Lehman's *Signs of the Times*, 90, 154. In "Why Do Multiculturalists Ignore Anthropologists?" Richard J. Perry examines the formers' tendency to bypass empirical research for a simplistic embrace of cultural difference (*Chronicle of Higher Education* (4 March 1992), A-52.

8. See Beth B. Hess, "Evolutionary Perspectives and Gender Hierarchy." The brain-centered research into sex differences carried out by Marie-Christine de Lacoste, Cecile Naylor, *et al* is summarized by Kathryn Phillips, "Why Can't a Man Be More Like a Woman...and Vice Versa."

9. Adrienne Rich, *Of Woman Born*, 39.

10. Penelope Shuttle, *The Wise Wound*; for more on hormonal cycles, see Winnifred B. Cutler, *Love Cycles*; Julia Kristeva *The Kristeva Reader*; Ann Rosalind Jones, "Writing the Body: Toward an Understanding of *L'Écriture feminine*"; Jane Gallop, *Thinking Through the Body*; "The Body Writing/Writing the Body." The above quote from Adrienne Rich may inscribe a naive essentialism as the passage is re-routed through cultural studies privileging mediation and representation; but the underlying question she raises of how the body, or the bodily self, impacts on creative processes is real and enriched by psychoanalytic data on early self-representations derived by pleasure zones, physical sensations, primitive fantasies, interchanges with primary caregivers, etc. In other words, while the body is always indirectly represented in texts, these representations also always have their internal sources as well as their cultural forms. For a critique of theorized bodies as sources of flows/outside the male libidinal economy as proposed by Luce Irigary or variously advanced by Judith Butler's performative selves and Elizabeth Grozs's "desiring machine" (*Volatile Bodies*, 167-8)), see Teresa Ebert's Marxist analysis of the breast as a "political economy" of labor exploitation ("For a Red Pedagogy: Feminism, Desire, and Need," 814-5).

11. Letter to the *NY Times Book Review* (12 June 1984) by the psychoanalyst Aaron Esman, addressing Harold Bloom.

12. Maxine Sheets-Johnstone, "An Empirical-Phenomenological Critique of the Social Construction of Infancy"; for an analysis of the spurious scholarly support, see my "Lacan and the Fate of Transference," *American Imago*

(1997).

13. Insisting that Lacan means what he says without saying what he means, Clement explains that Lacan's "Woman does not exist" does not apply to women, but only the myth of Woman (*The Lives and Legends of Jacques Lacan*, 63; see also Mitchell's and Rose's reading of woman as not-man in *Feminine Sexuality*, 49-50; and Snithow's & Stansell's, *Powers of Desire*. While one does get interesting analysis from Lacan's speculations on woman and femininity as (phallic) masquerade, what one doesn't get is a viable developmental line. On certain levels, especially in perverse scenarios, femininity may appear as phallic impersonation, but it may also be a compromise formation stemming from internal drive systems. Feminists who find Lacan useful take the Symbolic Order, i.e., the resolution of the male's oedipal conflicts by entering a sign-system of desire and by drawing on the culturally constituted *nom du père*, as a vehicle for interrogating patriarchal authority. Others, like Julia Kristeva, have privileged the Imaginary, the child's preoedipal dyad with mother as the realm of semiotic images. Margaret Homans' *Bearing the Word* strives to accommodate women's writing to Lacanian structures. A recent skeptical assessment of the mirror-stage occurs in Cynthia Willett's *Maternal Ethics and Other slave Moralities*, 65.

14. Sherry Turkle, "Dynasty," *London Review of Books* (6 Dec 1990).

15. By treating psychoanalysis as a totality, Foucault missed an opportunity to trace its own evolution, especially in respect to women and homosexuality. Michel Foucault, "The Repressive Hypothesis," *The History of Sexuality*, 1:17-49; in "Foucault's preemption of Freud's Sexual Discourse," chapt. 11 of *Enactments*, I have elaborated this perspective.

16. Irene Diamond and Lee Quinby, Introduction to *Feminism and Foucault* 16., xi; Sheila Jeffreys, *Anticlimax*, 167, 274-5.

17. This is not to endorse any current "gender system," which many feminists view as a "perniciously symbiotic polarity that denies full humanity to both sexes while meshing--and helping to create—their neuroses" (Coppelia Kahn, "The Hand That Rocks the Cradle"), but it is to foreground contributions of psychoanalysis to an evolving discourse of sexual difference (see Jon K. Meyer, "The Theory of Gender Disorders"). Questions of subverting gender through cross-dressing and other lifestyles as well as ones of transcending gender through art or philosophy remain open to further inquiry. But POMO (de)constructions of gender as confinement to be subverted/transcended need to be interrogated in less political contexts: individuals happy with their own gender arrangements need not be disparaged by elitist theories.

18. Elisabeth Young-Bruehl, *Anna Freud: A Biography*, 457.

19. Linda K. Kerber cites "feminist self-righteousness" and "romantic oversimplification" among the risks of "relying on women's allegedly 'different voice'" ("Interdisciplinary Forum," *Signs*, 304-33); Katherine N. Hayes contends that in "arguing that she hears women's voices correctly, Gilligan does not realize that her own voice has been distinctly shaped by the necessity to deny and disguise women's anger" ("Anger in Different Voices"); and the critique by Judy Auerbach, *et al*, "Commentary," *Feminist Studies*, 150-61.

20. Culture as ideology is "class struggle at the level of signifying practices," writes Terry Eagleton ("Ideology, Fiction, Narrative," 79). Ebert distinguishes between change as "merely a proliferation of differences" and as a "fundamental *transformation* of the economy of signification determining culture." But one never escapes ideology, for "to be outside one ideology is merely to be located in another one," and so even the unconscious "is determined and limited by ideology and the contestations over signification: the unconscious is inscribed in the social and political" ("Romance of Patriarchy," 54-5, 27, 25). In her more recent work, Ebert advances an "outside" beyond

cultural gamesmanship, based on a historical/materialist
inclusion of the real world of labor, but she still agrees with
Marx that "our wants and pleasures have their origin in society"
("For a Red Pedagogy," 814).

     21. Similarly in this hemisphere, when a Latin American
admits, "As a kid I was fanatical about baseball and U.S. music.
Babe Ruth and Elvis Presley are among my heroes," one may
assume he has been safely colonized by the dominant culture.
But when it issues from the Sandinista leader, Daniel Ortega,
by way of hyping his new book, one has to wonder who has
been having who on ("Ortega Looks to Write Himself into a
Fortune," Mike Graham, *Sunday Times*, 9 Sept 1990). However
skewed, he seems an improbable late convert to late capitalism.
Pleading that it's time to "challenge more strenuously the
application of exhausted Marxist categories to a phenomenon
like post-modernism," Ihab Hassan in a letter to the *NY Times
Book Review* concludes that the academy "has had its fill of the
intellectual fantasies and fiascoes of both left and right, and of
theories wholly unembarrassed by social fact or historical
development" (24 May 1992).

     22. It all depends on who defines "the folks." This is not
to deny that "quality" may have latent content, advance hidden
agendas, cement careers, oppress, or reinforce artificial
hierarchies; but disparaging form fetishizes content. The
problem is that the anti-hierarchical impulse, like all
generational struggles, carries its own hierarchical agendas, and
it is easier to kick out the props from quality than from
complexity.

     23. Ann J. Lane, *To Herland and Beyond: The Life and
work of Charlotte Perkins Gilman*, 255; Ellen Chesler, *Woman of
Valor*; Allen Chase's *The Legacy of Malthius* is cited by Don
Sloan who quotes Sanger's declaration, "More children from the
fit, less from the unfit" and notes her support for the "infamous
anti-Semitic and anti-Italian Immigration Act of 1924" (Letter
to *NY Times Book Review* [9 Aug 1992]). While the utopian
impulse in postmodern thought may be interrogated, doing so

need not preclude utopian/dystopian fictions from performing valid functions in challenging cultural assumptions about power and sex-roles; for more, see Jones and Goodwin, editors, *Feminism, Utopia, and Narrative*. On the face of it, the association, yellow/antisemitism, suggested to me by the Israeli scholar, Michael Yogev, may seem farfetched; but throughout the nineteenth century, the (white) Aryan/pure races were contrasted with the (yellow) Semitic/ugly "Asiatic" races (Paul Lawrence Rose, *Revolutionary Antisemitism in Germany*, 181-2).

    24. Psychosexual development should not be confused with or blend into socialisation, the "theoretical linch-pin of second-wave feminism," according to Carol Lee Bacchi (*Same Difference*, 236). See Louise Kaplan's discussion of "psychological femininity" in *Female Perversions*, 188-9, for a dimension usually glossed over in the postmodern. Feminist discourses (which replace heterosexuality with heterosexualism) and culture studies (which foreground the social production of sexualities) have contributed to a more complex understanding of sexual orientation. Being part of a dominant ideology, heterosexuality has been deconstructed (see Jonathan Katz, *The Invention of Heterosexuality*), but the other sexualities were protected by privileging their subversive quotient; similarly, homophobia could be anatomized but not its other: heterophobia. Soon, however, an inattentiveness undercut these formulations that had highlighted the artificiality, arbitrariness, and oppressiveness of gender categories once sexual-minority writers began objecting to *their* identities being so pejoratively inscribed. Belatedly, a recognition of "experience" was permitted into cultural discourses on gender; but *experience* addresses the *real*, which is literally unspeakable in postmodernism's language games that soon backfire on their own artificiality and arbitrariness. For if experience must be locked out lest it embarrasses theory, the real must be barred from discourse unless transformed into the Symbolic Order through language.

25. Allison Jagger, *Feminist Politics and Human Nature*;
Ann B. Oakley and Juliet Mitchell, editors, *What Is Feminism?*;
Karen Offen, "Defining Feminism: A Comparative Historical
Approach." Gender may be constructed, but the fact that all
definitions are biocentric suggests, perhaps necessarily, that
feminism, despite male tokenism, is an essentialist concept.
David Harvey in *The Condition of Postmodernity* seizes on 1972
as the moment of postmodern's arrival, but his reference-frame
is architecture; others have taken a more playful approach,
designating George Eliot as postmodern.

26. Marianne Hirsch and Evelyn Fox Keller, eds.
Conflicts in Feminism; Susan Ostrove Weisser and Jennifer
Fleischner, *Feminist Nightmares*; Rene Denfeld, *The New
Victorians* (see App. A).

27. But even this minimal definition is questionable
along its edges, for on the one hand women's self-realization in
any given society must be relative to similar aims embedded in
class, race, and ethnic groups, and on the other, a definition
drawing on egalitarianism is seen as ultimately mediated by
patriarchy, according to Teresa Ebert, "Romance of
Patriarchy," 49.

28. Lisa Appignanesi, *Femininity and the Creative
Imagination: A Study of Henry James, Robert Musil, and Marcel
Proust*; Thais E. Morgan, editor, *Men Writing the Feminine*.

29. Appignanesi, 15; see also "Henry James and the Uses
of the Feminine" by William Veeder and "Fictions of Feminine
Voice: Antiphony and Silence in Hardy's *Tess of the
D'Urbervilles*" by Margaret R. Higonnet; and "The
Counterdiscourse of the Feminine" by Rita Felski.

30. Judith Fetterley argues against antifeminist readings
of the novel as well as those of the "phallic critics" (*The
Resisting Reader*, 107-115).

31. Frances Restuccia, *Joyce and the Law of the Father*.

32. Donna Haraway's *Simians, Cyborgs, and Women* situates itself at the opposite pole from the matricentric: having no mother, the cyborg offers a "praiseworthy demystification of biological origins," according to Margaret Homans ("'Women of Color' Writers and Feminist Theory," 76).

33. In literatures of "erotic fantasy" (i.e., "male-oriented pornography and female-oriented romance novels"), write Bruce Ellis and Donald Symons, there is "little overlap in readership" ("Sex Differences in Sexual Fantasy"); Ann Snitow, "Mass Market Romance: Pornography for Women Is Different."

34. Mary Chamberlain, *Writing Lives*, 256.

35. Joyce Carol Oates, "Rewriting *The Scarlet Letter*: Hawthorne's Heroine Goes Hollywood," *NY Times Book Review* (15 Oct 1995).

36. Adrienne Rich, *Of Woman Born*, 21; representative of feminist psychology is Judith V. Jordan, editor, *Women's Growth in Connection*.

37. In "*Miss Julie* as 'Naturalistic Tragedy,'" Alice Templeton conducts a "feminist reading" of the play against Strindberg's own "deterministic, mysogynist" Preface, 470.

38. Sarah Lyall, "An Author Who Lets Women Be Bad Guys," *NYTimes* (23 Nov 1993), C-13.

39. Ibid.

40. Rukhsana Ahmad, "What's Happening to the Women's Presses?" and "Feminist Book Fortnight '91." Foucault has theorized power through a multiplicity of forces rather than a singular oppressive hierarchy.

41. See Judith Fetterley, *The Resisting Reader*, on Hemingway and Fitzgerald.

42. While discounting the sentimental idealizing of empathy in "mothering theory," Judith Kegan Gardiner (*Rhys, Stead, Lessing, and the Politics of Empathy*, 20) draws on Heinz Kohut's self-psychology for a definition of empathy as a "value-neutral tool of observation"; yet, without support and contrary to research, she places empathy in "twentieth-century Western culture" as a "specially marked female trait." See to the contrary, Eleanor Emmon Maccoby and Carol Nagy Jacklin, *The Psychology of Sex Differences*, 349. The fact that men and women share this basic human capacity but may express it in different ways and in response to different situations should not be construed as demonstrating an essentialist gender trait or be inscribed in a discourse of lack.

43. Louis Althusser, *For Marx*, 233. But when he claims that "Just as they are born 'economic animals' and 'political animals,' it might be said that men and women are born 'ideological animals,'" the political economy has bought out the libidinal economy (*Philosophy and the Spontaneous Philosophy of the Scientists*, 24-5).

44. That means a broad rather than a high church context; or, in Lehman's terms, soft-core rather than hard-core (*Signs of the Times*, 117-8).

Matricentric Narratives During the Sixties

One was, after all, oneself: one had a right to be
oneself. One moulded oneself to suit others, and all
failed, collapsing like a house of cards about one's
head. The thing was not to give a damn what other
people thought, but to take one's own path, pursue
one's own private adventure through the maze.
—Rose MacAulay, *Keeping up Appearances*[1]

Novels Discussed (pages cited in text):
The L-Shaped Room (1959), Lynn Reid Banks
Georgy Girl (1965), Margaret Forster
The Pumpkin Eater (1962), Penelope Mortimer
The Millstone (1962), Margaret Drabble
The Waterfall (1969), Margaret Drabble
After Julius (1965), Elizabeth Jane Howard
The Golden Notebook (1962), Doris Lessing
A Fairly Honourable Defeat (1970), Iris Murdoch
Henry and Cato (1977), Iris Murdoch
The Sea, the Sea (1978), Iris Murdoch
The Edible Woman (1969), Margaret Atwood
Surfacing (1972), Margaret Atwood

Gyne concerns women, but *matrix*, as womb, origin, source,
mother, concerns women in ways both more specific and
profound. *Matrix* spans biology, psychology, and culture,
depending on emphasis, tropologic intent, and author's gender:
e.g., wombs may in turn be inherent, emotionally cathected,
culturally constructed, or given to wandering as the mythical
source of hysteria.[2] There is also a certain banality of presence:
like Poe's purloined letter, the matricentric in women's texts is
frequently hidden in plain sight.[3] If ubiquitous and often too
obvious to be observed, it nonetheless addresses powerful
centralizing forces that recur consistently enough in women's
narratives to justify sustained inquiry. Three groupings obtain:
most traditional fictions of pairing-off/matching-up (womb as
procreative signifier); feminist-tinged narratives of quest for
origins/giving-birth-to-oneself (womb as symbolic life-source or

source of self-identity); many spinster narratives of ex/inclusion, marked by thematic variations on the odd-girl-out/in plot (womb as social envelope). These parenthetical connections are merely suggestive, for precisely how the matricentric distinguishes women's writing emerges only from careful attention to their texts.

The L-Shaped Room (1959) has been associated with the angry-young-man, kitchen-sink movement in British literature, though Banks disclaims any kindred impulses at the time of her writing—credit the *zeitgeist* then. Whatever the reason, the bedsitter bohemianism of West London marks the distance from Austen's gracious estates and the Brontes' gothic mansions; yet the narrative wavers between a comforting acceptance of traditional values and their abandonment. A young actress, Jane Graham, has gone on holiday with a fellow actor, yielding on one occasion to her erotic impulses. True to type, the actor's exit leaves Jane to play her seduced-and-abandoned role solo. Finding his daughter pregnant out of wedlock, Jane's Scotch Presbyterian father shows her the door; and she seems to be resigned to her new role of social outcast when she settles into disreputable digs in Fulham, though in fact she is choosing independence.[4]

Though out of synch with contemporary feminist scripting, Jane assumes stature by rejecting abortion and choosing to have the child on her own limited terms. Nor is there an anti-male stance, though things begin that way. On the one hand, she has been dropped by her lover, exiled by her father, and misperceived by the physician who assumes every woman naturally wants to abort a pregnancy rather than bear an illegitimate child. But on the other hand, she has been befriended on the far side of her wall by John, a black musician, and from the flat beneath by Toby, a starving Jewish writer. Their accepting her crucially helps her accept herself; and, as John performs a protective role, Toby becomes her lover.

Two late episodes bring out the novel's ambiguous relation to subsequent, more self-conscious fiction about women's lives. Addy, a maiden aunt from Surrey, arrives to offer support and income, by way of her own epistolary novel to be typed. This implicates Jane in a literary process where she is surprised to discover that the letters "created two people, two rare people complete in each other," but more remarkably, where the "writer was complete in herself"—being neither the young woman in love nor the lover, whose letters are omitted. After sharing a few moments of rapport with her aunt, Jane asks of the lover, "Why does he never write to her?" Aunt Addy bluntly replies, "Because he doesn't exist. Men like that never do. They always have to be invented." (245) It is unclear how this view should be applied to the characters in Reid's novel or to Jane's emerging awareness—its implications are potent but undeveloped. At least for Jane, it presents no solution, and so remains a feminist edge waiting to cut, or a new context in search of content.

A later episode also implicates Jane in the literary process by reason of a curious juxtaposition (which the author insists was purely accidental: trust the tale then, not the teller).[5] Differences had arisen between Toby and Jane, and as her time draws near they retreat to their separate worlds. As she is preparing to give birth, he is experiencing a complementary release through creativity. After writing 2000 words one night, he forces himself to work daily on his book, finishing his first novel and starting a second. When they are later reconciled, Toby remarks on "how wonderful it feels to be so totally in one's work that nothing else impinges at all," and Jane nods, recalling the feeling she had "while David was being born." (314) Conceivably, this playing off creativity/procreativity along gender lines has a Jungian import, with "Toby" being the female author's animus: the ideal man who has to be invented through which the woman writer at this time could produce a novel. If the novel were by a man, then Toby's writing could be seen as male mimicry of female procreativity—retiring in envy of female fertility, he gives birth to a compensatory word-child. But occurring here, it retains a curious ambience. At least it does until the very end when Jane returns to her more accepting parent and "dumped [baby David] unceremoniously into Father's arms," who becomes quite possessive about what appears in stock Freudian terms a daughter's love-gift. The matricentric pattern of a narrative turning on female procreativity, in which a revitalized self is born from the birth process, turns upon an ambiguous patricentric resolution: the rejected daughter sets off on her own to produce a child and overcomes her injured self-esteem by returning the newly acceptable child to a forgiving father. But, by pleasing him while satisfying her own needs for autonomy, she also deftly balances past and present.[6]

A similar milieu but different ambiguities entangle the plot of *Georgy Girl* (1965). At first George (*née* Georgina Caroline) seems one of those ungainly free spirits, witty and winning, as firmly in revolt against her mother's conventional marriage to a milktoast chauffeur as against her roommate Meredith's lusty liaison with Jos. George not only soon finds herself "odd one out" (148) in both domiciles but, in trying herself by prevailing standards (patriarchal, heterosexual, etc), finds herself ugly and unlovable. Only after Meredith has gotten pregnant and casually departs to have the child, leaving George to become Jos's mistress, do the heroine's real needs rise to the surface in the course of mothering the infant. Suddenly it becomes the center of her life and sets her future course. No longer playfully impertinent, she becomes doggedly practical and literal-minded. Losing interest in going out with Jos, she soon loses interest in Jos himself. When he calls her a shrew, the reader nods assent. George is next thrown into the lecherous arms of James, the contemptible family benefactor who provides her with marital respectability in return for sexual favors. What motivates George is nothing so simple as the sudden blossoming of maternal instinct because it is only as she learns that the baby is to be put up for adoption that her anxieties galvanize her to a rescue mission. It seems that there is a narcissistic component in her whole-hearted appropriation of this baby girl who is also odd-one-out: in the reclaimed child is something George needs to reclaim and reconstitute within herself.

Though following Jane Graham's story by only a few years, George's world is both hipper and bleaker—the compromises more cynical and self-destructive. Honestly assertive yet preliberationist, this quirky work presumes the traditionally important role in women's lives of making the right marital match, but opens onto something stronger and more basic than the mating games of popular fiction. George's uncompromising matricentric priorities—my child, my self—may have led into a patricentric trap, but her obsession with the child turns a suitable mate, Jos, into another odd-one-out. Her sexual aversion and circumvention of birth force her nurturing needs to stand out all the more sharply.

Another sort of matricentric obsession fuels the plot of *The Pumpkin Eater* (1962). Married three times and having delivered a "remarkable number" (12) of children, Mrs. Armitage at thirty-eight is plunged into a crisis, precipitated by her fourth husband Jake, who claims he has had too much of the kids and not enough of her. Unfortunately, he is often absent on film locations where she would only feel in the way. Meanwhile, he is erecting a tower on their estate, "overlooking the valley where they first met," and to which they can repair for privacy.

But Jake is "no longer lovable" in her eyes. In his sleep he "increased monstrously, became the sky, the earth, the enemy, the unknown." (44) She overhears him storming to the doctor, "We've got enough children!....When's she going to face facts? She can't go on having children for ever, anyway what for?.... She's got a bloody houseful already, and me, she's got me! Why can't she grow up, settle for what she's got, why can't she take some interest in the outside world for a change? I'm sick of living in a bloody nursery!" (51) Jake believes she is "obsessed" with having children and her doctor accuses her with losing interest in a man sexually who stops wanting to have children with her, as though sex for pleasure's sake were repellant. (64)

These sentiments are neither endorsed nor refuted in the text, and her motives for childbearing remain opaque. Still, a clue occurs when her father dies; and, as if to make up for the loss, she hints to her mother that she is pregnant—news which is more outraging than consoling. (130) Perhaps a case could be made for Mrs. A. as the victim of centuries-long conditioning of women as breeding-machines who no longer know how to stop, but it is not made here. And short of settling for some overriding biophysical urge, one is left to infer that child-bearing stems either from her wanting to please (an inherited cultural command?) or, on a more personal level, from avoiding painful loss. A sort of sexualized bulimia that binges on pregnancies, her having babies is not predicated on a love for the little things themselves, who remain uncounted and mostly unnamed. Still, from the way the consequences of this maternal disposition are played out, causes may be inferred.

Not surprisingly, the news of Mrs. A.'s (she has no first

name) pregnancy does not please Jake; and so with some misgiving but in hopes of winning back his love, she consents to an abortion plus sterilization. But instead of this removing barriers between them, she emerges from the operation with the "impression that Jake's world was wide open, longing to take me in, while mine was already disposed of, burnt up with the garbage." (152) It soon grows clear, however, that she has been living in a separate world all along. Going along and fulfilling her gender's agenda in a restrictive mode, she has been preserving an innocence about the ways of the world in a much larger sense. Jake's womanizing has been rampant, not just out on exotic movie sets, but under their own roof with a destitute actress they had cared for, and with the wife of their good friends, the Conways. Bob Conway arranges meetings with Mrs. A. where he details Jake's notorious "banging around," threatens Jake's life, and makes obnoxious overtures of erotic revenge. Worse irony, Beth Conway has conceived Jake's child to coincide almost to the moment with his wife's abortion. There's little to salvage for Jake's redemption here, while his wife has sacrificed not only her basic modus vivendi but lost all her illusions about human love. Suddenly she has been initiated into a horribly aimless world of lust, betrayal, and jealousy—from which her investment in the procreative side of life had hitherto protected her. In the last twist of the blade, Conway tells her that the idea for her abortion originated with Beth, who threatened to leave Jake if he became a father once more—or almost last twist because there are more.

In her confrontation with Jake, he admits to marrying her for "background." She laments that if he had only let her go ahead and have their latest child, none of the sordid business would have come out, as though her identifications with maternal processes would have shielded her from the horrible consequences of triangulated relationships wrought by entering male reality: "I realized," she remarks belatedly, "how completely I had been absorbed by Jake." (172) But this too is an illusion, for it has only been her misconstrued idea of Jake.

Desperate, she seeks refuge in the recently finished tower—less to await her knight's rescue than to hide out from his world. In the end, her children, set upon her by Jake like a pack of hounds, flush her out. Neither quite comic nor tragic, the finale is suitably modern. For how should readers respond to a woman who has lived conceiving not wisely but too well, only to find that, unlike the hapless Tudor lady, she has been condemned to life? After all, Jake has only come to take her home.

Apparently it takes a woman writer to demonstrate how a singleminded pursuit of one's matricentric endowment leads to her undoing; but if overinvested procreativity insulates some women, Margaret Drabble has entertained the opposite proposition. Since her novels typically begin with pregnancy, childbirth, or miscarriage, her narratives are thoroughly matricentric. Designated from early on as an exponent of women's concerns, she distinguishes between "women's issues" as being outside her interest and woman's "situation...being stuck with a baby, or having an illegitimate baby, or being stuck with a marriage where you couldn't have a job"—as the material of her early novels.[7] Accordingly, in *The Millstone* (1965), the dustjacket inscribes Rosamund as a "very modern heroine in a classic predicament": an "emancipated...clever cool, intellectual girl just out of Cambridge University" with a "self-detachment that shields her all too well from her own emotions." She has parlayed her student lifestyle into graduate studies and tutors to salve her socialist conscience. But she is far from emancipated in this calm before the storms of sexual politics and consciousness-raising; and too self-absorbed to reach out to anyone else, women critics have found her qualities "rather chilling."[8]

As much a career virgin as a career student, her story begins with an account of her supposedly conducting an illicit affair with a lad by slipping into a "cheap-smart" hotel but without their slipping into bed together. For a whole year, they "loved each other" without "making love," and only sometime later does she come to "realize that I had set the whole mould of my life." (9) A one-night-stand with her BBC friend George, however, leaves her pregnant. She does not inform him, and he exits her life until the end when he is shown their child, unaware he is the father.

Short on drama, the plot rises only with the heroine's rising belly, for it is only when she finds herself pregnant and decides to give birth that interest is sparked: "what begins to break down the walls of Rosamund's prison is, as she herself saw, becoming a mother."[9] Pried loose from her bookish lifestyle and her bohemian alliances, she discovers another reality where, in doctors' waiting rooms, for example, "were representatives of a population whose existence I had hardly noticed." (42) Her first visit to the Ante-Natal Clinic becomes a "memorable experience." (63) And giving birth is the "closest Rosamund comes to sensual pleasure"[10]: "sensations which though unbelievably violent were now no longer painful but indeed almost a promise of pleasure." (96) Octavia's birth compels her to care for another human being, and although she loves the child not for its sake but as an extension of herself, she does achieve something, perhaps a more substantial sense of feminine identity, no longer the neuter student or the fake mistress. Still, her final scene is a "retreat from communication, communion, and love."[11] At best, the heroine has completed narrowly a matricentric rite of passage from adolescent girlhood to young womanhood.

Along the way, readers are given a gloss on the dualism of creativity/procreativity in the life of a woman writer beyond that in *The L-Shaped Room.* Rosamund is not a simple self-projection of her author, who likewise was recently graduated from Cambridge and was experiencing childbirth (within marriage). Drabble recalls herself those days as being very "naive and straightforward." "I wrote about what was in my mind and it turned into a novel."[12] In other words, procreativity did not so much rival creativity as become its subject matter: "I had the confidence to think that what was under my nose was interesting."[13] Under her nose were typewriters and babies, needing in turn to have their ribbons or diapers changed. In the novel, Rosamund takes in a friend who is writing a novel which includes a Rosamund-character not very flatteringly depicted. While the would-be novelist is away, baby Octavia strays into the work room where she rips, chews, and otherwise savages the novel. Here, it seems, is life devouring art, getting some of its own back; however, the infant child does not have the last word over the infant manuscript—it can be restored. Drabble admitted that Rosamund "left the door open on purpose," partly to "illustrate the difficulties of living with a small child in a flat with a person who was writing."[14] But she also did so to demonstrate how life imposes itself on art, since Drabble is both the mother nursing and the artist creating an image of these processes.

Feminist psychology, in departing from male emphases on identity as self-autonomy consolidated during adolescence, holds that woman's identity is more continuously bound up with her relationships, especially in respect to sexual love and marriage. Traditionally, male novelists have awakened their heroines to self-realization through the preferred sexual mode of the moment, often privileging male agency. But feminist critics have noted that heroines in women's novels have different awakenings—often fatal in earlier times to their struggle to integrate inward/ outward selves or to inhabit private/public spheres. In feminist novels of the 1970s the awakening often coincided with the collapse of a marriage and the induction into a consciousness-raising group; but in less overtly political texts this also occurs matricentrically through the gender-affirming process of childbearing.

If Rosamund's development is severely circumscribed, Jane Gray in *The Waterfall* (1969) paradoxically escapes women's traditional confinement by embracing it. Here, character and narrative both begin in women's historically grim condition of maternity. Yet the defining imagery is not steely coldness but liquid warmth. The postpartum air is "heavy and warm and damp"; the "sweat of [her] effort [is] flowing unchecked"; the "blood [is] flowing from her onto the moist white sheets," underneath which are "warm and sodden" newspapers; the tea served by the midwife is "liquid and warm, like weeping." (4-5) This state of blissful immersion contrasts with her usual experiences of her body's "dry integrity" (180) and her growing-up problems in a sterile, unloving family, hypocritically invoking warmth while obsessed with the English vice of class: "They live in that small, self-justifying prep-school world, marooned in it: petrified, ossified, worse than that, mad—mad, dryly shaking their dry branches against the high gales of newspaper truths." (67)

More than pleasurably fulfilled, Jane thinks that "the strange confidence" she had discovered in handling her first child, "could have, perhaps, given me an identity," rescuing her from "inertia" and turning her into "one of those mother-women who ignore their husbands and live through their children." But she finds herself split in a "classic schizoid state"—between the anxious intelligent woman and the healthy efficient mother. Still, with the birth of Bianca, she begins to feel that "I was coming together, that I could no longer support the division, that my flesh and mind must meet or die." (123) Two factors conspire to bring about this integration. One is the tender attentions aroused in her cousin Lucy's husband James, who lingers beyond Jane's recovery period until he can join her in those cozy, moist, maternal sheets. The other factor is literary. Jane is a poet, but she is also reconstituting her life in a "fictitious form." (59) The narrative voice slips from first to third person in order to tell "the whole story," which comprises what "it means to be a woman," and "to be a woman novelist."[15] Thus, the narrative unifies in the *The Millstone*'s approach of separate characters—one having a child, the other writing about it as part of a fictional world. Moreover, Rose sees the "I"/"she" split blur by the end of *The Waterfall*.[16]

Drabble has called it the "most female of all my books," but is it also feminist?[17] Clearly not in any programmatic sense. Despite its liquefacting pleasures, it has been ignored by the Irigarian school of fluid/flow as *l'écriture feminine* as well as by Cixousian applications of *jouissance*, perhaps owing to the text being heterosexual, literalistic, and non-French.[18] Moreover, it begins in Confinement, goes to Sexual Bondage, and ends in Suffering and Doubtful Resolve. Yet as Rose's analysis shows, these negatives are accepted and transcended by being accepted and then turned inside out. Thus Simone de Beauvoir's view that woman's procreative destiny must "imprison her in repetition and immanence" is explicitly overturned in the novel's profoundly agreeable opening scene.[19] Jane's sexual bondage to James paradoxically allows her to find "reconciliation in willing her own subjugation to James and the flesh."[20] Some qualifications may be in order. True, after she and James have made love, she lay "drowned in a willing sea," (51) and she does admit that the word bondage "elegantly describe[s] [her] condition" (183); but she also actively desires and subjugates James to her needs. "I buried my fingers in his hair and tightened them, and his head fell obediently backward on the pillow, his mouth gently parting for me." (68-9) A "fantastic amalgam of Prince Charming and the demon lover," James, who races cars but little else, is too much the creation of feminine desire to impose any real threat of bondage.[21] In any case, after an auto accident forecloses their travel abroad and ends their affair by exposing it, Jane moves ahead toward an autonomous, productive life, for it seems that James "has put her in touch not only with her body but with her voice" as a writer.[22]

Yet a close reading reveals James's role to be less one of bondage than of bonding: "When James looked at me, he saw me, myself." (58) That is, in contrast to her family experiences where her mother in classical double-binding style would revere family warmth and flinch from any physical approach and her son-less headmaster father would tease the boys out of envy. (62-3) James "represented all that my family was not...an exorcism and an ideal." (60) "He redeemed me by knowing me...." (58) That is, he assumes the magic of the mirroring parent in the primary bond. So aggrandized, he is constituted to carry out more than a purely masculine role in the sexual relation, namely to midwife Jane into a second birth of wholeness. Initially, he provides the current to set her liquid sea flowing. He then performs the "waterfall" card shuffle which makes the cards fall "in an amazing careful rhythm, interleaving, dovetailing, one by one, joining and melting as they fall into one pack" (179) and leaves Jane in dazzled admiration. Later in bed she cries out to him "from such depths of need....like death, like birth: an event of the same order. Her cry was the cry of a woman in labor." At first when they start to make love, she is "alone and high up, stranded," then she "started to fall, painfully, anguished," until she achieves her own "deliverance ....in that strange sobbing cry of rebirth. A woman delivered." (180-1) Sexual love (with a little help from D. H. Lawrence) is represented as a matricentric event of self-birth.

After James has recovered from a near fatal car accident, the lovers return to their separate pursuits, she to writing, he to driving; and they see each other from time to time. What has changed is that the intensity of her need for him to help resolve her self-fragmentation has lessened. The setting for the climax is as spectacular as the Stonehenge slabs where Hardy's Tess was sacrificed on the altar of patriarchy, but the mood is far more modestly mutual as the pair take a quiet hike along the north Yorkshire moors to a cascading waterfall called the Goredale Scar. They enter a "rift" in the hilly landscape, a "roofless cave...where huge curved echoing rock sides stretched up above us, and water leaped down through the side of the cleft, pouring

itself noisily downward across brown rocks that are twisted and
worn like wood, like the roots of trees....a lovely organic balance
of shapes and curves, a wildness contained within a bodily limit."
(287) It is of course also a projection of her newly integrated and
reconstituted self—in vivid contrast to the "landscape" of her
original family, "civilized out of its natural shape." (65) It is a
stage of awareness and separation beyond that of immersion in a
"willing sea" of passion, beyond the "the ugliness of the near lethal
wound" of her sexual urgings, (180) and beyond the nearly fatal
injuries of the accident. It is also a cleft, an open cave, a scar, a
waterfall, a kind of psychic mandala; the path up alongside it is
a "route familiar to human feet," with cigarette butts and candy
wrappings that reconciles the lovers to ordinary reality. Along
the grassy meadows on top they find the "wild pansies" called
Heart's Ease.

But their encounter with "the subliminities of nature" (289)
is brief; and the lovers returning to their hotel room taste the
"dreadful, ancient, musty" flavor of mortality from the accidental
spilling of talcum powder into a bedside glass of Scotch. In a
postscript, Jane notes an existential decision that night to stop
taking her birth-control pills with their blood-clotting side-
effects, preferring neurosis to thrombosis, and therefore leaving
her susceptible to another pregnancy and confinement wherein
her life-in-the-text originated. Thus the characters' overriding
erotic aims are consistently negotiated via a matricentric subtext
that unconfines confinement.

Owing to Jane's rejection of patriarchal roles and her
"power to heal our inner divisions," Rose considers *The Waterfall*
"perhaps the most radically feminist of Drabble's books."[23] But
because there is no real male power structure, only a knotty
family conflict, and because James is so completely fitted to
Jane's needs, it might better be called radically feminine. Much
has also been made of Jane's referring to an anticipated,
unaccented "feminine ending," which Gayle Greene construes as
a "refusal of closure or enclosure" with an at least feminist accent;
but as in Jane's self-delivery through her lover, the same
openendedness attends Lawrence's *Lady Chatterly's Lover*, and is
the trademark of literary modernism.[24] Drabble also cites
psychoanalytic implications of Jane's namesake Jane Grey who

was beheaded ostensibly for sexual misconduct (see App. B).

Further distancing the novel from radical feminist politics is the way the woman writer in her text draws on literary tradition. Jane ends her postscript by dividing her inconclusive destiny from the "old novels" where the "price of love was death," paid by "virtuous women" in childbirth or by the "wicked, like Nana, with the pox." Readers are thus reminded that by writing her story, Jane has also been rewriting fiction about women: her "I" often corrects the constructed "Jane"-version of social and literary convention—both Austen and Eyre.

The impact of female gender on genre has generated ingenious theories within feminism. These contrast with a generational approach of males struggling ambivalently to appease or exceed their literary forbears as elaborated in Harold Bloom's celebrated anxiety-of-influence theory. Appreciating but objecting to the male-oedipal bias of this paradigm, some feminist critics have suggested a less conflict-ridden sequence of women reading back through their mothers where they perpetuate a literature of their own; and, since literary authorship has traditionally been a function of male authority, which pens-in and confines females to male texts, why not speak of women writers afflicted with an "anxiety of authorship"?[25] If true, Drabble is an eloquent exception, but she is not exceptional among women writers in learning from male precursors (D.H. Lawrence, Angus Wilson) and grappling with influence by writing her own variant on the I-Am-not-Jane-Austen novel. Of three overlapping models for fitting women writers to a distinctive tradition: gendered role-models, gendered oppression, and intra-gender conflict, Drabble opts for the third.

Several factors favor the role of literary influence over the more basic anxiety of authorship (which Drabble explicitly disavows; see App. B). Through *The Second Sex*, Simone de Beauvoir constitutes the strong parental literary authority from which Drabble, the "ephebe" in Harold Bloom's terminology, draws ambivalent inspiration. Rose effectively traces the influence through the characters and content of Drabble's earliest fiction, and as noted above, *The Waterfall* treats some of de Beauvoir's strictures about women as stereotypes to be subverted.

A second powerful literary mother closer to home is the

Doris Lessing of *The Golden Notebook* (1962), whose role Drabble
has noted as her "favorite experimental novelist," and whose
narrative techniques according to Rose were adapted to *The
Waterfall*.[26] With Jane already a poet, the anxiety-of-authorship
question doesn't arise, although the issue of females constrained
in male texts does. For Jane in writing herself realizes that she
must also rewrite women in fiction. But her quarrel is not with
the oppressive male author: it is with a female authority that
presides over English literary tradition, the indomitable Jane
Austen. *That* Jane is this Jane's imprisoning text—the voice of the
powerful, adversarial mother whom neither Drabble nor her
heroine can forget for long. In part, the hypocrisy and marriages
of convenience in this Jane's family provoke her into exclaiming,
"How I dislike Jane Austen." (65) "Her moral tone dismays me."
(66) Most offensive is the matchmaking in *Emma*. "What can it
have been like, in bed with Mr. Knightley? Sorrow awaited that
woman [Emma]." This Jane will leave that other Jane to "draw
those fine distinctions" between "morals and manners" (67) or
between "refinement and vulgarity," (109) which had blighted her
own childhood.[27]

To further underscore this Jane's disinterest in fleeing
confinement within male authorship, she evenly contrasts her
predicament with Hardy's Sue Bridehead and Eliot's Maggie
Tulliver. Between the one's going mad with sexual guilt and the
other's "abandoning herself to the water" (185) in expiation for
forbidden love, Jane "worries about the sexual doom of
womanhood, its sad inheritance," as she struggles toward a more
affirmative destiny. Her literary labors are corrective and
revisionary in accord with Bloom's reading of the modern writer's
belatededness; but the other Jane functions here, as in many other
British texts, as a literary mother to write against. Either way, a
case stands for the Novel's being a feminine form in England
from the very outset, one that accommodated women both as
creators and as characters.[28] But it is not possible to have things
both ways. That women for two centuries have exercised an
active role in shaping the genre through their gender disputes
totalising victim/oppressor models and affirms a degree of
matricentric agency. Finally, since intertextuality discovers in
every writing a rewriting (of which there are many varieties),

custody battles over the Novel are fundamentally moot.[29]

For her part, Drabble's interviews affirm a literary tradition of mixed—but preeminently English—genders. At Cambridge F.R. Leavis's grandnarrative of the English novel's Great Tradition was as impressive as Q. D. Leavis's essay on the Englishness of English fiction. The future direction of her own art is prefigured in her depiction of the actual waterfall which, unlike the fictional Jane and James, "exists." (286) But howsoever it exists out on the moors, in the text it is a "lovely balance of shapes and curves, a wildness contained within a bodily limit." More than Jane's projected inwardness, it represents a male/female configuration, a yin/yang sexual mandala. Implicit in this ideal is the recognition that the male principle is indispensable but needs further development in order to come into its own.

This is the direction of subsequent novels from *The Needle's Eye* (1972) to *The Realms of Gold* (1975) and *The Ice Age* (1977), by which time she is quoted as saying she has become "fed up with women" and makes a male protagonist central.[30] With *The Middle Ground* (1980), a sense of balance is regained by returning to the woman's viewpoint within a heterosexual milieu. What provokes the midlife crisis for the protagonist Kate Armstrong is matricentric—a therapeutic abortion. This, like childbirth in the earlier fiction, is the story's point of departure. An established journalist and feminist, Kate embarks on a quest for justifying her continuing existence and reviews along the way the key forces and figures in her past. Nothing dramatic or definitive happens, no breakthrough relationship formed or saving insight gained; yet at the end Kate's going forth to a dinner party of old and new friends is apparently the precise kind of moderate acceptance Drabble is seeking on this middle ground. The values affirmed are those traditionally practiced and preserved by women. "Why expect results, progress, success, a better society?" her social-worker friend asks her. "All we can do is to join the ranks of the caring rather than the uncaring. All we can do in this world is to care for one another, in the society we have." The need to go on caring, which is reified by the birth of a child at the end of the story to balance the sense of emptiness at the start, binds the biological, the cultural, and the psychological into a seamless matricentric whole.

The need for caring, which restates a traditional message for women and dovetails with trends in feminist psychology, allows an opportunity for widening the arcs around gendered fiction. It also distinguishes her novel from Angus Wilson's *The Middle Age of Mrs Eliot* (1958). Often construed as the female counterpart to the supposedly male *Bildungsroman*, female fictions of midlife crisis comprise a favored matricentric situation for many British women authors.[31]   That it need not be gender-bound is demonstrated by Tennessee Williams's *The Roman Spring of Mrs Stone* (1950) and Wilson's Mrs. Eliot; yet there are gendered differences. Kate Armstrong's crisis arises indigenously from a blow to her identity as a woman, specifically her child-bearing capacity—hence, its matricentric impact. Meg Eliot's crisis stems from the collapse of her identity as wife following her husband's murder—a patricentric event. Kate sublimates her losses through caring about others (more matricentric); Meg learns to stop meddling and to become more independent of others (more like a man).

Blending these approaches, Elizabeth Jane Howard's *After Julius* (1965), presents a woman who lost her husband during the rescue at Dunkirk and has some twenty years later invited her two grown daughters to her country house for a weekend. Here in this most traditional English setting, the narrative unravels and reravels the characters' lives. At dead center, the plot splits open to reveal diaries of the last days of Julius, a reticent unimposing man who yet suspends the tales of the living through their former ties to him.   Revelations about the parents produce a sense of wholeness out of which the fragmented lives of those surviving can better assemble themselves and face a future. It is a novel about society in transition, renewing itself by acknowledging past sacrifices. By the end the younger daughter in publishing leaves with her working-class poet in hand; the other daughter and a longstanding family friend, with whom the mother had hoped to resume her life, discover their love and plight their troth. With the younger generation paired off for a hopeful future, the mother is left alone in her country house to cultivate its gardens, still loyal to—still wed to—her husband's memory. Moreover, her bearing Julius's death makes her a life-bearer for the others.

Julius is a bit of Roman patriarch, citizen-soldier, and modern *pater familias* held together by memories of the recent war. His widow's role in mediating between past and present is to maintain the vital chain of continuity between the generations, and the garden she faithfully cultivates is England. Generous in its sympathies and loyalties, the novel's devotion to monogamy, concern with pairing off characters, and commitment to generational continuity are traditional signifiers of the matricentric imagination performing within a patriarchal ambience. If previous texts situate in the red, this one inhabits the purple.

In yet a different contrast, the works of Doris Lessing and Iris Murdoch, where diverse literary, cultural, and political influences impose, argue for either looser matricentric shaping or transcendence of gendered origins. Lessing's early fictions, e.g., the Martha Quest series, may be matricentric to the extent that they pursue specifically female quests for origins, values, and selfhood. *The Golden Notebook* (1962) is matricentric in its delving ever more deeply into women's experiences and to the sources of what has subsequently been called feminine *jouissance*.[32] But difficulties in this pursuit arise from two passages from different texts:

And he, in his dark, hot silence, would bring her back to the new, soft, heavy, hot flow, when she was like a fountain gushing noiseless and with urgent softness from the volcanic deeps. Then she was open to him soft and hot, yet gushing with a noiseless soft power.

The vaginal orgasm is a dissolving in a vague, dark generalized sensation like being swirled in a warm whirlpool....There is only one female orgasm and that is when a man, from the whole of his need and desire, takes a woman and wants all her response. Everything else is a substitute and a fake....

Perhaps both passages sound phallocentric today, but that may depend on who defines *jouissance*. The first passage is from D.H. Lawrence's *The Plumed Serpent* (1926), which deals with, among other things, the midlife crisis of Kate Leslie; the other is from *The Golden Notebook*.[33]   How Lessing's novel has been deemed the feminists' bible is no more surprising than why she has since disaffiliated from feminism.

Erotic exploration is a powerful drive in Iris Murdoch as well, and although her early characters invoked Lawrence's dark gods, she is more interested in ways that the Platonic triad of Good, True, and Beautiful mediates human desire irrespective of gender. Finding men more representative of the human condition, she opts for the perspective of her flawed male narrators; and while her novels are not preoccupied with marriage per se, they are deeply concerned with the related problems of love as the basis for human community. Her "typical plot begins with three or four couples living in the environs of London, to turn on Jane Austen's own formula for comedy of manners, but with this twist: each partner becomes entangled in the sexual lives of all he others."[34]   Admiring the centrality of these themes in the nineteenth-century novel, she blends a Dickensian affection for human oddity (her Bradley Pearson hearkens back to Bradley Headstone in *Our Mutual Friend*) with an Austenesque knack for matching-up, and throughout dispenses her madness and mendacity in equal doses among the genders. But many of her early plots grew out of a gothic (hence feminine) literary tradition, and therefore red shafts enter her purple prism.[35]   So situated, she is free to conduct matchmakings apart from traditional courtship scenarios by exploring how characters deal with the binding and blinding powers of eros that expand to occupy nearly all the spaces of her fictional mansions. Before the pill, Murdoch's fiction had exempted her characters from a biologically-bound sexual destiny.   Among them emerge three strategies or options. There is the aloof figure (usually male) who strives to protect his sterile autonomy by noninvolvement and eventually is forced to face his bottled-up, usually perverse, sexual desires.   There are the enchanters whose meddling in others' private affairs is a function of their unsavory power drives. Julius King, for example, in *A Fairly Honourable Defeat* (1970), attempts to carry off an Oberon brand of superior meddling when he wagers with his former mistress, Morgan, that he can separate a devoted homosexual couple so as to prove love

is not lasting and "anyone can be made to drop anyone." (234)
Self-described as artist and magician, Julian is only an artist
manqué (like Austen's Emma) who carries out the author's menial
plot labors through ill-conceived intrigues. But whereas Emma
comes to her senses, Julian King (*né* Kahn) has been too
emotionally damaged by previous Nazi persecution to recognize
that he is reliving his past by victimizing others. Morgan also
likes to stir people up and play them off against one another; the
love triangles always involve an injured third party. The retired
stage-director, Charles Arrowsby in *The Sea, the Sea*, is both
misanthropic and somehow a charismatic sorcerer, whose sudden
rediscovery of his adolescent sweetheart, Hartley, now a stooped,
grey-haired old hag wed to a conventional dullard, excites an
erotomanic passion revealed as a flight-into-reality defense
against the spurned homoerotic affection for his cousin James, an
embodiment of the Good and the True.

There are finally those who learn from experience or try
to fit their imperfect loves to some equivalent of Platonic
goodness (and usually suffer a "fairly honourable defeat"). On
these sublimated planes, matchmaking thrives and indeed
proliferates among a melange of characters, desires, values, states
of mind, and mixtures of gender. An enormous amount of plot is
consumed in *Henry and Cato*, for example, in awakening Henry's
libido for the presumed poor-girl/prostitute who had been his
glamorous brother's mistress, in exposing her as a vulgar
opportunist, then in shifting his gaze to the perky young girl of
his youth. A male writer might be content with the hero getting
the girl into bed, but Murdoch's matricentric urges in this
instance insist he get her to the altar first.

In Murdoch's relentlessly modern world, those still
doggedly pursuing their timeless quests must run a Freudian
gauntlet of aim/&/object-inhibitions, with existential voids
opening on either side. They don their intellectual fashions and
flaunt their chivalric codes, but neither do her ladies ever attain
their ideal Mr. Knightley nor do her males act very knightly. Yet
all the old visions of a higher—feudal, troubadour, religious—
order descend to haunt her characters and beleaguer, bewilder, or
bedevil the course of their perilous quests—their endless matches,
mismatches, and occasionally proper match-ups.

As women's fiction from the late sixties on grows more attuned to feminist dimensions of their heroines' lives, the question arises whether the matricentric may militate against the feminist or the feminist undermine the matricentric. Logically, one might accede to both possibilities, and the next two examples focus the rising tensions which on various levels were always present.

A comic variation on matricentric themes appears in Margaret Atwood's proto-feminist novel, *The Edible Woman* (1969), which deals with the attachments of Marian and her friends—married or single—in a not so swinging Toronto of the sixties. Wedged between a dull future in market research and a conventional marriage to Peter, Marian springs out of tight moments (rather like Updike's Rabbit) until she can concoct a more offbeat, appropriately feminine accommodation.

After visiting friends up to their ears in child-rearing, Marian's roommate Ainsley declares her intention to have a child solo and so to spare it the dreariness of growing up in a modern family. "Every woman should have at least one baby," she declares. "It's even more important than sex. It fulfills your deepest femininity." (40) But even as Marian mocks this pop anthropology, Ainsley schemes to select a fit father. However, Len, the young man she snares, is not your run-of-the-mill male primate who opts to copulate and run. "You've involved me psychologically," Len insists. "I'll have to think of myself as a father now." Ainsley too begins thinking about the "Father Image" and having second thoughts about homosexual sons reared in fatherless homes. But Len soon proves himself altogether too thin-shelled for the part. (165)

In fact, the narrative is virtually hatched-out of its food/birth themes. Eggs are continually being cracked, boiled, eaten, made contrapuntal to conversations—especially about conception—or played with metaphorically. Len's mother stirred disgust over biological sex by serving him an egg with an embryo inside; in parlor tricks, eggs can be squeezed without breaking, but Marian wonders if a less adept Len is up to the game; and her own edible egg cracks in the saucepan, releasing a "semi-congealed feeler like an exploding oyster." This image externalizes her fears of emotional immersion, because later while moving through tables of "eating women" to join her office-mates for lunch, she "felt suffocated by this thick Sargasso-sea of femininity" and responded like "some tactile sea-creature withdrawing its tentacles." (172)

Reacting to her fears of being "sucked down," she wants a man: Peter. But Peter is a pumpkin eater, and Marion is finding herself to be Peter's "delicious" pumpkin. She takes up with a poor-and-grubby but sensitive-and-decent graduate student named Duncan; he allays her fears of submersion and decay over the sight an Egyptian mummy under glass with a "peculiar floating drowned look," by calmly claiming that death is "perfectly natural." (192)

Whimsically downbeat and vulnerable, Duncan appeals both to Marian's rebellious impulses and her maternal needs. He is the ugly duckling and charming waif for whom someone like Marion needs to care; and after their timid lovemaking, he would meekly return to his "shell" if Marian didn't detain him. But ahead looms her engagement like a death sentence, and she has crawled into her own shell of anorexia. Desperate, she goes shopping for eggs and other ingredients for a cake. It is to be a sponge cake, pliable enough to be molded into the outline of a woman like herself and served up to Peter, who, failing to appreciate the gift or the joke, exits in haste. By this time Ainsley has been paired off with an acceptable father-image for her baby, and, after deciding to find herself a better job, Marian feeds the last of the cake to Duncan, a reluctant cannibal but a good-enough egg in the end.[36]

The matricentric narrative arising from Jane's preganancy in *The L-Shaped Room* that began this period of women's writing is reversed yet reinstated in Atwood's *Surfacing*. A deadpan prose style depicts the ersatz liberation of two pairs of American deadbeats who, during the Vietnam period, travel to a Quebec lake ostensibly to shoot a movie while one of the women, the unnamed I-narrator, pursues reports of her father's disappearance. During the couple's dissolution, the matricentric narrative surfaces. While the other three "disowned their parents long ago," the heroine has some unfinished business with hers. The quest for origins is hampered by the facts that her mother is deceased and her father's remains are fished up toward the end. What survives are memories, family scrapbooks, and his Indian drawings, which she seizes upon as signs of his sanity and legacy to her. But her origins quest is aborted, both literally and figuratively, when diving for traces of the now submerged drawings, she sinks into "pale green, then darkness, layer after layer, deeper than before, seabottom." There she visualizes a form "drifting towards me from the furthest level where there was no life, a dark oval trailing limbs. It was blurred but it had eyes, they were open, it was something I knew about, a dead thing, it was dead." Surfacing, she realizes the dead thing was what she had seen "curled up, staring out at me like a cat pickled; it had huge jelly eyes and fins instead of hands, fish gills, I couldn't let it out, it was dead already, it had drowned in the air"—her own aborted fetus. (167-8) Despite the abortion's approval by its father, she finds herself implicated in an all-encompassing death-system, figured by a hanging, mutilated blue heron, left by fishermen.

Her depersonalized condition ("I didn't feel awful...I didn't feel much of anything") is presented as disembodiment: when the "head is detached from the body both of them die." (91) "At some point my neck must have closed over, pond freezing or a wound, shutting me into my head...like being in a vase." (126) The bottled embryo which she sees and smashes after her abortion evokes the creatures she had freed from her father's bottles—both products of "pure logic" and symptoms of her schizoid ego. (168) Every interference with natural processes is now seen as detrimental. She allows her grossly insensitive boyfriend to impregnate her, tears up her past, and hides out in the wood as the others leave. Semi-mad in a totally mad society, she re-naturalizes herself and achieves—far too quickly—a semblance of integrated wholeness. At the end, she is poised, hesitating to be brought back. There are other equivocations: her final good pregnancy has been accomplished through bad sex, just as her earlier pregnancy was terminated by bad logic. To act in accord with the natural world is to act against reproductive freedom. Nothing is resolved by going back to nature, and the "return to the human community" makes for a "closed narrative."[37]

Thus exceeding former limits, the matricentric narrative highlights dilemmas women were beginning to face during feminism's new phase of liberation: breaking away from man as enemy, tuning in to the female body's voice, but glosses over other phases: where to go next? In many respects, the portrayal of women's situation has also grown bleaker. Sharply contrasting the supportive men during Jane's L-shaped confinement, Atwood's men are shallow, exploitive, lustful, grotesquely misogynistic. Nor is the female friend who talks up feminism a sister when it comes to fighting for her man (Atwood's own amivalence toward feminism will persist). There are in fact hints that these profound dislocations may admit no amelioration. But at the very least, while the body's ambiguities and sexual interdependencies do not disappear, matricentric narratives, spurred by 1970s-style raised-consciousness, launch new quests for origins in self and sisterhood.

Notes

1. Rose MacAulay, *Keeping Up Appearances*, 300. This admirable comic novel complicates the historical development of women's writing. The principals, two sisters—Daisy (who runs away from trouble, fibs, and makes a mess of things generally) and Daphne (the healthy cover-girl who shines through in every situation) are revealed along the way as the heroine's duality: the person she is most of the time, and the one she would like to be to please others as well as herself. The young man falls in love with Daphne only to discover Daisy, who, coming to her senses, sends him packing. Daisy, in effect, deconstructs the socially produced Daphne with all the finesse of femininity-as-masquerade *à la* Lacan; however, Daisy's deconstruction is not to expose patriarchal stereotypes but to reaffirm traditional encodings of honesty. In a more modern mode, Daisy earns her livelihood as "Miss Marjorie Wynne," a spinster novelist, a fall-back identity after the other two have been demolished. Its implicit egalitarian feminism thrusts it ahead of its time; its comic conventions, which rely on a stable social order, pull it back. Heading for an enthusiastic welcome in America, Marjorie Wynne is a liberated spirit, or would be except for one nagging problem: she isn't sure she exists. Nor is one certain Rose Macaulay's feminism exists. In 1957, she wrote, "Naturally I knew it was ridiculous to deprive half the people of the country of any voice in the laws they had to live under merely on account of a trifling difference in sex, but I did not think anything I could do about it was likely to be helpful." In reviewing a new biography, *Rose Macaulay: A Writer's Life* by Jane Emery, the reviewer concludes, "She seems to be a mixed case of emancipation and denial" (Claire Harman, "Tomboy Grudge," *London Review of Books* (27 Feb 1992), 9.

2. As is well known, the Greeks rooted women's emotional disorders and even madness in *hyster*: womb, which had become unmoored and wandered through the anatomy. This patricentric fantasy had its patricentric cure: sexual intercourse and pregnancy to re-anchor the womb (Jon

Solomon, "The Wandering womb of Delos," 104). When Freud
revived the term in a clinical context, he departed from the
ancient gender marker—some of his early hysterics were male.

3. It could be reasoned that men tend to see women
through desire and/or the defensive gaze of castration anxiety,
leading to aversion, fetishizing, splitting, etc.; while the neglect
of the matricentric by feminist theorists apparently stems from
other sources, although *l'ecriture feminine* evokes the fetish (see
chapt. 5).

4. Ruth Adam's history of British feminism, *A Woman's
Place, 1910-1975*, provides a social backdrop for this archetypal
event which threatened every young woman's coming-of-age.
"It was correct for a respectable family to turn a pregnant
unmarried daughter out of doors," Adam writes. "This proved
to the neighbors that they strongly disapproved of her
behavior," 61.

5. For more, see App. B.

6. This also anticipates concluding the Jane Graham
trilogy with *Two Is Lonely* (1974). In this updated world of
fragmented families and blended marriages, Jane is bringing up
her eight-year son David without benefit of male parentage.
She is operating a craft shop with a female friend in
Hampstead, while Toby has married, separated, and settled in a
Kibbutz. Enter Felix Andrews, a successful architect who has
lost his wife and resents his drifting son's hippie lifestyle.
Although Felix wants his relationships to operate as smoothly
as geometry, Jane looks through the "pompous" scientist to
determine whether there may not be "huddled" within someone
capable of bending her two-is-lonely theorem into a more
human triangle. But before launching into an uncertain future,
Jane revisits her past. She travels with John to Toby's Israeli
village. En route in Greece, she encounters Chris, Felix's
disaffected son, and comes to appreciate his notions about the
magical properties of water, without taking up his offer for an
oceanside night in his sleeping bag. John, meanwhile, finds

himself and a peaceful exit from the story through joining gay
vagabonds. Upon returning to London, Jane goes off on a
desperate search for David, who it is feared has run away to
find his biological father, now a dissolute actor making TV
commercials. But after David turns up at John's vacated digs
and Felix becomes a caring person, all obstacles are removed
for David to get the decent father he deserves and Jane to
complete the lettering in her L-shaped room to spell L-ove, at
last.

7. Ellen Cronan Rose, *The Novels of Margaret Drabble*, 2.

8. Rose, 17.

9. Rose, 17.

10. Rose, 17.

11. Rose, 19.

12. Joanne Creighton, "Interview with Margaret
Drabble," 25.

13. Creighton, 24.

14. Creighton, 24; for more, see App. B).

15. Rose, 59.

16. Rose, 62.

17. Rose, 49.

18. Gayle Greene's "Margaret Drabble's *The Waterfall*" is
the one exception.

19. Simone de Beauvoir, *The Second Sex*; See Rose, 49-53,
for relevance to Drabble.

20. Rose, 56.

21. Rose, 68.

22. Rose, 57.

23. Rose, 68.

24. Greene's recuperative feminist reading follows the postmodern mode by filtering *The Waterfall* through metafiction, intertextuality, the dialogic, the writerly model, and *l'écriture feminine* ("Margaret Drabble's *The Waterfall*," 307-332).

25. Sandra Gilbert and Susan Gubar, *The Madwoman in the Attic*, hold the "female artist['s]...battle...is not against her [male] precursor's reading of the world but against his reading of *her*." (49) This and other claims about the woman writer are advanced as transhistroical generalizations, although the cited writers are mainly 19th Century. A remark that "contemporary women do now attempt the pen with energy and authority" (51) confuses more than it clarifies (for more, chapt. 5).

Yet in one respect the authors' theories of female authorship is confirmed: Drabble's dual narrator in *The Waterfall* may be seen as a 20th Century device for the author to embrace the madness that in the 19th Century entailed the convention of a "mad double." Annis Pratt has drawn attention to parallels between Brontë's and Drabble's Jane, with the variation—"Reader, I loved him"—upgrading the latter heroine's quest for the "authentic sexuality" bestowed by Eros (locally residing in James) over the earlier heroine's quest for a suitable marriage (*Archetypal Patterns in Women's Fiction*, 91). However construed, the theme of madness persists in contemporary women's works.

26. Rose, 58-9.

27. "Her life is notable for its lack of events" runs Austen's entry in Drabble's new edition of *The Oxford Companion to English Literature*, 52; though cool and brisk, it is not so cold or curt as her predecessor, Sir Paul Harvey's 1932 entry.

28. Dale Spender, *Mothers of the Novel*.

29. James Tatum, editor, *The Search for the Ancient Novel*; Margaret Anne Doody, *The True Story of the Novel*.

30. Rose, 113.

31. Esther Kleinbord Labovitz, *The Myth of the Heroine: The Female Bildungsroman in the Twentieth Century* notes that female heroines have been absent from the traditional *Bildungsroman*, but her own reading of the genre as a lower-class hero's "using his vocation as a means of upward social mobility," excludes Stephen Daedalus's impractical "silence, exile, and cunning," Rilke's offbeat Malte Laurids Brigge, and Kerouac's Beats (251). Thus the conclusion that the male "completed his journey and arrived at momentous decisions while still a young adult" is unwarranted. Whether it is necessary for a female *Bildungsroman* to have the heroine delay "her direction in life...into middle age" is also a problematic if intriguing alternative (247); for there are many interesting examples within the traditional masculine time-frame, such as Doris Lessing's Martha Quest novels, Lisa Alther's *Kinflicks* (see Bonnie Hoover Brendlin, "New Directions in the Contemporary *Bildungsroman*: Lisa Althers' *Kinflicks*," in *Gender and Literary Voice*, Janet Todd, editor, 160-71), Maureen Duffy's *That's How It Was*, Rita Mae Brown's *Rubyfruit Jungle*, and Jeanette Winterson's *Oranges Are not the Only Fruit*. The heroine of Atwood's *bildungsroman*, *Surfacing*, has a nominal marriage in her past but is in other respects an adolescent going through a crisis of separation from her parents. A most notable American coming-of-age novel, Edith Wharton's *Summer* (1917), traverses the young heroine's Lawrencean love affair, her matricentric quest for origins, and

her entry into a Lacanian Symbolic Order via an implicitly
incestuous marriage with her adoptive father. Susan Fraiman's
study of 19th-century fiction by British women does not seek a
separate geneology for the coming-of-age genre but rather a
narrative of discontinuity, compromise, and contradiction
(*Unbecoming Women: British Women Writers and the Novel of
Development*). On the related subject of the *Kunstlerroman*, see
Jones' Introduction to *Writing the Woman as Artist*, 1-22.

32. Claire Duchen, *Feminism in France*.

33. D.H. Lawrence, *The Plumed Serpent*, 463; *The Golden
Notebook*, 216. The question was mooted in any case by Anne
Koedt's "The Myth of the Vaginal Orgasm," in *Radical
Feminism*, only to be revived by more inclusive views.

34. Steven Cohan, "From Subtext to Dream Text," 224.

35. Juliann Fleenor, *The Female Gothic*; Deborah
Johnson, *Iris Murdoch*.

36. In her study of eating disorders, Kim Chernin notes
Marian's transitory anorexia in connection with the cake of
herself which she cooks and partially devours as instancing
conflict-resolution. "By eating up this cake fetish of a woman's
body she assimilates for the first time her own body and its
feelings (*The Obsession*).

37. Sally Robinson, "The 'Anti-Logos Weapon':
Multiplicity in Women's Texts." Ironically, it is precisely
women's fear of compulsory childbirth under the New Right
intensified to compulsory conception under an Islamic dystopia
that Atwood's *The Handmaid's Tale* (1987) portrays. For
extensive feminist readings of *Surfacing*, see Hirsch, *The
Mother / Daughter Plot*, 140-5.

2

Matricentric Motifs in a Feminist Age

The acid test of feminist writing is whether it
names the enemy—men—and whether this enemy,
men, feels threatened in reading it.
                    —"Manchester Feminist"[1]

Novels discussed:
  The Seven Ages (1986), by Eva Figes
  The Passion of New Eve (1977), by Angela Carter
  Eve: Her Story (1988), by Penelope Farmer
  Praxis (1978), by Fay Weldon
  Puffball (1980), by Fay Weldon
  Hot Water Man (1982), by Deborah Moggach
  Daughter of Jerusalem (1978), by Sara Maitland
  Virgin Territory (1984), by Sara Maitland

Through the color bands of red/purple/blue, gender's
impact on the creative process may be visualized. With the blue
as distinctively male writing and the red its female counterpart,
the central purple spans the region where gender is subordinated
or dissolves into a priority of commonly-felt human concerns.
Here, many of the world's great writers—Tolstoy, Dickens, Austen,
George Eliot, etc.—may properly reside. But since for too long
cultural equations of Male=Norm/Female=Other have prevailed,
many male writers should be reshuffled to purple's bluish
periphery or further (e.g., Hemingway, Mailer, Kingsley Amis,
Kipling, and Conrad); on the other hand, the efforts of feminist
critics to retrieve prominent women writers from the rich purple
blend for the pure red may attenuate their texts.[2] But in the
absence of absolute norms and in the accuracy of literary
representations being questioned by normative ideals from both
ends of the gender divide, all such allocations must be tentative,
the Muses never having been equal opportunity employers; and
while the central purple may promise an ideally balanced vision
of normative sexuality, subjective values inevitably infiltrate the
color chart ("heterosexualism" along with other -*isms* subvert
notions of sexual maturity).
    In literature variety is paramount, and authorial biases
(e.g., sexism) are seldom easy to extricate from aesthetic strategies.

All the same, the extreme blue may shade into gender-specific writing like homoerotic fiction or subliterary genres like male-pornography, just as at the extreme red appear lesbian fiction along with romances and most gothics.[3] But these areas that conflate sex and gender may say more about the tastes and proclivities of readers than about gender influences on writers, since each gender can and has produced its counterpart's potboilers (American women, for example, have recently written war novels; males infiltrate the romance market; Anais Nin dabbled in porn). Still, certain gender crossovers *are* unlikely (e.g., lesbian s/m erotica).

Women's red shades into three tints: (1) fiction of woman's situation (e.g., Barbara Pym, Margaret Drabble, Anita Brookner); (2) woman-identified (lesbian) writing (Maureen Duffy, Jo Jones, Caeia March); (3) feminist fiction (Zoë Fairbairns, Sara Maitland, Michele Roberts). Not only do these categories overlap, but some of the best writers—Fay Weldon, Beryl Bainbridge, Susan Hill, Iris Murdoch, Doris Lessing—may sojourn among them at various stages in their careers while otherwise dwelling in purple. If the groupings blend at the edge, they also produce traditions and subdivisions. Woman's situation (1), for example, developed through a cluster of eighteenth-century conventions designated by Katharine Rogers as the feminine novel. With attention centered on the heroine as virtuous role-model, she and "sympathetic male characters" are "richly endowed with a sensibility that made them value emotions over practical considerations and be alert to the finer points of compatibility, love, and consideration."[4] The plot typically turns on the heroine's consensual options for marriage, with a predictably more generous field than society afforded, and on the "lengthy delays before the ultimate happy marriage," which "serve not merely to prolong the tale but also to express a resistance to man's dominion."[5] Lesbian writing (2) diverges into erotica and feminist (or, if one prefers, into libidinal and political economies). In light of its various sources, feminist fiction (3) is subject to a host of usages. It may be minimally signified as writing by avowed feminists or books issued from women's presses. Woman-centered narratives as in Isak Dinesen's *Babette's Feast*, the presence of a "strong woman protagonist" as in Willa Cather's *O Pioneers!*, or an affirmation of woman's erotic autonomy as in Drabble's *The Waterfall* have all been awarded feminist certification.[6]

Others may qualify by foregrounding feminist issues, but these are culturally relativized and variously historicized. Thus eighteenth-century courtship novels, "written by women and for women," are construed as feminist because, for a new breed of heroines, love leading to "companionate marriage" had become valorized.[7] Other definitions are more exclusionist. Writing as a committed lesbian feminist, Patricia Duncker desires feminist fiction to be utopian, oppositional, angry, the "centre of significant change" as being situated "between the women," and produced by as well as for "the community of women."[8]

Bringing rigor to the definition, Rosalind Coward writes that novels "with a surface commitment to feminism should be interrogated as to by what representations of sexuality, of maleness and femaleness, they achieve their version of reality." Thus consciousness-raising novels and narratives of woman's oppression are not sufficiently feminist. For her, feminist fiction, like feminism, should address the "'ideological' relations" where the personal and the political interface.[9] Similarly, Gayle Greene foregrounds the "analysis of gender as socially constructed and [the] sense that what has been constructed may be reconstructed."[10] Making both the political and the biocentric explicit, Carole Spedding defines a "feminist book" as one "written by a woman, in any genre, which is centrally informed by the author's critical analysis of her position in society as a woman."[11] Such restricting rigor may exclude all but a very select few novels, since fiction mostly eschews analysis and operates by inferences susceptible to multiple interpretations.

So contentious is this grouping that one is better advised to seek relative degrees of feminism in women's fiction rather than a totality. Unlike the woman's situation group wherein male authors like Richardson, Flaubert, Hardy, James, and the D.M. Thomas of *The White Hotel*, among others, could be included, all definitions of the third group assume only women authors could produce feminist fiction despite Gissing's *The Odd Women*, James' *The Bostonians*, Ibsen's Nora, the problem plays by Shaw, and the feminist moments in Brecht's theater (as well as his poem, "On the Infanticide Marie Farrar"), the gender deconstructions of *Ulysses*, etc. Moreover, sex-blind assignments are impossible: if the sex of the author of *Tess of the D'Urbervilles* were unknown, would Hardy be included in the retroactive reach of feminist scholars to expand the ranks of feminist fiction?[12]

Essentialist assumptions also affect the criteria of male/ female relationships being represented in a field of male hegemony, and while this may be unavoidable, it requires a stereotyping of male characters to suit the ideological aim. Put bluntly, in feminist fiction at its most ideological, women suffer, change, grow; men stay stuck or change for the worst. Seconding this scenario, Fay Weldon told an interviewer, "Men on the whole don't change. Women change because they have children" (she's probably thinking of Liffey in her *Puffball*, but all the same an extreme matricentric view, whose corollary would deprive childless women of change).[13] In feminist fiction, then, the reader is confronted with a procedure in which female characters struggle with constructions of their genders, while male sexuality remains an oppressive but uninterrogated essence. "Like the women in male pornography," for example, Andrea Dworkin's "men have no history, no psychology, no reasons for action; they are just knives that cut, arms that beat, penises that maim by the very act of penetration."[14]

Paradoxically, then, the more *literary* feminist fiction becomes, i.e., the more characters of both genders are created from the inside-out, the less feminist it is. Eva Figes' *The Seven Ages*, for instance, skims a millennium of English history from women's marginalized position. In this other-visioning of patriarchy, all males (apart from a few lines about a tender loving monk) are predators of one sort or another, be they warriors, doctors, generals, scientists, bureaucrats. Such retro-stereotyping may decenter the normative perspective of male heroism and hegemony; but by inscribing a biology of sex rather than a construction of gender, the work narrowly brackets woman's biocentric features—her generativity and rapability—at so elementary a level as to inscribe conservative essentialism.

But questions of whether, how, and to what extent feminist fiction may also be literature are better posed when Fay Weldon's and Sara Maitland's texts are shortly examined; through them the way gender impacts on feminist writing may assume new meaning when placed in a matricentric context.

Within the red, feminist criticism has foregrounded at least three basic creative strategies:

1) *Symbolic readings of traditional women's texts revealing subversive subtexts.* Assumptions that feminist encodings lurk within traditional texts hold promises not always fulfilled in practice (raising problematics taken up in chapt. 6). Briefly, retrospective readings violate the integrity of the literary work when so much in a text is revealed by even benign deconstructions as deceptive overlays, subterfuge, or inner-meanings, which, like dream-thoughts in an analysis, yield up their secrets only to a professional elite; inevitably, the decodings dovetail with the critics' contemporary agendas.

2) *Female (Re)visions of Male Texts.*[15] On firmer ground, feminist scholarship has uncovered a widespread strategy among women writers, practiced from the outset and still going strong. Eve's role and its implications in Genesis were reconsidered throughout the 17th Century, as, for example, this verse by Sarah Fyge: "Tho' Man had Being first, yet methinks She/In Nature should have the Supremacy;/For Man was form'd out of dull senceless Earth,/But Woman had much more Noble Birth."[16] This playing on the quality and order of origins ostensibly accepted woman as the "second sex," while countering conventional interpretations. Other protofeminists "thought women superior to men" and "turned upside-down the positions of male and female on the ladder of worth, status, and power."[17] More to modern taste, Michelene Wandor's *Gardens of Eden* (1984) revises Genesis to justify Eve and to include her sister Lilith. "You eat one apple," this disarming Eve laments, "and they remember you forever; you/only want to be left in peace, make/chutney, compote, dried apple rings/ on a string.../a snake? don't be silly/knowledge? you read too many Good Books/naked? so I like the sun. I tan easy."[18]

The deconstruction of desire as its own excesses turn one into the object desired is a theme of Angela Carter's *The Passion of New Eve.* Visiting New York, a young Englishman named Evelyn moves in with Leilah, a black girl of the streets, and when their love is terminated after a back-alley abortion, Evelyn flees across the continent to be apprehended by a matriarchal tribe of women living beneath the desert. In this magic land of Beulah, he encounters the primordial mother goddess: black, "bearded," and "breasted like a sow" with "two tiers of nipples," who, by the "sullen flash of Holy Mother's obsidian scalpel," sex-changes Evelyn to Eve. (59, 50) Like Philip Roth's Alan Kepesh who suffers a "massive hormonal influx" in transmuting into a female breast, the new Eve is given "massive injections of female hormones," but unlike Alan she does not really change.[19] Her voice and the ego through which it is modulated is unvarying. But she does have a woman's body, as evidenced by a rape under the auspices of Zero, a sadistic poet in the Charles Manson mode, surrounded by a masochistic harem of adoring groupies. Both Zero and the old Evelyn have been obsessed with the screen sex-goddess Tristessa, and when they invade her estate, she is revealed as a man. Thus when he copulates with Eve, she enjoys a perversely androgynous fulfillment of desire. After Zero is blown up and Tristessa is blown away, Eve finds herself among a Latin American guerilla force overtaking California. Among them is Leilah, revealed as Lilith, who, explaining that history is overtaking myth, takes Eve to visit the great mother, now exiled from Beulah and, like an ancient Greek oracle, dwelling among the crevices, pools, and caves along the coast.

This matricentric quest for selfhood through female origins takes Eve on a time-journey into her evolutionary past and returns her to an old woman on the beach who drinks vodka and sings blues incessantly. Eve takes the woman's boat and rows off to bear her love-child. Composed in the overwrought, apocalyptic style of modernism at its murkiest, Eve's text is resolved into lucidity only by recourse to another text: *The Sadeian Woman*. There, such formulations as "all myths of women...are consolatory nonsense" and "all archetypes are spurious" put period to ponderous passages of fictional myth-mongering.[20] By construing pornography as a "reactionary" text dependent on the "notion that the nature of man is invariable," Carter's deconstructive porno-parodies play with fluctuating genitalia as though they were floating signifiers.[21] If not obtuse, the feminism is oblique.[22]

In a more mundane mode, the Serpent in Penelope Farmer's *Eve: Her Story*, becomes a sort of Promethean instructor of womankind. With full shoulders and attired in a gleaming gold-green suit of scales, this notorious villain shows Eve how to use a knife, build a fire, and forge iron. But if Eve is naive, Adam is dumb, and Jehovah is just avuncular. After Adam goes off to dream up new ways of expanding creation, Eve explores paradise on her own. While espying her own reflection in a pond, she sights over her shoulder another figure whose features do not mimic her changing expressions. This is Lilith, Adam's first wife, who wearied of her subordination to his lust. She is a free spirit, roving the periphery of the garden—bitter, voluptuous, and given to sneezing as evidence of her fall from grace. Claiming a sister, Eve discovers her own sensual body, and eventually jealous rage; perplexed by Jehovah's prohibitions against the fig tree, she chooses its mortal sentence over the immortality of the apple tree. The knowledge that accompanies her fateful choice is of birth and death. But through it, she will be empowered to realize her life and to tell her story. At the end she is pregnant with a child and a tale to tell. Having chosen, she achieves character, and it is preeminently one defined by a matricentric identity that fuses narrative and female fecundity.

If there are advantages to the re-visioning approach, there are also complicating aspects. Hardly a feminist strategy, writers, regardless of gender, have immemorially and notoriously begged, borrowed, and stolen from others' works. Orwell's antipastoral *1984* ironically revises Lawrence; Atwood revises Orwell. Women revise women writers, as in Jean Rhys' *Wide Sargasso Sea*, and Eva Figes' *Nelly: Her Version*; and women revise characters, as in Tennant's *Tess*. Males ceaselessly revise earlier male texts (sometimes female texts as well, e.g., the opening of Lawrence's *Women in Love* evokes/inverts Austen) to such an extent that the revisionary impulse is very near the heart of the creative process as construed by Harold Bloom's anxiety-of-influence theories. Consequently, the attentive reader soon notices that Wandor's creation poems are closely modelled after Ted Hughes's revision of Genesis in *Crow* (1971), and Hughes is rewriting Milton, Hopkins, and Lawrence. Every variation on a theme is not de facto a subversion; just as often, (re)vision turns out to be plain revision or simple reversal which quickly grows mechanical and predictable. In any case, postmodernism's intertextuality renders all writing as rewriting, and women revise and subvert other female writers—e. g., Pym, Drabble, Brookner—as often as male writers; does that place such women authors outside the feminist pale? Even Austen's *Northanger Abbey* deconstructs female Gothics.[23] Subverting the past is not gender-determined, and depicting women writers fondly thinking back through their mothers is like calling cannibalism a love feast (which it is for the feasters, though not for the feasted).

Another difficulty is that, anthropologically speaking, at the headwaters of Western literature, male mythmaking springs from needs to reverse the biological priorities of female babymaking.[24] Thus most male myths reassign human origins to a fanciful male source of fertility, be it via Adam's rib, Prometheus's mud babies, Poseidon's spilled genital blood, or Zeus's fertile brow. One is reminded of Plato's cave allegory wherein art is the shadow of images several steps removed from reality, for such is the implication of considering female texts as revising male revisions of male texts which sprung from inverted revisions of female procreation. Perhaps a Lacanian discourse of lack and endless desire for the other would illuminate the processes. Some of the perplexities diminish, however, when culture is allowed its own priorities distinct from nature's; then an apparent copy may be experienced as an original by dint of being a vivid re-vision. Feminist contributions to this neverending process succeed best in foregrounding specific subversions of male dominance.

3) *Female Mythic Patterns.* The most prominent of these organizing structures, besides Eve/Lilith, are the Greek myths of Eros/Psyche, Demeter/Persephone, and the Amazons, along with folktales of Rapunzel, Cinderella, and others.[25] The operative assumption here is that within largely male myth-systems reside kernels for authentically female experience, and many studies have undertaken a sometimes Jungian reading along these lines.[26] Such archetypal patterns usually emanate from underlying matricentric processes, and the restoration, for example, of the lost daughter Persephone to the Olympian pantheon produces a "polycentric structure of consciousness."[27]

If women's fictions since the eighteenth century have inscribed a larger pattern, it is because they have most often been manifested through a *matri*-monial goal; however ambivalently represented, they may also partake of a more pervasive quest for *matrix*, less literally for mother than a matricentric quest for motherhood/selfhood conducted via womb/origins/source. In this context the ubiquitous marriage may have once served as goal, later as means, more recently as obstacle or irrelevancy, and most recently as re-invention. But while real, these developments can also be seen as variations on a more basic theme. Feminist scholars, exasperated by the monotony of marital plots in women's novels, have targetted the hopeless inequity of patriarchal marriage; but evidence suggests that they were sometimes led more by logic than by perception in establishing retrospectively similar misgivings and denunciations in earlier centuries of women's fiction.[28]

Formerly, women may have most often boarded the matrimonial bandwagon as merely the best matricentric vehicle then available, in society as well as in fiction; but that does not explain why marriage persists and even thrives. The fact that it is still so frequently being chosen raises questions less about the extent of women's oppression than about literature's ambivalent relation to it. Presumably, like men, women have conflicting or oscillating needs, and may turn at any given moment to outlets in romance or to solutions in feminism. Gloria Steinem, who once observed that women's interest in romance was a displaced longing for careers, reveals in her memoirs how she was preaching feminist salvation while sleeping with the enemy.[29]   But, whether the cloth of women's lives is being raveled in fictions of a traditional manner or unraveled in a more feminist one, it is the matricentric fabric itself which finally reveals the distinctive textures and dyes of gender.

Indeed, in Fay Weldon's *Praxis*, dualistic structures maintain an ambivalence nearly to the end when a transforming synthesis becomes feasible. As in Lessing and Drabble, the narrative voice switches from a wryly impersonal tone that accompanies the events spanning the fifty-plus years of the heroine's life to a first-person, present-voice. It belongs to Praxis Duveen, born out of wedlock to Lucy, who grows deranged over the years, and to Ben, a Jew who abandons the household after serving up various scenes of passion and violence to Praxis and her older sister Hypatia. Praxis means "turning point, culmination, action; orgasm; some said the Goddess herself," i.e., Aphrodite. (12) It also means practice, practicality, as other to theory, ideology. In the story it stands for the character's pre-socialized childhood, with which she never loses touch even when allowing herself to be called Pattie Fletcher, after her mother, or Pattie Parker after her last husband. Hypatia becomes Hilda as the girls are placed in various homes and schools in the wake of the mother's madness.

While Praxis is aligned with the sane force of the parents' original passions, Hilda internalizes her mother's madness while outwardly adapting to the rational expectations of a society in denial. The school authorities, referring to her proudly as "our very valuable head girl," reward her with medals and certificates. "She meted out punishment liberally, if erratically. She might give twenty lines or two thousand for the same offense: she invented crimes...as if a certain implicit insanity in the school...had become explicit in Hilda." She thrives in London's bureaucracy all the while writing letters of paranoid rage against her sister. Thus, along with dualities between practice/theory; male/female; proper/improper; Brighton/London, the central dualism is sane/mad as they are continually being inverted and redefined. If Hilda is calculating and superficially rational, Praxis is emotive and emotional. The one seems always to succeed, the other always to fail; yet a star in Praxis's visionary sky counsels patience.

While "Pattie" implies patience, Praxis also displays a certain Dickensian decency, which falls a bit short of conscience and leaves her susceptible to an array of worldly duplicities. After suffering the vicar's exhibiting himself to her and after being enamoured of a fellow student, she starts a diary, "part fact, part fantasy. She simplified the vicar's act of self-exposure into a rape...and described in detail how Louise Gaynor had kissed her." (43) Mother's reading of the diary transforms her into "some glassy-eyed, violent, mad stranger," who calls the police and taunts her child for being a "little Jewess, after all. Sly little lesbian. Little slut. Filthy...bastard." (44) Later, Hilda will slap Praxis for suggesting that their mother has been put away because she is mad and accuse her sister of causing the madness by her lesbian activities. When the first-person narrator meditates on the causes of Lucy's madness, she explicitly evokes Jane Eyre's madwoman-in-the-attic figure, by asking, "What is madness anyway? Throwing red-hot coals about a room, hating one of your children, worrying more about a lesbian kiss than a clerical rape?" (50)

Gradually the theme of madness interlocks with the condition of women and the construction of their gender in an androcentric society. Growing up traumatized in a nutty household, Praxis never evokes readers' pity as a simple victim; and while not taking the path of the madwomen in her family, she never resorts to blaming them despite their blatantly destructive behavior. Later married to Ivor, an upscale executive, who "wanted her life to have begun the day he met her," she tells him she has become "a figment of your imagination." (161) And when she leaves him, he tells her she is "mad, monstrous, unnatural." (187) But, staring "at herself in the mirror, at her doll's face, stiff doll's body, curly blonde doll's hair," she wonders if anything "could shine through the casing that Ivor had selected for her." Still, she does "not blame Ivor" because she had "preferred to live as a figment of Ivor's imagination, rather than put up with the confusion of being herself." (168) Having fled to Philip, the once handsome youth who had seduced her and then lost her on a casual flip of the coin to his friend Willie, Praxis comes to a similar conclusion about this now prominent filmmaker. Her life lapses "into black and white: as if she too were now some part of Philip's imagination" and he were "making an eternal square with his two hands and framing her through them." (189)

Thuswise is the theme of madness woven into the life-story of Praxis and threaded through a realized feminist consciousness (if not quite commitment). The tone is set by Praxis's early childhood memories. "Frigid bitch," cries Ben as he seizes Lucy's hair. "He is strong: she is helpless: if he wishes to rape her, he could, he would. It is in the air." (13) But at school the girls are told that they are "daughters of Eve and responsible for leading men into sin and for the loss of Paradise, and must make amends forever." (21) Upon getting her first period, Praxis laments, "five-twenty-eights of her life gone, stolen, and for no other reason than that she was a woman." (39) Later, she reflects, "If I was a boy I'd be allowed to get on with my homework—I wouldn't have to sweep floors first." (43) But this injustice is trivial compared to what she faces when she moves into the aggressively male-centered world of the university. While loving the unapproachable Philip and living with the ever-approaching Willie (a "mannikin, forever twinkling in front of her, white hairy legs" who casually impales her at will against the stove), Praxis finds she has to work hard at not doing well. (110) Cooking his meals and typing his essays, she still pulled an A to his C and suffered a humiliating rejection. After that she saw to it he got the A's and she the C's—"a flash in the pan" her tutor informs her. (92) But even this masochistic groveling to protect the all-important male relationship is framed when a classmate remarks, "If you behave like a whore, you get treated like a whore."

Prophetic words these, for Praxis, grown more desperate with her impaling mannikin of a lover, is later told, "the only way out is to sleep your way out." (119) And it is the practice of going off with bar-pickups that nearly undoes her when an elderly gentleman she turns a trick with turns out to be father. Yet paradoxically this unplanned but not undesired fulfillment of incestuous desires provides a boost to her damaged sense of self later on when she is bereft of everything. And, contrasted to the life-denying style of Hilda, Praxis—the active principle of Aphrodite—is as Ben says, the "centre of the universe." (128) She begins transcending her passivity (or masochism if it is) by acceptance: "she would take his guilt upon herself." (130) Perhaps this desire for the forbidden is part of the madness that splits humanity, but by allowing it and realizing that "she must be Praxis and Pattie, too, until the end of her days," (66) she may heal the fissures in the female psyche. She thus invites the madwoman out of the attic into her parlor and boudoir.

At least that is one strategy. But her dilemmas are not only personal. Praxis/Pattie is living through a major social upheaval in men's and women's lives, and her experiences are the practical living out of these forces as she embodies the author's evolving social awareness. Pattie works as a receptionist at the BBC and achieves a respectable marriage with Ivor. Ivor wants his nice Pattie and sexy Praxis in turn but only insofar as each fits into his emotional agenda. Soon she finds herself in bed with her first love Philip, having been summoned by Irma (her friend,

his wife) to look after the children while Irma gives birth (to
another's child, as it turns out). Now begins her longest and most
nearly satisfying relationship. She enjoys her work-career of
writing ad-copy for the electrical company, yet her life is split up.
"At home Praxis pretended she did not go out to work: never took
jobs home: never talked about her office day," while "in the office
she did not have a family: never talked about her home." (209-10)

By this time Irma has in Philip's eyes begun acting in a
"dykey" way by joining women's groups and going public over
sexism. Praxis is invited by her to a consciousness-raising session
ostensibly for coffee but in fact to be confronted for her sexist
ads: "God made her a woman. Love made her a mother—with a
little help from electricity." The reader sees the women at this
point through Praxis's colonized eyes: "a great many rather large,
shiny noses, strong jaws, with heads of hair, intense pairs of eyes,
pale lips, and rather dirty sets of toes cramped, stockingless, into
sandals." But the reader also sees how Praxis has come to be
socially skewed: "wearing high-heeled shoes, black mesh stockings
and a red-flowered Ossie Clark dress...her hair...dark and neat
across her face." (206)

It is a remarkable scene which confuses then disengages
the reader's sympathies and prepares for their realignment. The
women are rude and intrusive, confronting Praxis with her
unacceptable past, and Praxis resents the self-righteous posturing
of Irma especially in light of the fact that it is Praxis who has
been keeping up support payments to Irma and looking after her
children so that she can indulge her "strange behaviour...
eschewing the company of men and claiming that women were
oppressed." (208) It is later revealed that all the payments
received by Irma were donated to the women's movement, but for
the moment one is closer to Philip's views about Irma and her
friends as "basically unfeminine." Yet the fact that Praxis also is
being compromised becomes clear when she follows her next
assignment to advertise cigarettes. Accused of being "socially
irresponsible," She retorts from a position of faltering superiority:
"The trouble is I really can't take a roomful of women seriously."
(211) But if there was "something blackly depressing in the
notion of any all-female group," the "company of men was not
what it had been." (215)

The feminist catalyst occurs when Praxis is betrayed by

Serena, Philip's latest, just as Praxis had betrayed Irma; and after
correcting the grammar of a feminist broadsheet, Praxis is soon
throwing herself into "rousing editorials" for the movement.
Without realizing it, she has become a convert, operating through
practice not ideology. The odd women are not so mad after all,
but Philip's accusing them of being unfeminine lesbians sounds
rather too much like the deranged Lucy's rantings or Hilda's
paranoid vengeance cloaked in sweet rationality. And so the
women's movement offers a way out of the madness that comes
from denial and inner alienation as well as out of the madness
that comes from the socially-imposed nightmare of women trying
to live as figments of men's imagination.

Yet Praxis is still unreconciled. Having been released in
her fifties after a two-year prison term for smothering a
mongoloid baby to allow its mother a future, Praxis seems
forgotten by the society she had served. The liberated young
woman on the bus who thoughtlessly spiked her toe, causing an
incapacitating infection, is hardly sympathetic. Praxis is soon
turned into the madwoman in the basement flat, disregarded by
today's post-feminists. Ambivalence is alive and well as the first-
person narrator's lonely ruminations on madness and old age
provide a counterpoint to unwarranted enthusiasm over social
reform movements. On and on she talks until the very end when—
discharged under the unrecognized name of Pattie Parker—she is
rediscovered by her loyal followers and welcomed for what she
has become—a heroine.

No longer the other in sexist society, Praxis suits herself in
feminism. She is representative, she is oppressed, she is
continually being sex-typed by others in such ways as to deny her
selfhood and empowerment. To this extent, the novel is solidly
feminist; but her mother also mis-identifies her and confounds
male-made madness by her own manipulations; in addition, even
within her narrow confines, Praxis is implicated in her life by
being reminded she has choices. Mainly owing to this entrenched
ambivalence, however, and to its binary structure, the novel
remains poised between feminist consciousness and feminist
commitment, but the fulcrum on which it is poised is that of
highly accomplished art. Feminism is clearly validated because
it confronts a male power-system which meshes character with
destiny (one gets the impression that Weldon, who has disavowed

active participation in the cause, is here paying her dues in her own inimitable way). But along with this acceptance is a more profound and pervasive sense of the tough core in men and women of blind egotism and cruelty that renders our human condition if not hopeless, at best tragicomic: "I used to think men were wicked," Weldon lamented, "now I think *people* are wicked."[30]

Can the woman writer then have her feminist commitment and her creative license? Or are the two incompatible? Assume, for the sake of analogy, that you are lost in the Yucatan jungles with only the vague memory of a map to help you locate the nearest village. You have never been here, but having been lost before, you have acquired survival skills. You have your senses, intuitions, skills, and a bit of memory. If you manage to find your way out, you have created a solution to the problem. That solution is the creative process. If you had earlier met someone first and he/she pointed to anything from a donkey-track to a highway-sign, that is Feminism, Socialism, Existentialism, or any other -*ism* that promises a ready-made alternative. "Writing and *isms* are two different things," so Margaret Atwood muses over feminism's reversion to ideological correctness: "some emotions were okay to express—for instance, negative emotions against men. Others were not okay—for instance, negative emotions about women."[31] "I'm always wary of '-*isms*,' Wendy Perriam concurs. "They're usually too clear-cut, too 'cut and dried,' and I start getting uncomfortable, seeing the grey areas in the middle, the subtleties, the non-sequiturs, the unanswered questions or bits that don't fit the scheme."[32] "From the point of view of those who want a neatly ordered universe," Atwood continues, "writers are messy and undependable. They often see life as complex and mysterious, with ironies and loose ends, not as a tidy system of goodies and baddies usefully labelled."[33]

Simply put, writers grapple with the raw; -*isms* are the cooked. Academic theorists want their -*isms*; creative writers affirm their agency. To a greater or lesser degree, they appreciate the weight of personal and ideological baggage everyone bears but also realize that creativity entails ingenuity and mastery. They know that others have found themselves in similar plights before, that there are only a limited number of solutions and most have been tried, yet there are many clues to the careful eye and one succeeds only by finding one's own way—by trailblazing. In her own time and in her own way, Jane Austen accomplished it, but subsequent writers know that others who tread in her footsteps are likely to accomplish only oblivion. In Fay Weldon's words, "there is no correct way—you have to be open and receptive."[34] And you have to cast a cold eye on postmodernism's claim that even the raw has been pre-cooked and creativity mere culture-work. In the prevailing idiom, sex-work (prostitution) is to making love as culture-work is to creativity.

But if the creative process itself remains mysterious where every successful solution has to be unique, does this also mean that by definition it cannot be duplicated? Moreover, the creative writer's need to achieve mastery—however one chooses to express it—e.g., as making sense of oneself through making sense of the world, or vice versa—suggests that he/she is grappling with a certain amount of inner turmoil, chaotic confusion, and just plain private conflicts, which are resolvable at least partially or temporarily through mastery over the materials of the creative medium. "No man or woman from the outside could prescribe to me what to do," writes Edna O'Brien. "I have enough trouble keeping madness at bay."[35] Women writers who thus distance themselves from feminism have their reasons: it is to protect what no one else can give them. Postmodernism, which presides over the death of the author, also has its reasons: the writer's embodiment of the creative process confounds theory's pretense that creative activity is circumscribed by poets' strong readings of their progenitors and reduced to their adroit reshufflings of others' texts, much like critics. Why can't anxieties over oppressive hierarchies and an exclusionary ideal of quality be recognized without acceding to a denial of difference?

Chief among the problematic -isms for the present inquiry, feminism as idée reçue does not always share woman's creative space comfortably; but feminism as something to be imagined and as an ongoing problem for the individual or the society may be welcomed. If on the one hand, the writer maps for her characters' plights solutions that are already familiar and hence readily available to her readers, then it is fair to conclude that the creative task has been scotched. On the other hand there may be

various ways out of the wilderness. Jane Austen, for example,
seems to have radically doubted the nuptials she dutifully led her
characters to.   More apropos, suppose that—out in the jungle
again—one stumbled onto the wagon tracks of an old mining road
and stayed with it for awhile; then it might advance one's
progress by being put to a purpose different from the one
originally intended.   Thuswise may women's (re-)visionary
writing of men's texts become functional. Women would then
mine men's work for their own purposes. Never an absolute,
creative originality is construed in the postmodern as pastiche but
need not suffer from being experienced as patchwork—rough
textures better awakening the sense of touch—either as something
strange or, equally valid, something strangely familiar. Finally,
to extend the analogy, if gender affects the writer's way out of
his/her creative wilderness, women may be guided by a
matricentric compass—one which they are relatively free to
follow, fool with, or even fling aside.
        Certainly, no novel from a feminist hand tinkers more
mischievously with notions of what-women-want and their
vaunted biocentric destiny than Weldon's *Puffball.* Liffey and
Richard are contemporary urbanites lured to the countryside.
Liffey's dream of a rural cottage proves to be nature's way of
focusing her needs onto a nest, and Richard agrees to the move if
she agrees to a baby. Liffey at twenty-eight wants to produce a
novel not a child, but there is an outer Liffey at odds with an
inner one: a "cosmic Liffey, hormones buzzing, heart beating,
blood surging, pawn in nature's game." (15) Here the source of
madness arises not from a split between sexual affirmation and
sexual prohibition *à la* Drabble's *The Waterfall*, or between an
inner voice of sanity and patriarchal scripting *à la Praxis*, but
between the imperious forces of nature and the dalliances of self:
for the culturally-constituted Liffey knows little if any of the
biocentric Liffey. She has no sense that, far from a wise,
protective mother, nature is "but the sum of the genetic chance
events that have led down one evolutionary path or another." (16)
So when Liffey feels cross with Richard and then resents it when
he asks if her period is late, it is moot whether her hostility was
"caused by undue retention of fluid, or in fact the result of his
behavior." She naturally "assumed the latter," for "it is not

pleasant for a young woman to believe that her behavior is dictated by her chemistry." (15-17) It's bad enough when anatomy veers so dangerously close to destiny, but the countryside itself is rendered matriarchal by the rule of a cruelly meddlesome hag named Mag, who in a male text would betray entrenched misogyny. Mag is fiendishly jealous of Liffey's fecundity in contrast with her own recent sterility and uses all her spells and potions to rob Liffey of her newborn, until late in the game when her consort Tucker reasserts a welcome—in this context— patriarchal order. In the end, the characters' multiple plots yield to nature's singular one: "peripheral events leading towards the main end of your life, which was to produce me. You were always the bit-player." (240) Genetic transmission is nature's star turn.

It is readily observed but rarely noted that while women in society struggle for freedom from reproductive tyranny, women in fiction still struggle for reproductive fulfillment. However ultimately construed, the observation confirms a matricentric base to women's texts that picks up a few spins but remains remarkably unaffected by women's revolutions or cultural backlashes.

This is curious but not problematic unless the writer turns his/her gender into a gender-trap. It can happen when one's gender shifts from a facilitating role for accessing experience to becoming the object of the creative quest. The mirage for men may arise from the overflow of the psychic energies marshalled in escaping from woman (originally mother) that bestows upon them an ideally-tough autonomy or that aggression does not entail reparation; for women the illusion may be that by accessing their child-bearing properties life's major obstacles dissolve.

Deborah Moggach's *Hot Water Man*, a contemporary Passage to Pakistan, veers toward but narrowly averts this danger. When a young company-man, Donald Manley, last of a family prominent in the days of empire, relocates with his young wife Christine to Karachi, occasions arise for clashes among the cultures, classes, and sexes. While Donald grows a blond (please note) moustache and embarks on various nostalgic trips seeking family origins, Christine gives vent to her restlessness and boredom by shopping excursions among the native quarters and

by job-hunting. Soon the exotic culture has widened the gulf
between the sexes. Donald wants her to act the proper role, while
Christine, who has previously had her consciousness raised, taunts
Donald with his sexual colonialism—an example of how a
nonfeminist work absorbs feminist politics.[36] Before long the
Manleys, whose marriage is laced by happy memories of courtship
and a wish for family, are subjected to some evenhanded satire.
Donald's sterile marriage is underscored by his company's
product—the Pill; and his eventual quest to relieve the white
man's burden by locating a missing half-brother turns up a quite
prosperous, urbane tailor. Christine is lured into posing for a
commercial photographer only to find her own larger-than-life
photo on billboards for tampons, something no self-respecting
Pakistani woman, she soon learns, would ever consider doing.

More ominously, the sexual politics chafing her marriage
bonds leads her to an ill-advised sexual rendezvous with one
Sultan Rahim, a business entrepreneur with an Oriental macho
appeal. By the time she finds herself pregnant, her distant
Donald has come around. Since they had earlier engaged in one
of their baby-making sessions, the suspense in the final pages
turns on paternity. The moment of truth is also the moment of
birth, and when enough of the baby shows—that is, its blond hair—
their marriage is saved. Whether one remarks on how odd an
ending for "an emergent feminist" as the jacket has it, or on the
great power of childbirth and motherhood in women's lives, the
matricentric mechanism for releasing the plot-springs is visible.

How gender-inflected wishes can fuel creativity as well as
direct narrative and how well fiction can grapple with feminism
may be best instanced in Sara Maitland's *Daughter of Jerusalem*,
which occurs entirely within the new cultural spaces of feminism
and almost entirely within the character of a committed feminist.
Feminism is a firmly established reality—present and accepted
from the first page on, never doubted. Yet nothing is smooth or
easy about this work that promises to be a feminist novel but
succeeds by breaking the rules of the feminist novel. Liz Jones's
female friends are all staunch feminists. Around their
consciousness-raising group they sort our their differences and
provide mutual support. Except for her husband Ian, men are
either peripheral or problematic like the formidable Dr. Marshall,

who advises Liz to consult a psychiatrist because she may be
rejecting her feminine role (in good-humored defiance, Liz wears
an "I-Am-A-Humourless-Feminist" tee-shirt).   Good male
chauvinist that he is, the doctor disapproves of feminist displays
and adopts a paternal attitude toward his patient. But he also
operates a prominent sub-fertility clinic, and Liz is seeing him
because she and Ian desperately want a child. Since there is no
biological barrier to her pregnancy and Ian's sperm count is
healthy, the doctor concludes that "sub-consciously" she is
rejecting the idea. In fact the only time she has ovulated in
recent months was while Ian was away (the "symptom" will repeat
itself later in the story). So the complacent physician may be on
target, and Liz is compelled, over the nine chapters named for the
months, to reflect on her motives for wanting a child, the kind of
person she is, the kind of man she wishes to conceive with. At
full term, she delivers something—product of her creative labors
and the promise of a reproductive future.

The novel, which is the immediate product of her labors,
also delivers: a complex grasp of the human dilemmas of an
inwardly-torn feminist who realizes that the wish for a child was
a "craving...in her gut" that "could only be alleviated there." (74)
Adoption is thus ruled out especially in respect to "ex-gays with
Marxist tendencies" like Ian who need to feel sexually adequate.
But then if there is nothing wrong with her and if the doctor
knows so little about women, why can't she conceive? Doubting
her desires, she revives a childhood memory of maternal rejection
based on her mother's wanting a boy. If she had wasted her
childhood wishing she were a boy, would she now squander her
adulthood "trying to prove she was a real woman"? (12) Or was it
all for Ian? To give him a child in order to keep his love, "while
secretly denying him because she was jealous of him for being a
boy," seemed on reflection an unlikely scenario. (13) Taller and
older than Ian, she has delivered him from his love for other
males as well as from "his fear of women." Missing the secondary
sex-characteristics of some of her friends, Liz is flat-chested, and
seems to have deflected her maternal tendencies onto him ("I like
to mummy Ian. It's true. My little boy who I, only I, can
introduce to the beauties of heterosexual love"; 160). Still their
sexual love for each other is convincing. Moreover, Ian is
sensitive, considerate, devoted, and not pushy—a type usually

typed out of feminist fiction. Yet on both, the strain becomes obsessive, unbearable, and finally bursts into a violence of name-calling and blows. Liz reverts to her promiscuous past long enough to have sex with her companionable boss, following which the extremity of Ian's and her passion, returns them to a saner course. Other events have also left their mark. Not wanting to march at an abortion-rights rally, Liz has a temporary falling-out with her more militant sisters over strategy.

At this point the narrative seems to swerve into a moral context: individual conscience versus communal good. But the cause is never seriously doubted, and Liz manages to join in despite her jealousy and resentment over women who have the luxury to conceive and to terminate at will. Women's collective right to choose (abortion) takes precedence over the individual's right not to march (for abortion). Her spirited defense of this right may win a bit of grudging respect from Dr. Marshall, who had seen her photo in the media, but he kindly warns her against overexcitement—fecundity is weighed against sexual politics.

As a literary agent Liz also questions her chosen career as a kind of midwife for productive writers, all the more so when Amanda, one of her successful authors, gives the issue an edge with her book about the blessings of motherhood. At the coming-out party, Amanda places Ian's hand on her swelling tummy where the sensation of tiny kicking feet sexually excites him. Liz is also driven into her own past to confront her feelings of guilt about sex aroused by her sexual initiation at college; ignoring an urgent telephone message from her mother, she belatedly learns her father has suffered a stroke. Sex signifies fatal betrayal: psychologically, loss of the father relation. (102) Perhaps her tie to needy Ian is a way of avoiding these feelings, though the otherwise insightful Liz never considers this, and her having bedded down with him for ten months before engaging in sex could be taken as self-punitive measures against forbidden pleasure.

With her mother Liz is equally unreconciled. A memory about menarche focuses her guilty embarrassment for starting later than her peers and failing to notice when it belatedly began between classes. On an emotional level, it was her punishment for her previous pleasurable explorations, and her mother showed no sympathetic interest. Now, an auto accident that hospitalizes her

mother occasions a tentative reconciliation. When mother later on
gives the couple a large sum of money from the sale of the family
home, Liz and Ian are faced with moving out of the small
apartment without the pretext of moving to larger quarters in
order to start a family. Such a move would have to be based on
mutual commitment. Ian locates a suitable house, but it is too
large for two. They will take it anyway and invite in a feminist
friend who is about to give birth. Through facing infertility, the
couple begin coming to terms with larger uncertainties, yet desires
for a child persists. A Christmas gift to Liz of a warm puppy
only makes her miserable, and later returning home, Ian bitterly
doubts his masculinity. At least they have become clear about
their love for each other; but in other respects, the author seems
to have painted herself into a corner. Liz's craving for a baby
persists as her way of affirming her womanhood; but if a baby
can make one feel a happy and fulfilled woman, then what is
feminism about?

A way out comes through a prevalent theme in feminist
and woman-centered fiction, one that is firmly if obliquely
developed here. It could be called the quest for a matrix in all its
variants: as womb, origin, mother, source, self. Paradoxically, it
is the disparaged Dr. Marshall whose incessant examinations puts
Liz most directly in touch with her womb. Stretched out with
"her feet up in the stirrups," she submits to what Dr. M. call his
"nasty little procedures," and acquires a "strange knowledge" of
those parts of her which have no knowledge of their own: "the
pear shape of the womb, the fallopian tubes waving, delicately
inviting, at the ovaries." (35) Later in radiography, she watches
the television screen reveal the dark "secrets of her bony pelvis":
the "fine cliffs of bone and the harbours between them where the
baby could lie and wait, protected by the craggy pier of her
spine." (71-2) A liquid is poured in and "suddenly, appearing on
the screen, the shape of the magic organ—the Garden of Eden and
the seat of madness—it looked moonlike, so close to the moon in its
moods and fluctuations." She thinks back when her former macho
lover had accused her of being hysterical (evoking the Greek root
and malady—*hyster*=womb; hysteria as a flying womb), "and
watching her womb bathed in inner light, the sting had fallen
away from the word, it meant only that she was the possessor of

this perfect thing, glowing in the dark....Beautiful." And it is not
wandering as in the mythical aetiology of hysteria, but rooted in
its proper center. Through the miracle of technology a woman's
womb is restored to her as her evolving self-consciousness, and she
thanks the technicians profusely for the magic show. Safe to
assume then is that the earlier "panic and fear" over menarche,
the sense of being punished for pleasure, the guilt over loss of
virginity, have been alleviated by this innerspace voyage into
positive selfhood. Barrenness may be a curse still, but it is not
one she has brought on herself; moreover, the promised land of
fertility is within her. But the classical patricentric cure of
conception to anchor the unmoored womb can be negotiated only
after being transformed through matricentric self-discovery. It
is also equally clear that the child-bearing wish is susceptible to
all the emotional experiences of one's past—it may be felt as a
simple craving, but along the way it has become severely
overdetermined. In Liz's fantasy-system, the womb signifies the
inner mother, an internalized good-object, which the father-
physican validates.

Woven into Liz's matricentric quest for gendered origins
are set-pieces on the lives of strong women out of the Bible,
models to bolster modern women in analogous situations. Liz is
not very religious (her father was), but these passages nonetheless
focus her conflicts in a religious frame that aims to deepen them
and provide strength (though more for the reader than for her).
The title also suggests that modern woman may be a "daughter of
Jerusalem," in contrast a son of David—in other words that women
can find themselves in Christianity. Supposedly, this tells Liz to
relinquish any male-oriented and rather grandiose claim as Ian's
"saviour" (62) and settle for saving their marriage by mothering
their child instead of him. The last of these Biblical prototypes
closes out the story by evoking the Virgin giving birth at
Bethlehem, counterposing Liz's Christmas-party discovery that
her normally punctual period is twelve hours overdue. The
"craving," the "lust," (12) the uncompromisable wish to have a
child has finally become a "hope." After nine months (and nine
chapters), she has found the strength to conceive.

Liz's matricentric quest has taken her beyond feminist
messages that the "desire to have children is imposed on women,
externally, by a sexist society," (12) yet less away from feminism

per se than toward a fuller recognition of the legitimacy of
woman's right to choose even if it means not to bear a child
(including abortion). It has led her into the vortex of male
technology where she paradoxically discovers her own fertile
center and where male labels of madness as female hysteria are
pursued to a supposed source that turns out to be an organ
innocent of blame. Between woman's traditional place and her
liberated spheres, from her conscious longings to her most private
spaces, the narrative has woven its quest. It expands in time as it
takes her and the reader back through the situation of her own
mother and Biblical analogies. When she finally stands on the
brink of motherhood, her matricentric concerns have merged with
her quest for matrix.

Liz's voyage-in suggests that woman's quest for values or
selfhood need not be set adrift in a sea of narcissistic absorption
or smashed against the rocks of masochism. Nor need it be fatally
mapped out by a cutthroat crew aboard the pirate ship Patriarchy.
But it does suggest that, however differing from male patterns of
coming-of-age novels or returning-home epics, this woman's
odyssey will have the kind of distinctively circular pattern
inscribed by matricentric.

Maitland's *Virgin Territory* is both a struggle against
helpless rage, guilt, and masochism and a "stategy of reclamation"
that is securely bounded by matricentric time frames.[37] It
begins with the rape of an American missionary by the "Security
Forces" in a South American village. Immediately the focus shifts
from the victim (who soon recovers) to her fellow nuns—to Sister
Kate, whose initial anger over their impotence precipitates her
into revolutionary tactics and a violent death, and more centrally
to Sister Anna, whose initial detachment and lack of response
signal a more profound emotional breakdown. No longer able to
cope, she is sent to her Mother House in upstate New York and
then packed off to London to carry on a research project on
colonialization. As her travels end her journeys begin. These
cover an exhaustive exploration of the inner meaning of
sisterhood, the implications of virginity tied to spiritual
commitment within a male hierarchy, and the tenacity of
internalized voices of authority. Out of these issues emerge a
quest for the origins of self and the means for its renewal;

conducted within a lesbian feminist ambience, this quest is as profoundly matricentric as the earlier one.

Two years before, Sisters Kate's and Anna's journey down the Amazon had placed them into direct contact with nature's steamy profusion and each other. At the end of the novel, Anna reflects on her father's not wanting the five daughters he had raised to go searching for their mother—an individual instance of her Church's patriarchal point: "The Fathers [her voices] do not want the daughters to leave them," and these patriarchs punish in subtle ways acts of disobedience and disloyalty. In counterpoint, Anna thinks of Demeter searching for her child Persephone, who once found she could "stroll easily between heaven and hell and gather flowers wherever she desires." Feeling herself an orphan needing rescue, Anna reverses her condition; but she will seek the mother she never knew or the home she never had. Somehow, "she must go back to the womb and be born again in the power of the spirit." This being literally impossible, a metaphorical solution is found. She will go back "to the dark damp belly" of the "Amazon valley where she has once been with Kate. She will go to the headwaters and float down the great river until she comes to the land of the mothers and she will stay there and learn to be a grown-up woman." (204)

Before reaching this stage, she undergoes a series of agonized awakenings inscribed in matricentric time. At the end of the year, she was told by Mother Superior, she can decide what to do: "'nine months,' she smiled, 'like a pregnancy.'" The prefigured birth will be into her renewed self. And while dallying at the British Museum, she is advised to get outside herself and so volunteers to help a family with a brain-damaged child, Cara. She must be exercised continually in order to stimulate her brain to develop new centers and circuits of growth. Cara becomes another Voice that speaks to Anna of the chaos of life before a self emerges, of the resistance to change, finally, of a more primordial wisdom than the counsels of the morally vicious Fathers. Anna's psychodrama is further enriched by Karen, a feminist intellectual who falls in love with her. It is Anna's growing realization that she also loves Karen but cannot carry through until her spiritual and emotional dilemmas have been resolved. Concurrently, Cara's mother Fiona has given birth to a healthy son and refuses to return home until Cara, who has made marginal progress, is placed elsewhere. The burden of this painful decision falling upon Anna and the child's father epitomizes the interlocked loss-and-gain that life exacts from the living. In near despair, Anna drifts to the tattooist whom her feminist friends had visited and bares her breasts to receive a sacrificial cross between them; but he introduces alternatives, and Anna settles on the figure of Christ as fish to be drawn over her heart. With this ambiguous act, she readies herself for her matricentric quest for the mythic sources of Amazonian womanhood where a new synthesis of feminist and Christian values may be conceived.

Although Weldon's and Maitland's women inhabit the same world, biocentrically pivoted on pregnancy and birth, their subjective experience differs substantially. Praxis struggles over several decades to realize her own matrix in opposition to powerful, sexually-charged naming forces. In her constructed roles, Praxis encounters an emergent feminism negatively, which only through a gradual assimilation is validated. Maitland's narratives begin where Weldon's leave off: feminism is an accepted dimension of her characters' selves and milieu, and so the emphasis is less on a dialectical struggle than an internal conflict with religious and moral complexities. The gender system recedes in order to explore subjective aspects of women's continuing needs to bear children, to affirm sisterhood, to chart the gendered self.

Taken together, the deconstructing of desire through a quest for origins in Carter's new Eve, the splicing of story-telling and impregnation in Farmer's Eve, the reproductive plot-twist of Moggach's Christine, the traditional moral dilemmas of Maitland's women in a feminist age, and the abiding humanism of Weldon's Praxis collectively affirm the diversity of feminist narratives and their solid literary appeal. Composed in an age when women are freer than ever to write as they choose, they are especially informative. The tenacity of matricentric features insures an inner cohesion that suggests enduring dimensions to women's writing. Their earlier texts are thus rendered less restricted than had been thought and their more recent texts apparently more conservative than would have been predicted.

Notes

1. From a letter to *SpareRib* 209 (Feb, 1990): 5, signed by "Manchester Feminist."

2. Instead of telling all sides of the story, for example, women would end up as the title of Molly Hite's study proposes, telling only *The Other Side of the Story*, 5-8; Deborah Johnson's gynecentric reading of Iris Murdoch concludes that she "reveals an in-touchness with some vital feminist issues, and can speak to the feminist need for re-readings of the world, even though she cannot be claimed as a feminist writer" (*Iris Murdoch*, 112).

3. Though still largely a male enclave, pornography for women or its more respectable sister, Erotica, occasionally appears, as in Lonnie Barbach's anthology, *Pleasures*; lesbian erotica has also begun mainstreaming. Meanwhile, feminist scholars like Ann Snitow hold that romances remain women's preferred equivalent to pornography.

4. Katharine M. Rogers, "The Feminine Novel," in *Feminism in Eighteenth-Century England*, 150.

5. Rogers, 151. Similarly, the novels studied by Nancy K. Miller in *The Heroine's Text* follow a pattern of social incorporation through marriage. Nicola Beauman's survey of the "Woman's Novel" from 1919 to 1939 discerns a "category of fiction written for [though not always by] women," which "have little action and less histrionics." It is about the "drama of the undramatic, the steadfast dailiness of a life that brings its own rewards, the intensity of the emotions and, above all, the importance of human relationships" (*A Very Great Profession*, 5).

6. James Woodress, *Willa Cather: A Literary Life*, 245; Marleen Barr, "Isak Dinesen's Female Artists as Precursors to Contemporary Feminist Fabulators," *Feminism, Utopia, and Narrative*, eds. Libby Falk Jones and Sarah Webster Godwin, 21-33; while Margaret Drabble calls *The Waterfall* "the most female   of all my books," Rose (*The Novels of Margaret*

Drabble) goes her one better and calls it "perhaps the most radically feminist of Drabble's books" (68).

7. Katherine Sobba Green *The Courtship Novel*, 1-2, 7.

8. Patricia Duncker, *Sisters and Strangers*, 17-8; Deborah Silverton Rosenfelt similarly locates feminist fiction in "the *bildung* and the utopia," and although her examples are American, she traces a "mythic progress from oppression, suffering, victimization, through various stages of awakening consciousness to active resistance and, finally to some form of victory, transformation, or transcendence of despair" ("Feminism, 'Postfeminism,' and Contemporary Women's Fiction," *Tradition and the Talents of Women*, ed. Florence Howe, 270. Both *A Piece of the Night* and *Praxis* fit this paradigm.

9. Rosalind Coward, "Are Women's Novels Feminist Novels?" in *The New Feminist Criticism*, 237-8. Judi M. Roller (*The Politics of the Feminist Novel*) requires that in feminist novels, the central character(s) "must be female and must represent women in generally as well as woman specifically." These works "portray women as a group oppressed" and "relationships between men and women are shown to be power-structured"; the "situations" are shown to be dependent upon "economic, political, and social systems" (4-5).

10. Gayle Greene, *Changing the Story*, 2.

11. Carole Spedding is quoted as one of the Feminist Fortnight organizers for 1990 in Zoë Fairbairns' "It's a Feminist Fortnight!" *Everywoman* (June, 1990): 12.

12. Kathleen Blake (*Love and the Woman Question in Victorian Literature*) considers another Hardy novel in "Sue Bridehead: A Woman of the Feminist Movement," 146-70.

13. John Haffenden, *Novelists in Interview*, 314.

14. Martha Nussbaum's review of Andrea Dworkin's *Mercy, Boston Review* 17:3-4 (1992): 26.

15. Adrienne Rich in *"When We Dead Awaken*: Writing as Re-Vision" (*College English*, October, 1972), advises this "act of looking back, of seeing with fresh eyes, of entering an old text from a new direction" as an "act of survival" for women writers.

16. Moira Ferguson, *First Feminists*, 157.

17. Richard Harvey, "Early English Feminism and the Creation Myth."

18. Michelene Wandor, *Gardens of Eden*, 2.

19. Philip Roth, *The Breast*, 13.

20. Angela Carter, *The Sadeian Woman and the Ideology of Pornography*, 5-6. Her interpretations of pornography owe much to Steven Marcus's *The Other Victorians*.

21. *Sadeian Woman*, 16.

22. The text's vision of America seems to derive from someone traveling West, watching lots of television, and reading *Time* magazine along with Donald Barthelme. In an interview, Carter recognized the great disparity between her intentions and her readers' responses (Haffenden, 85-87). But the United States tends to refract strangely in the texts of this study. Sara Maitland's Americans slide into English idioms in *Virgin Territory*; the peaceful Hopis in Jeanette Winterson's *Sexing the Cherry* behave in the worst Hollywood fashion by kidnapping Spaniards.

23. Nancy Armstrong, "The Nineteenth-Century Jane Austen."

24. Sherry Ortner, "Is Female to Male as Nature Is to Culture?"

25. Elizabeth T. Hayes, *Images of Persephone*; Huang Mei, *Transforming the Cinderella Dream.*

26. Grace Stewart, *A New Mythos, The Novel of the Artist as Heroine*; Nancy K. Miller, *The Heroine's Text*; Annis Pratt, *Archetypal Patterns in Women's Fiction*; Carol Pearson, *The Female Hero in American and British Literature*; Alika Barnstone, "Women and the Garden: Andrew Marvell, Emilia Lanier, and Emily Dickinson"; Stevie Davies, *Emily Bronte: The Artist as a Free Woman*; Estella Lauter, *Women as Mythmakers*; William Tyrrell, *Amazons, A Study in Athenian Mythmaking*; Lee Edwards, *Psyche as Hero*; Clarissa Pinkola Estes, *Women Who Run with the Wolves.*

27. Hayes, 3.

28. The "myth is always the same: innumerable variants on Falling in Love, on courtship, on marriage, on the failure of courtship and marriage, How She Got Married, How She Did Not Get Married" (Joanna Russ, "What Can a Heroine Do?" 9). DuPlessis also maintains that the traditional "romance plot, broadly speaking, is a trope for the sex-gender system as a whole" (*Writing Beyond the Ending*, 5). Rosalind Miles, on the other hand, argues that from "its foundation the novel has been and remains *the* female form" and therefore giving women readers what they wanted (*The Female Form*, 208). Moreover, for her, romance is privileged as "that form within the novel which is women's and women's alone" and thus "women writers must order, interpret, dramatize and heighten these events and preoccupations of women's lives, because if one thing is certain, it's that the boys won't." (34) DuPlessis's totalizing of culture as site of oppressive ideology excludes the bio/psycholgical dimensions of women's experience.

29. Gloria Steinem, *Revolution from Within.* DuPlessis also views romances as a "compensatory social and narrative practice" that women turn to when they "lose economic power," but the strong sales record of romances throughout the recent decades of women's progress argues for a principle of simultaneity as evidenced in Steinem's life *(Writing Beyond the Ending*, 2).

30. Fay Weldon interviewed in the *Washington Post* (24 April 1988). London feminists, especially Sara Maitland, who have insisted in conversations on excluding Weldon as a feminist writer, may have preferred her sensibility to be filtered through a more consistent socialism rather than through the skeptical liberalism inscribing *Praxis.*

31. Margaret Atwood, "If You Can't Say something Nice," 21.

32. Wendy Perriam, interviewed by me in June, 1984.

33. Atwood, 21.

34. Weldon, *Washington Post* (24 April 1988).

35. Edna O'Brien, *Writers at Work, Paris Review,* 251-2.

36. For example, Rosalind Miles writes in *The Fiction of Sex,* "Women writers were more influential than men in keeping women" in place: "their colonization by male supremacists was complete; they policed each other" (62). "Several feminist critics have recently used Frantz Fanon's model of colonialism to describe the relationship between the male (parent) culture and female (colonized) literature" (Gilbert, *Madwoman in the Attic,* 74).

37. Andrzej Gasiorek, *Post-War British Fiction,* 125.

3

Writing Beyond the Matricentric?
Feminist to Post-Feminist Narrative

The grand narrative has lost its credibility,
regardless of what mode of unification it uses,
regardless of whether it is a speculative narrative
or a narrative of emancipation.   I define
postmodern as incredulity toward metanarratives.
—Jean-Francois Lyotard[1]

...the frequency [of postmodern] attacks on reason
(and also on Enlightenment universalism) has been
used to discredit feminist attacks on local
traditions that subordiante them.   These
experiences have confirmed me in my conviction
that feminism needs to be able to avail itself of
robust notions of reason and objectivity.
—Martha Nussbaum[2]

I

Michele Roberts: Deconstructing the Lacanian Body

Feminism has done lots of things for me. All my
strength comes from it.   Through it I have
reclaimed being feminine....I have learned I can be
anything I like. I have reinvented myself.
—Michele Roberts[3]

An exemplary work of feminist determination is Michele Roberts'
A Piece of the Night (1978). Written in the high-precision prose
style of modernism, it is finally less painterly prose for art's sake
than literary pointillism for a purpose: modernist style serving a
feminist cause. Unless this is granted, the Joycean influence, for
example, would be too intrusive. In the Joycean *Portrait* manner,
for example, Roberts eschews quotation marks for dashes, and
adapts a modified interior-monologue/impersonal-narrative
technique, allowing her to weave in and out of her central figure,
Julie Franchot, who grows up in a hothouse climate of French

Catholicism and English convent schools. Moreover, Julie brings
a Joycean retinue of guilt ("monstrous desires" to confess to a
"ghostly father"), ambivalent authority figures, and power's
seductive lure in a religious vocation. Even the resolution affords
a Joycean variation: Julie will forge the conscience of her gender
by writing about a ghostly mother, literally a heroic nun of the
previous century, whose spirit Julie will continue into the present.

In the theory of women's authorship as (re)visionary of
male texts, the line between revision and derivation continually
criss-crosses.[4]   In the present instance the line dissolves
differently because Julie's real coming-of-age is distinctively un-
Joycean, though not singular.[5] Moreover, this text has a more
pervasive original vision to revise. If Joyce provides an aesthetic
model for this Portrait of the Artist as a Young Feminist, the
psychological model derives from the French psychoanalyst
Jacques Lacan's theory of the mirror stage.[6] All told, Roberts'
text is richly overdetermined.

On the eve of departing from "the chaos of London for the
well-ordered terrain of family" in Normandy, Julie gazes from
her room near her young child Bertha and her lover Jenny into a
window that only "gives her back herself, solitary spectator." (20,
18) Separated from husband Ben, Julie is now in her late twenties
and living in his house with their child and her lesbian friends.
She is caught in several binds: about to go off ostensibly to "nurse"
her "dangerously ill" mother, she is in competition with Bertha, "in
need of comfort, of consolation as much as any child"—that is, the
undeveloped mother-within needs nurturing. (15-16) Meanwhile
she is as upset over having to share Jenny with another as over
her own possessive jealousy. To top it off, Ben, whom she left for
female friends, has taken a mistress and would like to put the
house (a turtle-shell version of mother) on the market. The news
hit her like fists "in the face": "the skin on the front of Julie's
body rips off like rags, the air is raw on her exposed flesh, she
huddles like a foetus." All the same, in Normandy, she insists that
her conventional parents accept her lifestyle and treat her as an
adult while she clings to her childhood entitlements. News
accidentally broken that her parents are soon to move away
intensifies her odd-girl-out feelings and panics her into dropping
the family soup tureen where it smashes into "twenty odd
fragments." (152) Thus externalized is her susceptibility to inner

fragmentation along with fears and anxieties excited by rage.

A memory sequence from her tenth year clarifies these liabilities. Following a fainting spell at Sunday Mass where she is kindly assisted by her grandfather, she is sitting at the family dinner table and indulging a grandiose fantasy of flying about the countryside with her much admired Tante Juliette when her grandfather's voice startles her into spilling her glass, drawing attention to her, and provoking her dismissal in tears of humiliation. It is one of those everyday events whose ill-timing can elicit far-ranging, even traumatizing, effects.

Lying on her bed, she "stares at the mirror facing her two feet away" on the wardrobe door, and does not see her own image. Over the mirror a "knot of formal flowers" turns "into an owl, and then into a hideous face, leering at her, mocking her." (34) Feeling helpless and abandoned, she fears a ghost will enter when it grows dark. She sits up and "remembers the mirror downstairs and its route to forbidden places." Inside the wardrobe her mother keeps the sheets that "belong to the bed her father sleeps in with her mother," where sometimes Julie would be allowed to slide in, "curl against her mother," and feel whole.

Sexual issues, however, have arisen, stimulated earlier by her emotional interest in her grandfather whose stern reproof at the table has disrupted a fragile new alignment and propelled a regressive quest to regain the security of her mother's body when she could fit "herself into the curve of her mother's breasts and stomach, soft under her nightgown" and listen to her father harmlessly "splashing" in the nearby cubicle. She remembers that when "her mother started trying to tell her the facts of life," she "resolutely shut her ears."[7] But behind the protective good mother is the child's own destructive rage which terrifies her as it reshapes the mother's image into something monstrous. This is what transpires in the wardrobe mirror as the "frightening face" dissolves to owl then into flower knot; alone and unrescued, Julie hardens her heart against her aunt, and in a revenge fantasy sees her "boxed up in a barrel of spikes" like the goose-girl's wicked step-sister. With the rage externalized and for the moment at least bound up in fantasy, a new "girl looks out of the place beyond the mirror, silent, determined, sad. She is very like Julie, but taller, and thinner." This idealized double "does not look as though she ever cries, gets angry, upsets her parents or loses her mother's love. She is hard and brave and clever, admired by everybody for being so grown-up."

Julie "tells her feelings to nobody"; only her double "knows what she is feeling," and this twin is "Jules, even tougher than a boy." (35)   Replacing Tante Juliette as ideal-I, Jules defends against self-fragmentation, protects Julie's fragile self-esteem, and assists in regaining through this newer, mixed identity the love Julie needs from her mother. Never quite the whole-self, Jules transforms the jeopardized narcissism into an ideal-self to be submerged until she materializes in the sisterly bond with Jennie—for Jules per se does not reappear.

As signifier of the Lacanian ideal-I, Jules is the child's *méconnaissance* (misperception) taken for a "true" identification. For Lacan, this idealized self-image enters the child's subjective repertoire of the Imaginary. The mirror image is false because it mistakenly represents (replaces) the messy, awkward, and ill-coordinated child as a unified whole and shields it defensively from its segmented body—*le corps morcelé*—the child's own frightening other, creatively distorted by rage. But in the present (fictional) context, the false or imaginary I assumes adaptive capacities beyond Lacan's paradigm (which in their overly mental formulations slight affects).

This clinical subtext clarifies the method of naming in the text. Julie believes she is so-named because her father Julien had wanted a boy with "curly hair and straight strong limbs" (2): as the child's desire to realize the parent's desire, Jules fulfills both the father's ideal and the mother's longed-for phallus as posited in Lacanian discourse.   Jules functions, however, as Julie's idealized inner strength gained from a measure of good-enough care. But Julie's full name is Julienne, which the frontispiece tells us is a "French culinary term referring to a mass of vegetables cut up into small sections and then made into soup." Here is a rendition of *le corps morcelé*, with the English link in morsels (partial self-images) apparent. Thus when she drops the soup tureen at the shock of her parents' imminent departure, archaic fears of abandonment along with unfocused rage are reawakened and the terror of self-fragmentation is enacted in the smashing of the fragile vessel (container of self-images and identifications): in effect, she feels shattered.

That Julienne is the "mass" of "small sections" contained but not integrated within Julie is confirmed by two passages. After a mental breakdown on the heels of her sexual initiation with Ben, Julie is advised by a token woman not to be so vulnerable: "Don't talk so much; become a kaleidoscope instead, dazzling them with varied images of who you are, might be." (74-5)   In Lacanian terms, she is to accept the masquerade of femininity—i.e., an absence or a self-alien gender constructed by male desire and projected castration anxieties.   In a sort of defiant compliance, she wears instead a black suit, which intrigues Ben into asking, "Why black, Julienne?" ("blackness" had fallen over Julie in her cradle as her father and grandfather enter and interrupt the sunny maternal household. (6)   Not only do males signify loss and lack as absence of color and self-compromise, but Julie in the company of men is apparently nothing within herself, only something for them to project their dreams and fetishistic desires onto and love "like an angel of the Pre-Raphaelites, mysterious and bored."

Pre-feminist as well, Julie "has no existence yet as defined by herself or other women." (68) She sleeps with Ben "in order to discover herself," but at the "final moment with her lover and her mirror, vision distorts: she is presented with a fractured picture of herself." (67) She doesn't know which picture to trust: "the splintered yet separately concrete vision of herself Ben offers, or the hidden whole self that struggles to say that his vision of her is distorted and moves in fantasy." But if she continues to "live his fantasy, she can no longer reach out even to distorted splinters and does not know where to begin to look for herself." Her convent-school friend Jenny, appearing at her wedding, "presents her with another mirror into which she is now afraid to look." (67) She lives a shadow existence: "A pretty boy in drag; a woman sexily boyish," who dons and hates the "only image offered her of femaleness and beauty...terrified of male responses to her body." (75) It's as if the alienating effects of male desire sensitize her to her own self-alienation.

Out of touch with the potential strength of Jules, the shadow-person known as Julie comes to mean a fake-I as it is force-fitted to the heterosexual masquerade where women must "stay beautiful" or else the man's "eyes will wander." (76) But the times have been a-changing. Julie and Jenny meet two other women fresh from a conference and begin exchanging ideas in a pub while some men start flirting. At first Julie feels excluded by the independent women who are rude to the men towards whom she feels some sympathy, but she also hears a new voice that tells men, leave us alone; we don't need you; get lost. Put off but also intrigued, she invites the feminists home where they are met by long-suffering Ben ready to complain about her absence but soon finding that he is the excluded party. The perspective shifts toward the women who in male eyes are witches: "heads bent together under the lamp and around them darkness. He turns up the stereo to drown their muttering that beats at his heart like fists. They have been brewing and hissing all day, Julie, Julienne stirring them up, showing off, puffing all their accomplishments boiling over in that bloody huge family of hers, and swimming, swimming on new ideas....plotting." (100) But Ben in construing power as domination can only envision his own drowning in their "bottomless cauldron" and so fails to appreciate power as empowerment.

The second evoking of Julienne in the context of a witch's "bottomless cauldron" also speaks to Julie's underlying need to come to terms with the mass of inner segments (*le corps morcelé*) that can neither be contained within the original family nor find an outlet in heterosexual marriage. But now, by having these accepted, she will experience the strength simmering within her as Jules. "She clutches for support at the other three women, unable to stop talking, spilling her personal life like a vegetable soup that simmers from day to day on the back of the stove, the soup stirred by generations of Fanchot women." (101) As she "ladles out the soup" of herself to others, the mass of inner segments becomes the overflowing "mess of words."

She discovers wholeness in a feminist container. At the end of the novel, after she has exchanged with her mother some words of kindness that suggest reconciliation, and after talking back to Ben on the phone so that he is impressed by her strength, she turns to other women, urging them to talk about their past and overcome their isolation. But as the strong Jules gains the upper hand, a new militancy breeds military analogies: "They are passing telegrams along battle-lines...recognizing allies under the guise of femininity, no longer smuggling ammunition over back

garden walls, no longer corpses in the church and mouths of men."
Female empowerment begins to resemble male models of power-
over.

If this is still a strong ending for a brave book, giving men
the final word produces an odd effect: it reminds one of their
virtual absence from the story. The only male character is Ben
whose gender/class-bound scripting poises him somewhere
between a nerd and a wimp. Apart from pushing her out of bed
one night after she returned drunk and sick, he does little to earn
the formidable classification of Enemy. On reflection,
Julie/Jules/Julienne is the only real, only multifaceted character
in the story. Jenny matters only relative to Julie. Her mother is
endowed with minimal individuality; her father delivers stilted
speeches about "Love. You don't know the meaning of the word."
And in fact other authority figures deliver still-born speeches as
in the case of Mother Superior chastising Sister Paul for tolerating
affection among the female students: "You have broken your vow
of obedience to me, your Superior, by not letting me know about
this much sooner. Spiritual arrogance, Sister Paul, is a very grave
fault." This officious put-down occurs even though readers know
that the two "understand one another's elliptical communications
perfectly, sensitive after years of community life built on
silence." (50-1)

In sum, a Lacanian reading foregrounds narcissistic-injury
issues centering on mirroring, the self-core, self-esteem, unstable
identifications, as well as post-Lacanian separation/
individuation issues—play wholeness off against fragmentation.
By (re)envisioning psychological processes, Roberts shows how the
ideal-I (Jules) contributes to the strong feminist self and how
feminism is woman's path to wholeness. Certainly, narcissism and
its transformations comprise as valid a base as any from which
the imagination may operate, but narcissism can also unbalance
a work unless counterweighted by empathy—and that is in short
supply (true also of Joyce's *A Portrait*). In reply to Jennie's
question of what next, Julie is content to "look in the mirror, see
wrinkles, start growing old," so long as it reflects "me stronger."
(178) But it is unfortunate that Julie, who is in touch with so
many of her feelings and knows what it is to be excluded, cannot
empathize with Ben when he is left out, instead of turning him

into a symbolic enemy whom she fears and hates. Perhaps this inhibition of a valuable affect is overdetermined by Julie's childhood resentment at being replaced by her baby brother Claude: "I watch him sucking my mother's breast, a greedy baby, she laughs at him, a proper little man." (152) And although the two become friends as he grows up, she remarks, "He has money I envy, he will have the parents I mourn." (153) And so his taking away the parents once again may further explain her rage and symbolic fragmentation via the shattered soup tureen. Jealousy or envy over men's lives and their prerogatives as she enters Ben's world may have been too strong to overcome given the opportunity to turn the tables on them, but it remains an unacknowledged conflict for the heroine and an unresolved issue for the novel.

In rejoinder one may argue that men are not supposed to be sympathetic in feminist novels, which bears all the force of a growing literary convention behind it, and thus self-validating in its fashion. Yet the question of empathy is a real sticking point in assessing these texts. Does, for example, lack of empathy *for* men get translated into lack of empathy *in* men? Will empowered woman be kinder as well as more capable? Fay Weldon wonders, and replies, "It depends on the degree of her imagination. And her capacity for empathy."[8]

II

Wendy Perriam: Deconstructing the Sexual Other

...I'm always wary of 'isms,' be they Communism, Catholicism, atheism, feminism, or even pacifism. They're usually too clear cut, too 'cut and dried,' and I start getting uncomfortable, seeing the grey areas in the middle, the subleties, the non-sequiturs, the unanswered questions, or bits that don't fit the scheme. Often I feel I ought to join some cause, march behind a banner, lobby the government about the price of sanitary towels, but I'm more concerned with those basic questions you're meant to have worked through during adolescence, but which still continue to haunt me:

> how did the universe originate, what is the nature
> of good and evil, is there a God, is morality
> justified?   To be perfectly honest, I'm more
> interested in who made the world than in whether
> Tampax should be subsidized.
> —Wendy Perriam[9]

Reflected in her mother's eyes, Michele Roberts' Julie sees
the "witch whom you call your crazy daughter," and in Ben's Julie
is the "crazy woman, loved and feared at a distance." (108) Wendy
Perriam's *After Purple* is lucidly written almost entirely inside the
madness of a modern woman, except that the madness emerges as
something closer to the Life Force itself.   Inhabiting a post-
Portnoy, post-Jong world, Thea Morton is the Dame Folly that
Erasmus praises for being the bane of fools, Dostoyevsky's
Underground Man's other half, and the Wife of Bath in a movie
by Buñuel. As her name weds divinity to mortality, she moves so
freely between the subjective spaces of daydream and delirium
that while one may know where she is one never quite know how
to take her. It's as though her narrative is telling men, you think
we women are illogical?—try this out one out; you think we are
emotional?—try this; dependent?—try this; amoral? humorless?
conniving? sex-obsessed? love-crazed? masochistic?—try these
scenarios on for size and then say something sensible.   Until
stretched to the breaking point, all one's male notions about
women—residual ideals about the feminine along with the worst
fears, fantasies, and stereotypes—exceed their limits and snap,
split apart, revealing no longer madness or anything so appealing
as a higher sanity, the wisdom of the body, natural affinities, but
what at this point may simply be called *elan vital*, or whatever it
is that, despite anyone's best efforts to define, classify ('obviously
a classic hysteric') limit, contain, or otherwise domesticate, can
finally be neither accepted or rejected.   In the end even Dame
Folly is spun around and made dizzy enough to land on her head.
But, however one eventually responds to Thea, she succeeds in
trashing stereotypes of women by embodying them and
performing them till they explode and disintegrate in absurd
laughter. Polymorphously transgressive, she achieves for ideas

about women what *Finnegans Wake* achieves for ideas about language.

Of course, she is also a literary character, in the the odd-girl-out mold of *Georgy Girl*. But blissfully pre-ambivalent and militantly anti-maternal, Thea sails through a post-feminist world where the men like Leo her erstwhile lover and Adrian her former husband leave little to choose between in their maddening mix of sexual brutality and lustful cowardice; on the other hand, the Franciscan "pop priest" Ray, who turns up along the way, is portrayed with genuine sympathy for his fallible integrity. The all-male world to which Thea awakens began at age four when her father abandoned her along with her mother for a mistress and Thea was dumped at a Catholic convent school where God became the target of her free-wheeling libidinal energies. There, among the 300 "blessed girls" who "feasted on His flesh and blood and wore His naked body on a chain around their necks," Thea, being unbaptized, is only a "step-child," though her passion for Him is unlimited and undying. (13)

Finding herself thwarted in her morning-after attempts to compel Leo's interest after a turbulent night of lovemaking and breakage, she masturbates on the subway to Adrian's flat, seeking an ultimate thrill: "You soar beyond you own confining body and hit the electric fence which runs round heaven. It's all shock and heat and sparks—an angel or rocket-launch zooming out of space and time boundaries" before the Luciferian fall. (18) Eliciting an arousal from Adrian, she thinks, "Sex is like masturbation. It makes you feel sacred—at least for an hour." (22) It also unites her with "another human being" and lets her feel less "alone and frightened" when a "bit of male is corkscrewed right inside." Men are sex-objects for Thea who "can never really tell where men stop and their pricks begin." (24)

Men are also difficult to keep, inside or otherwise. Made intriguing by his mysterious Russian background, Leo is too often deep in the pages of *The Listener*, consulting with his friend Otto about art dealings, or at the piano "communing with the souls of dead composers." (13) Sometimes she has to go to extremes, like smashing a Chinese phoenix, in order to provoke his interest. It is no better with Adrian, his head being filled either with student essays or unfinished monographs on European history. Preferring

"randy" over "sexual," Thea ponders the language of men: how the
-*ity* words come out sounding alike, even bestiality and
spirituality; and Adrian's -*isms*—Feudalism, Scholasticism, etc.—
also get in her way. Understanding only sensualism, she would
like to lie down under Leo's piano—a "smug, preening slob of a
Bechstein" he makes love to—and enjoy his thundering hands
pounding out "Eroticism. Barbarism." Thea has no trouble
making language serve her desires.

Her trouble comes in getting her desires satisfied. She is
odd-girl-out with respect to more than her males' distancing
devices. Instead of making up after a quarrel, Adrian leaves and
marries Janet ("I didn't even know he had a Janet!"). Thea's
nemesis as well as her antithesis, Janet is the stereotypical
respectable wife whose virtues derive from reaction-formations
against filth. She "had one of those television commercial
complexions which never need to use the lotions they're
advertising. She'd grown up in the country with extra milk and
ballet lessons and badges from the Girl Guides for Stitchery and
Housecraft." Her eyes were the dreamy blue of Mills and Boon
romances. Everything about her and around her was "cream—her
blouse, her teeth, the thick pile rug, the hession-colored walls" of
her office. Double Devon cream "spilled down her cleavage to her
soft, swelling breasts," making Thea's look "smallish and
unspectacular" in comparison. (33) Janet is culturally constructed
male desire in female flesh—a highly-processed dish; Thea is raw—
Lacan's *le corps morcelé* —to Janet's ideal-I.

Adrian's unwelcome news of Janet's pregnancy makes
Thea imagine a "pastel-coloured baby...lilac nappies...on a
primrose-crocheted doily." (p. 28) "Things," Thea ruefully reflects
later, "always came in threes: mummy, daddy, Rutherford [his
mistress]—Adrian, Janet, baby." (356) Reality is oedipal, but that's
only Freudianism, another -*ism* in Thea's path not worth dwelling
on when strong measures are called for. Expelled from the
blissful bower of Adrian, Janet, and baby-to-be, Thea returns to
Leo, after pausing to pray for the baby's death, pay for a special-
intention Mass, and glimpse the statue of St. Bernadette, "a
shabby, homely person" corresponding to her own step-child
image. She has also made token gestures toward the Janet-side of
life by accepting an office job and assembling an extravagant

meal for Leo and his friends. But Leo is meanwhile waiting for
her at a restaurant, and later in the night when they do connect,
she provokes him into a jealous rage with her tales of Adrian's
secret visits to the flat. Finally, Leo grasps a glass paperweight
"with tiny scarlet flowers painted on it in dainty little clusters"
and with a single blow converts her mouth into a "smashed,
pulped, purple flower." (70)

Recovering in a Catholic hospital, she meets the
Franciscan chaplain, Ray, falls for his spirituality (of which she
simultaneously conspires to relieve him), and works out a plan to
join him over Easter at Lourdes where he will chaperone a party
of handicapped boys and she will be among the other "wrecks and
write-offs." (p. 127) Along with Ray's sexual/spiritual healing,
Thea guiltily attributes Janet's recent miscarriage to her own
murderous wishes and seeks absolution.

Meanwhile, the secular males have become solicitous of
Thea's welfare, but not for the noblest of motives—Leo, fearing a
lawsuit, tells her she had a fall; and Adrian, upset over receiving
the bills, tries to get her quickly signed out. The fervor of Thea's
love for Leo, however, remains unabated—if only he would just
apologize. But when she makes erotic advances, Leo makes a
tragic discovery—no arousal. Thea thinks, "some terrible justice
had descended and disarmed him, so that by maiming me, he had
somehow maimed himself." (166) Thea's loony-logic exposes an
even crazier male-logic in which women are to blame even for the
violence men inflict on them. Leo sulks over the piano, and Thea
realizes, "If Leo could play like that, he was a god, a seer, a
conjurer, and had no need to make amends. I was the one who
had inflicted all the damage—wounded his pride, disabled his
prick, turned my knife in his limping self-esteem. I fell on my
knees in front of the piano, paying homage to them both. 'I'm
sorry, Leo,' I sobbed." At the saint's grotto she prays for a second
miracle: "bring him back...a new and resplendent prick." (177)

But Thea's ever-mixed motives also aim at getting Ray into
bed. At the hospital, when she held back from confessing to sex
with 47 men, he had reassured her, "Even if you're screwing
around, you can still be OK with God...You've got a lot of love in
you, Thea, even holiness"—fatal words from a celibate. (139) She
bares her breast for his touch, and when he refrains, she
reproaches him with, "you just said screwing didn't matter, so why

all this fuss about one small breast?" Ray wriggles out of this theological conundrum by saying he meant that so long as "you strive for good, then sex is less serious. The important thing is to want God rather than screwing." To which Thea replies, "I want to screw God." Not to be bettered, Ray replies, "Well, at least you want Him. That's the only way you know how to love at the moment, so God accepts it." (141)

So far, the nearest Thea can approach divinity is through the earthly servant Ray. At Lourdes an opportunity arises to draw Ray into her designs when one of the boys makes a pass at her which she inflates into an attempted rape, thereby putting Ray on the defensive. Ministering to her alleged injuries in her guest-house bedroom, Ray takes up Thea's invitation to talk about himself—now he is the one confessing. But it is more an act of discontent than of repentance. Ray is an idealist who wants to serve in the literal mode of St. Francis, and join the Franciscans, an order without walls. "But our vows are walls, cutting us off from all the real problems and responsibilities, from sex, from parenthood." (215) With that verbal slide, he is well along toward slipping the rest of the moral distance into bed with Thea, who has gotten jealous again because he "is more interested in his soul than my body." His "priestly shine was already tarnishing"; his "famous holiness had cracked like a half-priced halo." Thea didn't "really fancy him" as a man: "it was the priest I craved." (216) And she reassures herself, "Christ Himself may well have been plain and scrawny with thinning hair and hammer toes," but it was his "soul and sanctity" she "lusted after." She "had imagined him screwing me purely as a pastoral duty...his prick like a bishop's crosier, proud and tall and sacred...divine passion." (222) But all she provokes into a sexual lunge is a "lascivious" man who feels "small, slimy, apologetic almost." He proves to be not a "noble Vestal, just a premature ejaculator." Her "forty-eighth man" is last "not only in number, but in order of achievement." (223)

There is still St. Bernadette, whose wall photo has been observing the recent scene, not frowning, or looking cross or disappointed, but smiling. The two females look alike and have "lots in common," but there are also differences: "Bernadette was a saint. She didn't swear or nick things. She'd never had sex and I doubt if she'd even masturbated. She prayed for poor depraved

sinners like myself. I felt, though, she could have been a sinner."
(111) But the saint is difficult to locate among the crowds,
"gabbling and jostling as if they were about to visit a circus or a
zoo." (239) Candles were being sold for five francs,
commercialism was rampant even though Bernadette had "told the
townsfolk not to turn the shrine into a corner shop." She would
be "furious." At the twenty Holy Water taps there were long
queues "like check-outs at a supermarket." "Bossy women with
shopping baskets full of empty bottles were shoving each other
out of the way, as if they were fighting for bargain sales." A man
was splashing water over his chest; someone else was "struggling
with twelve Pepsi bottles"—the faces "showed greedy self-
absorption."

    The river running through the place Bernadette had called
her paradise is "tamed and castrated": "nature and beauty have
been banned." (240) The famous statue of the Immaculate
Conception depicts "a taller, older, simpering, Gothic matron with
a pious smirk and dead marble eyes." Clearly there will be no
Easter miracle on this "tarmac wasteland."

    But awaking in the middle of the night and returning to
the shrine, Thea kneels in the darkness, gazing up at the statue
only to find it missing. Blinking and gasping, she discovers in its
place a "short plumpish girl with a broad oval face (no
cheekbones) and a pale rather blemished skin like mine when I
have my period. Her eyebrows were heavy, her dark hair almost
hidden beneath a coloured kerchief. She had a full, generous
mouth" and was "wearing the local old-fashioned Pyrenean dress
of coarse striped cotton with an apron and a heavy patterned
shawl."

    "Bernadette!" The saint gets right down to business: "Thea,
I want you to help me, please." The request, notwithstanding its
miraculous portent, puts Thea on guard, knowing that "when
people ask for help, it's often something dodgy or even dangerous
which they shrink from doing themselves." (249) She begins
having second thoughts about the saint who "was there to help me,
for heaven's sakes, not the other way around." It was "fine to
have her as a sister so long as she stayed flat and two-
dimensional, made no trouble or demands." (250) What the
apparition wants is for Thea to take her message and spread it
throughout the world, starting with the clergy. The message is

simply that she did not see the Blessed Virgin. (How could she have in light of the travesties made of her vision?) Thea feels unworthy of this grandiose calling. "Look, Bernadette, who...er...did you see then?" But the saint isn't geared to small talk: "I'm sorry, Thea, I can't say." At least it's no one evil, but too difficult to explain, and so the saint vanishes. With her miracle in hand and her mission awaiting, Thea realizes that in the eyes of the world, someone in her situation—"no fixed address, scarred, sick, starving and divorced"—would be locked up and labeled a "madman." (253) Nonetheless, she tries, but no one wants "truth or science, only miracles and Masses," she ruefully concludes, an outcast once more. (282)

With madness so compounded, the psychic terrain shifts to a no-man's-land between delirium and delusion as the locale switches to London. Leo, it appears, has sped off to the Orient with Otto perhaps to find the missing mate for the phoenix Thea has smashed earlier. Adrian and Janet grudgingly take her in, and Thea finds herself in the guest-room using the no-longer-needed infant's apparel for insulation. "All I wanted was to be a baby," she thinks as Adrian comes to wake her and foreclose even this desperately innocent wish. (237) Where to go next? She returns to the hospital, thinking she may become a nun, only to find the wrecker's ball was making it look as if the hospital was having "an operation on itself." (335) Briefly joining with the construction workers, she ends up submitting to a gang rape, and here delirium dissolves into delusion as she crawls toward the restoked blazing fire. "I was torn, exhausted, filthy. I needed to purify me, burn me down to ashes. Things were always burnt in winter, to make way for spring...soaring like a phoenix." As she walks into the flames, her wound opens and streams with blood, her mouth is full of lava, her eyes were "scarlet holes." (344) In this perverse Pentecost, following the purple of her Lenten mortifications and her Easter vision, Thea is faithful to her sacrilegious rubrics.

What follows can only be her assumption into heaven after the workmen rescue her and she is about to be operated on by the National Health. Before that, Ray has come to see her and explain his reinstated vow of obedience would condemn him to a desk in Glasgow, but so be it. A postcard with its message smudged arrives from Leo with an Eastern phoenix on it. An

omen of hope, it becomes her holy-card, an "icon." She is clothed
in white and surrounded by more white as an anaesthetic is
administered. With the operation imminent, her final apotheosis
is realized: "I was a phoenix now, a white one, rising from the
flames of pain and violence, flying away from purple, from the
colour of pomp and penance, the shades of Lent and sin. I had
left pain and death behind, scorched through fire and furnace,
and come out hallowed on the other side where the pure cold light
of heaven smote scalding on my eyes." As she is put to sleep by a
silver "javelin gleaming in the green god's hands," the "sky came
hurtling forward, and as I soared, rushed to meet it, I saw my
father sitting up in heaven, holding out his arms."

This final wish for fusion with the Almighty
Parent/Godhead, which is incredibly granted, implies that for all
her displays of voluptuous sexiness Thea's desires are more
primitive than erotic, more homey than sexual. But if the life of
the narrative is not fueled by Eros, it is hardly driven by
feminism, which, along with sexism, Freudianism, and
Catholicism, is absorbed the way a cyclone absorbs shopping
malls, trailer parks, and town centers, swirling them helter-
skelter, scattered at your feet to be rediscovered in strange new
relationships. Yet undeniably the narrative stems from a woman's
point of view on the odd-girl-out theme raised to a creative
principle. Desperate to woo Leo away from his piano-playing and
"prove I still existed," Thea sets herself up as a female daimon of
creation/destruction equal and opposite to that of the male in
present-day society. (14) This may be why she often seeks less to
secure a stable and satisfying relation with a potent, loving male
than to compel the self-centered, self-contained world of maleness
to take note of the female other. But even this transgressive
perspective recedes to reveal a radiantly original celebration of
the imagination's flight toward apocalyptic oblivion.

Juxtaposed with Roberts' novel, Perriam's becomes more
revealing. If Roberts' feminist fiction is a modernist
metanarrative whose liberating energies preempt male models and
deliver her to herself, Perriam's fiction is postmodernism's rebuff
to the liberationist project. Neither Christian transcendence nor
Enlightenment humanism escapes her withering, parodistic vision.
Feminism succeeds only in heightening one's awareness of male
mendacity, and female oppression falters before the forces of the

irrational. Perriam's Bernadette plays on a type of Freudian humor termed the "degradation of the sublime"; in Lacanian terms, the Catholic saint is the ideal-I, promising transcendence, while the peasant girl who appears to Thea is the segmented body, professing immanence. Together with the scenes of sexual debasement and erotic apotheosis, Thea puts "forward the unpresentable in presentation itself; that which denies itself the solace of good forms, the consensus of good taste which would make it possible to share collectively the nostalgia of the unattainable."[10]

On the other hand, Roberts' text is modernist in its evolution of consciousness leading to social commitment (à la writers of the thirties), but it also postmodernist in arriving at this position via deconstruction of male theories of woman that stem from an interplay of desire and fear. Julie is (re)constructed by deconstructing Lacan's patriarchal theories which deny women's access to agency within the Symbolic Order. Both she and Thea are odd-girls-out, but in feminist fiction, this dilemma is resolved less through social incorporation or "honourable spinsterhood," than through affiliation with an alternative society.[11] Yet if Roberts' means is deconstructive, her end is circumscribed by an essentialism in respect to men who are assigned formal roles as the enemy in an all-out holy war.

Perriam's text deconstructs not only the sexual and the religious other, but the privileging of the victim within the feminine subject as well. Julie's quest is a variation on the Enlightenment narrative that leads to liberating knowledge—feminism incorporated on a deep inner level to complete the mandala of her self and generate activist agendas. But in Lyotard's sense of the postmodern condition, "knowledge is no longer principally narrative."[12] Hence, narrative is no longer linked to knowledge. Thea's narrative, then, paradoxically liberated from liberation, deconstructs itself and bares the dark side of Enlightenment. She is the ultimate odd-girl-out whose destabilized self recenters the oddness of desire.

If Julie's desire is for wholeness through a healing, empowering, but ultimately fighting community, Thea's desire is for wholeness through a transcendent, but ultimately annihilating sexual *jouissance*. The site of turmoil for one is the female psyche, for the other the female body. Both play out the self-fracturing consequences of male desire and parlay the woman's condition as other into searing discourses of difference. Both ultimately plunge into the origins of the female/feminine self through a matricentric medium that only women writers can access. For despite their contrasts, the texts are joined by gender: the ways that Julie is reborn into sisterhood and Thea is blissed out of mortal existence would stymie any masculine imagination.

Notes

1. *The Postmodern Condition*, 37, xxiv.

2. Martha Nussbaum, "Feminism and Philosophy: An Exchange," 48.

3. Brenda Polan, "Myth Perfect," *The Guardian* (27 May 87).

4. Gilbert and Gubar, *Madwoman in the Attic*, 73-90. Two of Michele Roberts' subsequent fictions are explicit re-visions of male texts: *The Wild Girl* (1985) is a retelling of Mary Magdalene's story; *The Book of Mrs. Noah* (1987) is as the title indicates.

5. An oscillating narrative from the new cultural conflicts of young adulthood in London and the old childhood conflicts reawakened by a visit home is close kin to Lisa Alther's Ginny in *Kinflicks* (1976). In both instances, the daughter's need to affirm an offbeat lifestyle is caught in a rapprochement crisis involving an invalid mother. Ginny's mother dies, and Ginny goes off into a future with something maternal within; Julie's mother recovers but leaves Normandy for Switzerland, and Julie returns to London a stronger person and more committed feminist. Despite some narratives of women's coming-of-age after marriage, female *bildungsromanen* in the supposedly male mode of coming-of-age during adolescence abound: Lorrie Moore's *Who Will Run the Frog Hospital?* (1994) is a case in point.

6. Jacques Lacan, "The Mirror Stage as Formative of the Function of the I as Revealed in Psychoanalytic Experience," in *Écrits*, 1-7. Lacan was well-known in England before his prominence in American literary circles and had figured in Juliet Mitchell's *Psychoanalysis and Feminism* (1974); given Roberts's French background, she was likely acquainted with the French Freud. However, in her piece in Wandor's *On Gender and Writing*, she singles out Freud and the

loss/reparation theories of Melanie Klein as indigenous to her
creative work. She also alludes to her mother's not wanting
"twin daughters, but a son" (64) and refers to her own
"terrifying feelings: burning hate, sizzling despair, rage that
tears you apart" in respect to her mother: "the fantasy image of
her I constructed inside myself." If this sounds Kleinian, she
has also expressed attraction for Jung's theories, and her second
novel, *The Visitation* (1983), begins with boy/girl twins
(Felix/Helen) and ends with the woman writer's struggle to get
beyond the "warring archetypes exhausting her energies" to the
"twins" that "lodge simply deep inside her, as images of
different parts of herself, as needs for different sorts of
activity." (175) Earlier, Helen had entered a sort of magical
garden or labyrinth with her friend Beth. Their "words are like
statues"—one is of Adam and Eve "so closely interlinked that
they seem to be one." (170) It is the androgynous ideal of
creative wholeness espoused by Woolf and the Romantics. Soon
the garden composes itself into a Jungian mandala of the
psyche. It also turns Lacanian as Helen gazes into the pool of
tears she has wept and sees not a "Minotaur" in a labyrinth, but
"herself: a woman." (172) The Minotaur, one of the warring
archetypes pursued by the Hero to form a complementary pair,
probably has more immediate origins than ancient Crete. It
stems in part from the moral monster of Stephen Daedalus's
guilty conscience and from Dorothy Dinnerstein's study of preoedipal development along Kleinian lines (*The Mermaid and the
Minotaur*). Witnessing these symbolic processes, Beth, who is
pregnant, pushes symbolism to a further extreme in giving
birth to Helen, or in midwifing Helen's re-birth. All told, it is
an intricate piece of psychological mythmaking which
regressively attempts to reorder outer reality by rearranging
the components of inner reality. Ending with a dream while
sleeping in her male lover's (Robert) arms, Helen seeks her lost
twin Felix. At his address, he approaches her through her own
reflection in the grey glass of his front door—i.e., as her own
created fantasy, in the Jungian animus/anima pair. How
successful a resolution this is depends on one's attitude toward
subjectivism. A fictional character's dreams, a critic said once,
are like doors painted on the walls of real rooms. By and large,

readers prefer to have conflicts played out in at a least semblance of reality—it's one thing to summon Jungian mandalas from the deep, another to talk through one's problems with them. The two novels are themselves rather like twins in their techniques, inwardness, themes of artistic becoming, and especially in the heroine's need to overcome through rebirth past deficits centering on faulty sex assignment—it's what sends Julie, after her own child *Bertha*, back to family origins and Helen to her Jungian assimilation of male/female self-components (see C. Goodman, "The Lost Brother").

Finally, a feminist author's utilization of a patriarchal analyst's theories is intriguing. Some feminists have objected to Lacan's views because he essentially bars women from the Symbolic Order of the father accessible to males via the absences made through the castration complex (e.g., Estella Lauter, *Women as Mythmakers*, 8); but it is also possible from the revisionary strategies of feminist authors like Michele Roberts that feminism becomes its own Symbolic Order and masculine heterosexuality inherits the masquerade role. Lacan's sexism is sympathetically interrogated by Mitchell and Rose in *Feminine Sexuality*; the question of his relation to literature has been explored by me (in "Lacanian Mirrors and Literary Reflections") where I found his theories about the mirror-stage to be more useful than true.

7. A more orthodox Freudian model of the child's discovery of adult sexuality and experience of the male as intruder, disrupting the maternal dyad, opens an intriguing line of inquiry for the inherently negative male-role in a burgeoning feminist's development, but cannot be taken up here. Suffice it to say that it is the primal scene that implicates every child in the mysteries of both male and female sexuality (Ikonen and Rechardt, "On the Universal Nature of Primal Scene Fantasies"; Dervin, *Creativity and Culture*).

8. "Fay Weldon, Fancifully," *Washington Post* (24 April 1988).

9. From an interview taped in June, 1984; both her questions and her text dovetail with the ontological emphasis given the postmodern in Brian McHale's *Postmodern Fiction*: "What is a world? What kinds of world are there, how are they constituted, and how do they differ? What happens when different kinds of world are placed in confrontation, or when boundaries between worlds are violated?" (10).

10. Jean-Francois Lyotard, "What Is Postmodernism?" in *The Postmodern Condition*, 81.

11. Patricia Thomson, *The Victorian Heroine*, 114.

12. *The Postmodern Condition*, 26. Sabina Lovibond in "Feminism and Postmodernism" struggles to reconcile the two terms of her title.

4

Mediations of the Matricentric:
The Material Culture of Women's Writing

I have always wanted to write for as many people
as possible. I want my books to be on the general
fiction shelves as well as the feminist shelves.
—Zoë Fairbairns[1]

The material culture of women's fiction—its production,
distribution, and reception—forms a complex feedback system that
extends the matricentric perspective to discover ways in which it
is continually being culturally mediated. In analyzing how
women interface with systems of power, Margolis devises an
interlocking model of (1) *exchanging*, (2) *pooling*, and (3) *placing*.
Food is exemplary: a woman enters the marketplace by shopping
(1); then shares her food among her household (2); and defines her
social status through her guests (3).[2] By analogy with food,
fiction circulates through three analogous zones that continually
constitute and reconstitute it.

Exchanging means that for the literary system to work
effectively, the commercial marketplace (1) must be accessible to
the author (who is assumed to have access to the skills and means
for producing). This two-way track presumes a supply/demand
economy that encompasses agents, editors, publishers, networks,
media, and outlets on the one hand and viable consumers on the
other. Authorial accessibility is then balanced by product
availability and customer demand.

Pooling spans into three directions of distribution. Books
are (a) commodified in capitalist economies and fluctuate in price
value as they move from new to used outlets, although an older,
counterbalancing economy (b), a socialism of the circulating
libraries, co-existed from early on. Prior to these, women's
domestic reading circles formed a "literate, nonscholarly textual
culture of minimally educated bourgeois and moneyed readers,"
which, although male participants and male texts were included,
tended to develop gendered readings.[3] Circulating libraries
originated in the early 18th Century when booksellers would "lend
to their trusted customers volumes which they wished to examine
before purchase." Mainly "patronized by women" and maintained

by modest subscriptions, they sprang up in the wake of the "flood
of novels that followed *Tom Jones* and *Pamela*." They were in
turn inspired by the "profitable market prospects" of the many
book clubs whose middle-class members "met for a monthly dinner
and exchange of books." These clubs were sexually exclusive as
well as mixed. So popular were the circulating libraries that most
fiction after 1775 was purchased by them rather than by
individuals, and along with bluestocking circles they functioned
for women as coffee houses did for men.[4] Finally, books have
always been passed freely among readers in an egalitarian
economy of mutual interest (c). Thus while authors' profits may
decline as readers' alternative distributions rise, *pooling*
compensates by keeping the author in circulation and thus looping
into the model's third area, *placing*.

In respect to the work, *placing* is negotiated through
critical estimates, best-seller lists, book clubs, popular tastes, and
loose systems of prizes, awards, and grants. In respect to the
author, *placing* is affected by education, class, gender, age, race,
as well as by adaptability to the marketplace and the ratio of
productivity to demand—which loop the process around to (1).

This model may now be set in a larger context. The
material culture of literary publication is a microcosm of the
macro-economy to which the former is beholden. Writers
participate both in publishing's micro and in the macro of the
national economy (though at best indirectly so for early women
writers). And since for only a fortunate few men or women is
writing a fulltime occupation, most writers engage other facets of
the economy for financial support. Here cultural as well as
gender differences arise. Today, writers in America are likely to
be sustained by teaching, whereas in England by ancillary
writing, e.g., adapting radio and television scripts. More
consistently in the past, women writers operated within another
micro of domestic economy as wives and mothers. Ultimately, the
tri-partite model, financial-support models, and the economic
system are all bound together by feedback loops in which author
or book can be centrally situated.

It may be seen from the outset and in virtually every
aspect of these processes that gender plays a key role. Formerly
it was assumed that the absence of women writers in earlier

centuries offered proof for oppressive/prohibitive practices; then the rediscovery of earlier women's texts demanded newer explanations. Lewalski finds among the writings of Jacobean women, for example, not only patterns of resistance to the "patriarchal construct of women as chaste, silent, and obedient," but also a "strong sense" of themselves as authors and producers of texts.[5] Thus while they were embedded in their culture and its institutions, they were not defined by their oppression. Due in part to the disruptions of family life during the English Civil War, a remarkable expansion of women's writing coincided with their new roles and responsibilities in the 1640s. Although mostly producing religious tracts, children's books, and manners manuals, women wrote out of their experiences as wives and mothers, and while affirming traditional values, they reasoned from their Christian base for dignity and full mental development. This pamphleteering represented women as "political animals...as likely to comment on the public issues of the day...as male authors."[6] Following the monarchy's restoration in 1660, another material change had farreaching consequences: the initiation of a postal service fostered letter-writing as a training ground for the epistolary novel.[7] And as the next century witnessed the emergence of a new class of female readers, the marketplace geared its products to newly gendered tastes.[8]

But if gender affected production, the reverse also held. Class privileges and whatever leisure afforded women by marriage purchased an essential raw material for producing literary texts: time. Those who wrote for their livelihood sought other options. To offset men's advantages from patrons, women in the eighteenth-century often relied on subscriptions. This practice of pre-selling a work among the author's friends, however, also presumed social leverage.[9] "The women of higher social rank could pay for their work to be published, unlike Aphra Behn who sought to make a living by her writing"; but to some extent even literary women "lacked access to the literary world" and were too few to form an "alternate literary society."[10] Partly, this was offset by subscription publishing and subscription libraries.

Production affected gender in other profound ways, for as writing fiction became viable for women, they were brought at least indirectly into contact with a public sphere of exchange.

Though a male-system, capitalism's supply-and-demand values could nevertheless threaten to override male prerogatives; so, if from the first, women's access was regulated by gender, class and economy must also be factored in. Aphra Behn is again a case in point. After Dryden, she was the "most prolific and popular writer of her time," and the "evidence does not support the contention that her career was hindered by general prejudices against" women playwrights, bawdy or plain; indeed, her complaints of a double standard suggests "an elaborate rhetorical interaction that dictated the very terms in which she was conceived."[11] If sex would become commodified, she would trade on her notoriety. She capitalized more on house receipts for her plays than on her published fiction, and it's been calculated that novelists of whatever sex would have to publish a dozen works a year to be self-supporting, a prospect that would likely have exceeded public demand.[12] However, popular demand for trendy subgenres like gothic fictions could quadruple payments, regardless of author's sex.[13] In the literary marketplace, genre tended to neutralize gender, as name-recognition would in later centuries; and early on consumers of popular culture began dictating the terms—if not also the nature—of producers.

Women's newly, if circumscribed, literary access thus looped through profit via the rise of a capitalist economy, as well as through education via the spread of girls' academies. And while upper-class sons were still privileged by the school system, the emergence of circulating libraries from booksellers' putting new books in the hands of potential buyers meant that the many new works of fiction would be accessible to young middle-class women with minimal investment—and with optimal return as burgeoning writers. Literacy could also be self-taught, especially when the new fictions rendered reading pleasurable.

As a harbinger for other fields, the English stage at the end of the Restoration offers a striking model of the battles between art and commerce, license and restraint, and the competing tastes of men and women (it was also a new job market where women entered as actresses and sometimes ended as playwrights, though never as managers).[14] The comedy of manners as conceived by Etherege and Wycherly had by the 1690's succeeded all too well in imposing a macho-libertine sexual ethos, and a loose coalition of excluded gentlewomen, reforming clergy, and prosperous bourgeoisie were demanding change. Sensitive to these shifting demands, the shrewd actor-manager, Colley Cibber supplied *Love's Last Shift* (1696), which served up hardcore satire for four acts, then did a turnaround to repentance and forgiveness in the fifth. Venting long overdue tears, audiences begged for more. This combination of morality and sentiment appeased all three critical factions: the stage was saved from the puritans, women returned to enjoy scenes of romantic triumph, the middle-classes were confirmed in their belief that virtue would be rewarded in this life; and as male writers mimicked matricentric values, sentimental comedy was born. Yet when Congreve's masterpiece, *The Way of World* (1700) played to empty houses, John Vanbrugh's hilarious but cynical rejoinder to Cibber, *The Relapse* (1699), was a hit. This split in taste, which divided the cultural market through the century, with Farquhar producing toned-down manners comedy and Steele catering to the fashion for sentiment, enjoyed its point counterpoint in Richardson's *Pamela* subverted by Fielding's *Shamela*.

The tone as well as the terms were also set for women's fiction to serve a more conservative market, for which some would claim they were temperamentally suited. Without dismissing this essentialist approach (aired more fully below), one may observe that it was a male in both cases who adjusted the gender dial to a more pleasing tone, while the premier female playwright of the period, Mrs. Aphra Behn mimicked libertine values by penning boisterous Cavalier comedies with Hobbesian heroines pursuing suitable marriages to please female as well as male palettes: "For as 'tis true, all men are stark mad for wenches, so 'tis true, however custom pretends otherwise, that we wenches be as inly stark as men."[15] In other genres, she has been praised as a "poet of love," who played her part in the "soft passion" becoming "established as women's subject."[16] All the same, "rape-celebrations in Behn's *oeuvre* outnumber the arguably more feminist poems."[17] Thus are gendered selves both externally constructed by literary culture and inwardly cultivated.

Subsequently, the bourgeois moral sensibility that women authors brought to novels stemmed from a fervently matricentric matching-up energy that was channeled into the courtship novel and epitomized by Austen's *Emma* and her made-to-order Mr.

Knightley.[18]   Although there was a marketplace for the anti-sentimental narrative, women writers eschewed it, sensing that "at its best, sentimentalism humanized and enriched the picture of sexual relationships" and "did more than rational argument to improve the position of women."[19]   In addition, their novels favored matricentric themes over patricentric variations by "emphasizing the situation of the afflicted [heroine] rather than that of the responder [hero] to affliction."[20]

Eschewing both sentimental formulae and progressive politics following the French Revolution, Austen, who used her brother as her agent and signed on her novels as a Lady, adapted a shrewd blend of aesthetic and business decisions.[21]   In Kelly's analysis, the name of the placing game was to elevate one's work from the disparaged modern or fashionable fictions of the circulating libraries to symbolic or cultural capital of the classics, which one purchased for personal libraries. As books to be re-read, classics were to be owned. Austen took over courtship plots, satirized romantic excesses, and made her narration more problematic by what Kelly terms an "omniscient but not all-disclosing narrator" combined with "inward thoughts and feelings of the protagonist." An ironic distance between the two opens up possibilities for the protagonist to misread her society, and so the reader must be alert and careful through rereadings—thus her texts aspired to the higher capital of literary or classical status.

Later in the century, as the "domestic fiction actively sought to disentangle the language of sexual relations from the language of politics," according to Nancy Armstrong, there were major consequences: the privatization of desire based on gendered qualities, and the production of the "domestic woman," who introduced a "whole new vocabulary for social relations."[22]   For cultural critics, this privatizing and domesticating project expresses the dominant ideology of moral discourse, but the growing power of the marketplace advances a counter-ideology of economic practice. In fact, women's fictional production parallels their sisters' acting professionalism: "the roaringly successful commodification of feminine sexuality within the theater gave the economic lie to attempts to construct the actress's sexuality as private and domestic."[23]   Thus as material culture expands images of dominant ideology, a new dynamic in the development of women's fiction legitimizing matricentric representations suitable to the age is also brought into focus.

The converging factors that favored women authors early in the 18th Century thus include not only epistolary skills and educational opportunities, a congenial literary form amenable to domestic labor and an expanding bookselling/circulating-library economy, but also a public desire for narratives per se and an "increase in the legitimating power of print."[24]   These were aided and abetted by a sexually conservative turn in society that privileged domestic zones of privacy, shunning the vogue for seductive, amatory fictions and yielding only in later decades to more politically liberal agendas.[25] Despite some anachronistic stretching and straining in feminist criticism for proto-revolutionaries (see chapt. 5), women authors by and large played an occasionally ambiguous but overall moderating role within those perimeters. As in the previous century, doctrines of the immortal soul could be interpreted to further their cause, so in a new era would Shaftesbury's philosophy of innate moral sense be constructively deployed to legitimize tearful tales of repentant rakes and virtue embraced. But the production of morality was accomplished through a privileging of privacy, by which sexual segregation in households inhibited sexual knowledge and promoted curiosity, prurience, and the private voyeuristic pleasures of novels, especially when their subject or their authors were women—it need not matter which.[26]   Privacy thus inadvertently promoted an objectifying of gender: in Foucauldian terms, the proliferation of women's presence (writing and acting) pivoted on a Freudian repression of their sexuality. In economic terms, the scarcity of the one increased demand for the other. This blended model may help account for disparities in the dominant ideology: cultural production of sexuality presumes psychological repression of sexuality (specifically, the wishes and fantasies of childhood with incestuous overdeterminants).

But despite the uneasy trade-offs, in the first half of the 18th Century, a woman could make her living by writing— "provided she was prolific and versatile."[27]   Thus a powerful motive force behind this expanding cottage industry was economic. From *Camilla*, Frances Burney "built a home for herself and her penniless husband"; for *The Italian*, Ann Radcliffe, cashing in on the gothics market, received 900 pounds

(commensurate with Fielding's 1,000 pounds for *Amelia*).[28]
Literary trends were now profoundly implicated in literary
production as highlighted by the decline of romances around mid-
century and the rise of gothic romances at century's end.[29] In
the latter half of the century two-thirds of epistolary novels were
written by women (some, as Goldsmith suspected, by a
pseudononymous male hand).[30] The "professional female author
was by the late 1790s pretty much established in England, and at
least three to four hundred women published during the
decade."[31] On an average, a new woman author was published
every year throughout the century.[32] By 1840, "most novelists
were probably women" and were well on their way to cornering
the fiction market.[33]

Then men invaded the field, reconstituted fiction to better
accord with purse and palette, and gradually tilted the scales
toward a male enterprise by century's end. Though Tuchman and
Fortin find this reprehensible, entrepreneurs would shrug. It is
apparent that previously the novel had been held in low esteem by
critics while simultaneously flooding the market.[34] With supply
greatly exceeding demand, an artificial creation of scarcity was
achieved by redefining the product and assigning it a more
upmarket (masculine or at least gender-free) identity—for this
winnowing-out project was not essentially male after all.

Whether serious women authors were harmed by upgraded
marketing is rendered moot by George Eliot's diatribe against
"Silly Novels by Lady Novelists" and the lucrative deals she cut
with her publishers: collecting 7,000 pounds for *Romola* and
netting over pounds 9,000 for *Middlemarch*. Stateside, Willa
Cather's similarly scathing critiques put inferior authors in their
place. In "The Hundred Worst Books and They That Wrote Them,"
she complains about the "enormous output" from "reputable
publishers" that pose a "herculean task of selecting the hundred
worst from the thousands sufficiently poor."[35] Most of these
poor things come from women. Inveighing against agencies of
mass production and distribution (printing press and public
library), she cites a phony duchess, a prolific sentimental novelist
(Laura Jean Libbey), and directs her strongest contempt to Marie
Corelli, the "raving sybil" who "hypnotizes sensible people until
they accept her ludicrous philosophy, distorted ethics and

sophomoric pyrotechnics of style."[36]   However, when Cather exceeded the economics of winnowing and joined other critics in trashing *The Awakening* for taking up a "sordid and trite theme," Kate Chopin abandoned fiction entirely.[37] In this context, *idées reçues* that women authors are generally more communal than competitive and in the 19th Century required male *noms de plume* may be reexamined (practices often revealed the opposite).[38] Even in the present, Emma Tennant clearly has her eye on the fiction commodity market rather than sisterly community when she remarks "the new Brookner or the new Murdoch is relatively similar to the last, and readers know roughly what to expect, and they buy."[39]

Although women's writing advanced along various slopes during the period 1640-1840, the circulating libraries as the "chief encouragement" and "chief outlet" for women novelists suggests that their key contacts with power were mediated through *pooling*.[40] As the 19th Century progressed, efforts by novelists and critics to upgrade the novel as an art-form and women as serious writers (conducted by George Eliot and Henry James and continued by Virginia Woolf, *et al*), record an emphasis up to the present on *placing*.

Placing encompasses such elusive forces as the relatively new mass media that arbitrate taste, academic selectivity that privileges great traditions and sacred canons, and those elite circles that occasionally coalesce into an Establishment.   But establishing what and who exactly comprise an Establishment gender-wise is no easier than agreeing upon its spheres of influence.   Received ideas that English literary establishments were a male hegemony, presumably run on the model of men's clubs, is an essentialist trap awaiting the unwary.   Starting with the 1880's, one would cite James or Wilde as centers of a brilliant literary society, followed by Shaw, H.G. Wells, Ford Maddox Ford, and Rebecca West, and succeeded after the War by such Bloomsbury luminaries as the Stracheys, the Woolfs, Lady Ottoline Morell, and E.M. Forster.   Then there arrived what has now been grouped under the rubrics of the Brideshead Generation—Acton, Waugh, Powell, Greene, Betjmann, *et al.*[41] If they were upstaged in the thirties by Auden, Spender, and Isherwood, a continuing center was sustained by Cyril Connolly,

Elizabeth Bowen, and Rose MacAulay until *Horizon*'s demise in
1950. By now several problems have begun to emerge from the
male-hegemony premise. Class is a powerful determinant; the
population is mixed by gender; most of the great moderns—Joyce,
Lawrence—are missing or unwelcome—"underbred" was Virginia
Woolf's tag for them. And, far from being literary fathers, most
of the males belonged to a beleaguered sexual minority
(aestheticism sprang from gay men like Pater, Beardsley, Wilde;
others, like Waugh, struggled over their sexual identities). The
truly heterosexual male is but another minority—if a reflexively
privileged one.[42] Bereft of its ideological greatcoat, the (male)
Establishment is not only a highly problematized term but an
obsolete one as well—at least in the eyes of today's writers—and
placing operates through various other channels such as the
serious media and literary awards.[43] Nowhere is this better
illustrated than in the case of Muriel Spark. Having written
biography, served as a poetry editor, and won a national short-
story contest, she was commissioned by Macmillan in 1954 to
write her first novel.[44]

But even with "Establishment" deconstructed, if one
factors in publishers, critics, and reviewers, a male hegemony,
measured by crude essentialism, has undoubtedly exercised
disproportionate powers; and it would not be until the 1970s that
women would gain control over their literary destinies in the key
exchange area of ownership. Previously, women had enjoyed
relative positions of power as editors both at presses and the
newer literary journals.[45] And while Virginia Woolf's feminism
embraced women's having a room of their own, it did not extend
to their accessing a press of their own when she and Leonard
founded Hogarth Press.[46]

Decades passed before an almost overnight revolution in
publishing occurred. Virago (1973), Women's Press (1974),
Onlywomen (1974), Sheba (1980), and Pandora (1983) were
established by women for women.[47] A turning point in *pooling*
came during the 1984 Feminist Fortnight and Book Fair held in
Covent Garden, an international exposition which opened the
channels of mainstream distribution. Late 1980s estimates,
including Black Women Talk and the ever-struggling Journeyman
(which in 1978 brought out *Tales I Tell My Mother*, the first

anthology of feminist fiction), ran to eleven women's presses. Radiating from these were a supportive culture of media (e.g., *Women's Review* [1985-87], *Women's Review of Books, SpareRib,* and *Everywoman*), public readings, regional feminist book fairs, book shops, and book clubs.[48] Suddenly, it was enough to "call a book feminist and it was bound to sell."[49]

Commercial houses began tapping into a gender-enhanced market with their own lists of women authors and women's studies; while in other respects, women's presses have operated as stepping-stones for successful writers like Michele Roberts and Jeanette Winterson en route to larger houses. Although presses like Virago can be "authoritarian" in their insisting on "Virago books instead of Zoë Fairbairns books," as this author wryly laments, and the larger commercial houses "can afford to treat a writer well," the former retain a commitment to their authors' "accessibility."[50] All the same the marketplace spoke: "the feminist publishing boom has not been caused by feminists publishing books as a way of being nice to each other." But rather, a "number of talented feminists working in the publishing industry realized, *because* they were feminists, that there was an unfilled demand for a certain kind of book, and linked up with feminist writers (many of whom had been struggling for years to write feminist literature and get it published) to meet the demand."[51] Still, women's presses often served as buffers between the emerging author and the turbulent marketplace of astronomical advances and frenetic buy-outs rampant in today's international capitalism analogous to the circulating libraries during the rise of capitalism. In the end, "they are *our* market forces," declared an upbeat Fairbairns: "why shouldn't we make use of them?"[52]

But eventually, in feminist publishing as in other enterprises, the eighties' boom led to the nineties' bust. The collapse reverberated through both feminist presses' micro and publishing's macro economies. Signs of the recessive times in the macro was the plug-pulling of *Punch* and more seriously the long-standing cultural guide, *The Listener*. One crisis within the micro of feminist publishing epitomizes the conflict between the values of art and capital. Internal struggles broke out at The Women's Press over wages and philosophy, in which the editors were accused of "only paying lip-service to...principles [of] breaking down hierarchies and genuine power sharing."[53] As a result of declining sales, walkouts, and resignations, the press was sold to Mr. Naim Amallah (head of the Namara Group of businesses to which the press had belonged).[54] A similar fate overtook Virago in the fall of 1995 when declining sales and disputes among the top staff led to resignations and a buyout by Little, Brown.

The phenomenal rise and relative tenacity of women's presses, however, never claimed more than a modest portion of the market. Of the 35,720 books published in Britain in 1990, Virago issued 26, The Women's Press 15, Pandora 14. An average first printing at Virago would run from 5,000 to 7,000 copies, with the rare movie tie-in (e.g., *The Handmaid's Tale*) bolstering the number fourfold.[55] Although feminist fiction continued to be displayed in mainstream bookstores, read, and circulated, Virago's flagship bookshop near Covent Garden closed in 1991, symptomatic of a shift away from hardcore feminist narratives to softcore erotica, women's detective fiction, and a surge of pop-psychological, self-help books. More dramatic has been the rise of gay and lesbian studies, accounting for 2,000 new books in 1994 alone. Yet, despite the fads and fluctuations, mass-market romances continued to thrive, with Harlequin publishing over 144 titles annually from 1973 to 1980 and selling over 30 million copies per year.[56] Feminist arguments for these romances as reenforcing gendered readings or privileging women's emotional life over other cultural representations offer cold comfort to strapped feminist editors watching their readership decline. The uttermost pinnacle of mass-marketed fiction has been reached by the once-upon-a-time Yorkshire typist Barbara Taylor Bradford, whose 1992 $37 million three-book deal with HarperCollins may make her the world's highest-paid author.[57] Running a close second is Danielle Steel's $12 million advances per book.

Factoring in anti-feminist backlashes and market surfeit, one can see why women's writing has again turned problematic. Writing of "lesbian sleuths" as one of the trendy dilutions to satisfy public taste, Irene Coffey admits that the "genre raises the same question that is raised every time we produce lesbian erotica, fiction, art—lesbian culture—is it enough to just reproduce the same old and weary picture of the world, simply replacing heterosexual presence with a lesbian presence?"[58]

It is a question that may be modified and posed for women's writing from Aphra Behn on down, within a context not only of male hegemony but of marketplace and other feedback systems. On the one hand, with feminist presses flourishing for a time, it was possible for more women to write more freely than they had ever dared in the past in any culture; yet on the other, it must be admitted that very few memorable works emerged, and in the end readers' preferences decisively shifted. Often contrary to the best marketing research or politically-correct theories and policies, art thrives more in adversity than in congeniality—a loose loop, *sans* feedback.

A related question asks to what extent is the production (and occasional overproduction) of fiction by and about women also the cultural (re)production of women? As feminist critics have noted, the publication of women's fiction historically foregrounded the author's gender as part of the package.[59] Moreover, Spender maintains that the distinction between *Novel* and *Romance* was gender deflected—male/female respectively.[60] However, the *Novel* label also evoked negative associations, and Frances Burney spurned both terms for *Camilla*, preferring "sketches of Characters and morals, put in action," while Austen interrupted *Sense and Sensibility* to defend the term.[61] In the next century, *The Scarlet Letter* would be subtitled "A Romance," as Updike would follow suit with *Marry Me* (1976). If the success of Byatt's *Possession* (1992) carries any lesson for quality fiction by women in the post-feminist nineties, it is one of gender hybridization. Not only does she claim Hawthorne's model of historical romance but Emily Dickinson's poetic voice, not only Umberto Eco's detective conventions but George Eliot's passionately individualized letters—all topped off by Henry James's plot idea of a lesbian feminist from *The Bostonians*.[62]

Even more problematically than her genre, the woman's moral character was from the outset read through her text, while more positively, the acceptance of women's fiction may have also contributed to the gradual social acceptance of women as gendered persons.[63] Thus postmodern's conceit about the author's death cuts two ways: on the one hand all texts may profitably end up neutered and immune from male hierarchy or gender bias; but on the other, signs of woman's capacity to write in her own name (or her hard-won right to) are erased in the name of intertextuality.

Yet despite or due to marketplace fluctuations, women's fiction will likely continue to mutate into new hybrids. Will this relatively new system of freedoms and constraints, amid such diversification, find matricentric determinants a binding imposed by past gender-tailoring or will women authors continue to write though a matricentric identity? In short, what will happen to moral concerns seasoned with sentiment, to meliorist shapings of relationships relentlessly working toward suitable matchups, and to a vision of humanity governed more by reproduction than by rebellion? Any response will be skewed by whether one takes matricentric uni-dimensionally as culturally constructed, or includes its psych/bio dimensions. Ultimately, artistic freedom can accommodate woman's flight from matricentric constraints when culturally imposed as well as her deeper implication in them when not. Yet the matricentric is not bound by an oppressive dialectics of self/society but implicated in a tri-alectics of bio/psyche/culture.

While such issues transcend material culture, they do address another aspect of women's literary lives. The present emphasis on contractual relationships may have upgraded women as persons in their own right, but these also downgraded sisterhood as women must compete with women.[64] Women authors' mixed experiences with various women's presses have shown that favoritism and insensitivity transcend gender. In fact, one questionable influence of material culture has been to reshape woman's relational identity of sharing/caring into a more autonomous one of competing/contending.

Other questions impinging on the relation of the marketplace to women's communal investment must be held in abeyance in order to explore more particular feedbacks within the processes of literary production and consumption: the distinctive ties that bind many women authors to their reading public and protect a matricentric mode against male incursions and exclusions.

That women have had "a literature of their own," as Elaine Showalter discovered, does not so much imply that they have been excluded from the larger culture as implicate a peculiar

condition.[65] Similarly, if an "anxiety of authorship" afflicting
the woman author proves either too hypothetical or dated,
something else less dramatic and more pervasive, like anxiety over
exclusion, can be better documented.[66] In her history of British
feminism, Ruth Adam referred to the "odd woman out" as the
post-World War II mother without a supporting male.[67] Of
course, from a modern feminist standpoint all women, but
especially combinations of lesbians and feminists, are the odd-
ones-out in patriarchy, but there are degrees of designating who
is out and who in.[68] Growing up in working-class poverty, D. H.
Lawrence could gaze with outsider's eyes onto the dazzling
literary complex of Bloomsbury with Virginia Woolf or Lady
Ottoline very near its center—was it a mirage? Yet Virginia
Woolf herself could feel excluded from the charmed circle of
Oxbridge and refer in *Three Guineas* (1938) to professional women
forming their own Society of Outsiders. In or out, then, is less a
question of place than of placement relative to power systems.

As a case in point, what Ruth Adam addresses is an advanced
stage of long-term trends in society's objectifying of single—odd—
women. By the end of the eighteenth-century, a quarter of upper-
class women were never to marry; as their ranks grew through the
nineteenth-century they were the old maids; following World War
I they were the spinsters.[69] This surplus of unmarried women
in England resulted from various socioeconomic factors, e.g., late
marriages, the high rates of male emigration, wars, etc. The old
maids who were expected to live with and be provided for by
relatives were accordingly subjected to a great deal of
ambivalence and undeserved resentment. The spinsters could earn
but not quite enough to live alone, nor would society sanction
their doing so; and so, beholden to others, they were
marginilized.[70] It was only in the 1920s and 30s that spinster
teachers could earn enough to support themselves in a society that
was beginning to tolerate changes. Consequently, for many
decades in England there have been large numbers of literate
women whose energies were not only forcibly constricted in
various ways but who had sufficiently large amounts of time on
their hands to read. Naturally they wanted to read about what
bore on their lives without being unduly bored. However
discerning and discriminating they may may have been in their

literary fare, taste and intelligence are not the issue here; rather
it is literature's more basic function of sustaining emotional life.
This purpose would have been realized in various ways. Perhaps
most obviously kept alive were readers' hopes that they would
eventually fit into a satisfactory marital union as traditional
heroines mostly did, or that traditional marriage might be
modified along more humane lines to include everyone. Perhaps
they also needed a species of fiction that knew better.

Whether   literally, as   someone   outside   marriage,   or
figuratively, as someone inside a less than satisfying marriage, the
odd-woman-out links the woman author to the woman reader in
a strongly-bonded feedback loop. Though not the first, perhaps
the purest spinster novel is *The Third Miss Symons* (1913) because
it is about little else and could be subtitled, The Making of a
Spinster. Born in 1872 into a family of clergy, classical authors,
and historians, its author, Flora Mayor, who never married, had
various role models, including seven maiden aunts. She
matriculated at Cambridge, and before settling on a writing
career, performed on the professional stage. Her heroine
Henrietta may embody less the new freedoms of the day than the
external constraints and inner failings of a previous time, as
Susan Hill writes in the Virago Introduction; but changes have
been exceedingly gradual, and a lifestyle of rare proposals,
disappointing suitors, restless visits to foreign spas prevails.

Only briefly does Henrietta escape the feeling of being
"odd-man-out," a phrase that changes to odd-girl in *Georgy Girl*
(1965), and in Elizabeth Jane Howard is elevated to the title of
her *Odd Girl Out* (1972).[71] When the odd-one-out is integrated
into society via marriage, friendship, or work, historical
circumstances have been addressed and transformed by a
gendered story. Modern women's fiction continues to explore and
expand the alternatives. Not only is there still the prospect of
reforming marriage but that of transforming society; not only are
there traditional romantic themes but also themes of female
friendship; not only are there plots similar to male oedipal
scenarios that represent erotic love outside marriage (Flaubert,
Lawrence, *et al*,), but there are plots wherein women deliberately
choose a single career with or without a love interest, from Ruth
Adam's own *I'm not Complaining* (1938) to Anita Brookner's *Hotel*

du Lac (1984).

In between lies one of the most extraordinary British writers in this century, Barbara Pym (1913-80). Like Austen, Pym grew up among the middling gentry of the provinces and in her fiction skirted the major social upheavals of her day. The following description fits her well: "The key to her characters, therefore, is their immersion for art's sake in the tedium of existence. Where most novelists have to heighten the feeling of living in the interests of their art," she "deliberately lowers it and, by so doing, gives its quotidian dullness an unexampled vitality. Her lively sense of the ridiculous makes all kinds of tedium amusing....Not the extravagances but the deprivations of being are the deepest spring of her comedy"—the passage is not about Pym, but about Austen.[72]

Perhaps in homage to Austen's meddlesome Emma, Pym's own Jane, a fortyish Oxford grad improbably wed to a clergyman, sets about matching up her former pupil Pru, whose twenty-ninth year has brought her to "an age that is often rather desperate for a woman who has not yet married."[73] With an almost brazen irony of the kind only Pym can sustain, marriage is both affirmed and negated as the reader gradually realizes that Jane's fervent matchmaking efforts scarcely conceal the reality of her own mismatch. Pru's escape from Jane's grand designs precipitates her comic fall into a more suitable match.

Akin to Austen's comic plots, Pym's gratify her readers with happy endings, but more often the Austen matching-up method is eschewed for seeking alternatives that are closer to the lived experiences of single women who know better than to believe in a happily-ever-after, yet do not despair. Pym effectively reverses Austen by showing how ostensibly unhappy endings may become tolerably happy. Even that most somber work, *Quartet in Autumn* (1978), about senior citizens facing redundancy, lonely retirement, and the end of the line, patiently affirms that hope springs eternal, tomorrow is another day. Less traditional than appears, Pym is a sort of modern minimalist *sans* Samuel Beckett's relentless irony. A spinster *malgré-elle*, Pym's first published novel, *Some Tame Gazelle* (1950) displays an uncanny prescience when it projects her sister and herself into a middle-aged future that finds them both thoroughly enjoying their single lives. At the time of the writing (1933), she clearly assumed she would marry someday, though very soon after her Oxford years she began referring to herself humorously as a spinster; and although her sister Hilary was married for a time, eventually the two of them lived out their lives in an Oxfordshire village.[74]

The other extraordinary aspect of her career is an eclipse from the published world from 1962 to 1978, due to an apparent change in taste, and her rediscovery largely through the pieces on her written by Philip Larkin and Lord David Cecil in *TLS* (1977) on the century's most underrated writers. (It goes without saying that this male-rescue effort puts a peculiar spin on theories about women having a literature of their own or inhabiting a more humane community; Henry James had also sustained and inspired such Victorian novelists as Mrs. Humphry Ward and Vernon Lee in their difficult labors.)[75] Fortunately, Pym never abandoned the career that seemed to have abandoned her, and her final novel *A Few Green Leaves* (1979) manages to be mainstream Pym and matricentric in the best Austen matching-up sense. Suitably named Emma, a female anthropologist of thirty-eight takes a cottage in a country village where the handsome, widowed clergyman is at loose ends after having just lost his sister, if only he would forget about his quest for deserted Medieval villages and really look at Emma, which of course he eventually does—so the last of her spinsters gets her man in the end.

Yet in British women's literature, the specter of the spinster endures: positively as a spiritual presence joining woman author and woman reader, negatively as a threatening spirit to the author—her unfruitful fate unless her work be wed to the reading public. For the woman writer herself is—perhaps both as writer and as woman—an odd-one-out who overcomes this liability through her literary success. And yet she never quite allows herself to forget the odd-one-out's condition, for, generously or obsessively, she sets out to remedy or eliminate that stubborn piece of reality. Pym's achievements fulfil that late Victorian ideal of "honourable spinsterhood."[76] For Laura Doan, Pym revises and transforms the spinster stereotype into an "alternate lifestyle."[77] In either case, Pym can be credited with bringing into maturity a distinctive creative mode of spinster fiction.

Several features distinguish spinster fiction. Constructed

around a single heroine, it begins at a low point in her affairs, with a faint whiff of promise. She is taking a cottage in Wales to get over an unhappy affair (Alice Thomas Ellis), or embarking on a solo holiday at a Swiss lake (Brookner), or sojurning in a remote village for study (Pym).[78] This initial low point coincides with the low mood or depressed affect of the reader-spinster when she in turn looks away from her present impasse and picks up the novel. Interesting things of a comical or romantic nature soon begin for the spinster-heroine, offering the prospect of realized desire. But once awakened, desire is dispersed in various directions, away from its troublesome sources, and a new set of conflicts arise to be resolved, so that by the end there may emerge a better-off feeling, a sense of forward movement, or of feeling better about fitting back into the scheme of things. If the reader had suffered a prior break in connections and a lowering of self-esteem, these ensuing moods have been acknowledged, objectified, and given new imaginative form. So immersing herself, reader may experience a release of pent-up energies or a restoration of relatedness through fictional companionship. More to the matricentric point, the spinster-reader overcomes the odd-one-out syndrome by being adopted by the spinster author (who is in turn adopted by her public).

Nothing akin to spinster fiction exists outside of Britain, and it may not have been accidental that Pym's loyalest and certainly most famous reader, Philip Larkin, was himself a sort of spinster librarian in Hull (which rhymes so well, as Wendy Cope can't resist, with Dull).[79] There is no theory to explain the male reader's appreciation of this genre within a genre (John Bayley finds Pym "soothing").[80] But the few moments of high hopes and waning expectations, the dreary return to the kettle on the cooker in the bedsitter (or in Brookner, the spike-heeled trudge along the rainy pavement to one's damp flat with the single lamb-chop to serve with the last of the summer wine), the reliance on friendships with one's own sex to tide one over, the dense and disappointing lovers, the consoling love of poetry and art, the capacity for finding whimsical amusement amid the most prosaic details—most of these may dovetail with many an English male's sense of insularity, his cultivation of privacy, and his lonely self-containment. Ultimately, the appeal of Pym's art is no more gender-bound than land-locked, and a viable theory would have to account for her transcending national boundaries. Such a theory might be called Gender, Genre, and the Gentle Reader; it would also have to account for how readers authorize their texts— for spinster fiction suggests the author is not so much dead as a moveable feast.

Notes

1. Zoë Fairbairns, *SpareRib* (February, 1991), 220: 29.

2. No gender stereotyping is intended in Diane Rothbard Margolis's, "Considering Women's Experience: A Reformation of Power Theory," which emphasizes woman as consumer, and I have expanded her model to include her as producer as well.

3. Louise Schleiner, *Tudor and Stuart Women Writers*, 15.

4. Raymond Irwin, *The English Library*, 234-49; Alison Adburgham, "Circulating Libraries and Mid-century Magazines," 110-27; F. Alan Walbank, Intro. to *Queens of the Circulating Library*, 9-18.

5. Lewalski, *Writing Women in Jacobean England*, 2-3; Tina Krontiris, *Oppositional Voices*.

6. Janet Todd, *The Sign of Angellica*, 8.

7. Ruth Perry, *Women, Letters and the Novel*; however, Eva Figes argues the method was too subjective to suit women's needs for irony and distance (*Sex and Subterfuge*, 17).

8. For a revisionary view of the "construction of a female reader," see chapt. 2 of Ros Ballaster's *Seductive Forms*, 31-42.

9. Dale Spender, *Living By the Pen*, 240.

10. Patricia Crawford, "Women's Published Writings, 1600-1700," 213-4.

11. Catherine Gallagher, *Nobody's Story*, 3, 6-7.

12. Cheryl Turner, *The Growth of Published and Professional Fiction Written by Women Before Jane Austen*, Ph.D. dissertation, Univ. of Nottingham, 1985), 299, quoted by

Spender (1992), 240.

13. Turner, 291.

14. Kristina Straub, "The Construction of Actresses'
Femininity," in *Sexual Suspects*, 89-108.

15. Aphra Behn, *The Rover*, Scene Two, 24; on male
prejudice against her, see Antonia Fraser, *The Weaker Vessel*,
333-6.

16. Jane Spencer, *The Rise of the Woman Novelist*, 30-1.

17. Caroline Moore, "First Lady of English Literature,"
London Times (14 Jan 1993).

18. Katherine Sobba Green, *The Courtship Novel*; Louise
Schleiner locates only three gendered discourse modes in Tudor
and Stuart England, all oppressive: the "superior-female-
chastity discourse"; the "extramarital-seduction discourse"; and
the "female-demonization discourse"; but various courtship
discourses had already been present in Renaissance drama that
readily lent themselves to matricentric shaping by women
novelists in the 18th-Century (*Tudor and Stuart Women Writers*,
16-17).

19. Katharine M. Rogers, *Feminism in Eighteenth-Century
England*, 119 & 143.

20. Patricia Meyer Spacks, "Oscillations of Sensibility,"
505.

21. Gary Kelly, "Jane Austen's Real Business," 154-67.

22. Nancy Armstrong, *Desire and Domestic Fiction*, 3-4.

23. *Sexual Suspects*, 101.

24. Ros Ballaster, *Seductive Forms*, 25.

25. Ballaster, 197; see also Paula Marantz Cohen, *The Daughter's Dilemma*.

26. Nancy Armstrong, "The 19th-Century Jane Austen," 240.

27. Spencer, 9.

28. Spencer, 9.

29. Ballaster, 197.

30. Spencer, 7; Adburgham, 114-5. A similar practice continues today in male-penned Mills & Boon romances. A mini-scandal blew up when a male fobbed off a collection of Asian stories by "Rahila Khan" to Virago (Rosalind Coward, "Looking for the Real Thing," wonders what constitutes an "authentic voice"); in other respects, it was a case of supply meeting to demand.

31. Todd, *The Sign of Angellica*, 218. On the role of the Minerva Press, which catered to the popular craze for gothics, see Dorothy Blakey, *The Minerva Press, 1790-1820*.

32. Dale Spender, *Mothers of the Novel*, 119-37.

33. Gaye Tuchman, *Edging Women Out*, 7.

34. Spencer shows that women novelists were receiving serious attention long before 1840 and traces their disparaging as far back as Alexander Pope (*Rise of the Woman Novelist*, 4).

35. Willa Cather, "The Hundred Worst Books and They That Wrote Them," 961—2.

36. Cather, 963-4.

37. Willa Cather, "Four Women Writers," 697-9; this silencing of a woman writer by a woman writer goes against the sexual polemics of Tillie Olsen's *Silences*, which includes both Eliot and Cather but misses their strategies.

38. The Brontës' choice of Currer, Acton, and Ellis Bell was deliberately gender-neutral, as Lyn Pykett writes, quoting Charlotte, an "ambiguous choice...dictated by a sort of conscientious scruple at assuming Christian names positively masculine, while we did not like to declare ourselves women, because...we had a vague impression that authoresses are liable to be looked on with prejudice"—being either chastised or flattered due to their sex (*Emily Brontë*, 13). Gerin relates the names to local acquaintances (*Emily Brontë: A Biography*, 186); but Sharon Marcus demonstrates that Bell was a prominent media name, and that such ambiguous usage was known as the "puff mysterious," even though reviewers surmised the author's true gender ("The Profession of the Author: Abstraction, Advertising, and Jane Eyre, 213-15). Like the Brontës' George Eliot's name-change had less to do with market-access than with false *placing* by sex, which for her had both personal and literary implications (Ruby V. Redinger, *George Eliot: The Emergent Self*, 3-4); Jennifer Uglow, "'George Eliot' and the Woman Question in the 1850's" in *George Eliot*, 65-81. Ina Taylor portrays Marian Evans as a shrewd business woman with powerful social ambitions, who was "prepared to indulge her lover by playing the part of the fragile genius, reliant on a clever business partner, and quotes her admission, "I am a very calculating person now—valuing approbation as representing guineas" (*A Woman of Contradictions: The Life of George Eliot*, 157-8]). Moreover, as Tuchman notes, "literary historians have usually ignored the use of female pseudonyms by men...to emphasize the theory that nineteenth-century authors were expected to be men or that women novelists felt that publishers gave preferential treatment to male authors" (*Edging Women Out*, 53). The ideological version, on the other hand, claims that the above authors "employed male pseudonyms and at times male narrators in an effort to legitimize themselves within a literary patrilineage that denied women full creative authority"

(Gilbert and Gubar, *No Man's Land*, 1:185). N.N. Feltes intriguingly speculates that Marian Evans' adoption of George Eliot was predicated on her recognizing the distinction between amateur and professional (*Modes of Production of Victorian Novels*, 41); finally, Maryline Lukacher argues that the French writers Stendahl, Sand, Rachilde, and Bataille used pseudonyms as "part of a subversive effort to challenge patriarchal authority and to reinscribe the suppressed relation to the mother" (*Maternal Fictions*, 2).

39. Olga Kenyon, editor, *Women Writers Talk*, 183.

40. Adburgham, 113.

41. Humphrey Carpentar, *The Brideshead Generation*.

42. The collapsing of all men into a heterosexual totality signified as Patriarchy is then another case of the "Problems of Exclusion in Feminist Thought" (the subtitle of Elizabeth V. Spelman's *Inessential Woman*).

43. In conversations with representative women authors ranging from Elizabeth Jane Howard to Margaret Drabble and Sara Maitland, I was often told that writing had become too dispersed to congregate under an Establishment umbrella.

44. Muriel Spark, *Curriculum Vitae*, 205.

45. Jayne E. Marek, *Women Editing Modernism*.

46. Quentin Bell, *Virginia Woolf: A Biography*.

47. On women's presses, see Patricia Duncker's *Sisters and Strangers*, 39-54.

48. Meiling Jin, "Feminist Publishing from This Writer's Point of View," *SpareRib*, 202 (June, 1989): 29; Allison Hennegan, "A Demand That Is not Being Met," 28-9.

49. Ros de Lanerolle, editor of The Women's Press, quoted by Nicci Gerrard, *Into the Mainstream*, 31.

50. Nicci Gerrard, *Into the Mainstream*, 30-31. For an account of Zoë Fairbairns' misadventures with publishers after her Cinderella debut with Macmillan at age seventeen, see "I Was a Teenage Novelist," *Women's Review*, 8 (June, 1986):8-11.

51. Zoë Fairbairns, "I Was a Teenage Novelist," 11.

52. Zoë Fairbairns, "It's a Feminist Fortnight!" *Everywoman* (June 1990), 12.

53. "Feminist Book Fortnight '91," *SpareRib*, 224:29; Rukhsane Ahmad, "What's Happening to Women's Presses?" *SpareRib*, 223:12.

54. Duncker, 47-8.

55. *SpareRib*, 223:12; according to Dale Spender, women comprise 25% of the general writers in print (*The Writing or the Sex*), and various countings of women reviewing and being reviewed in the media are somewhat lower. Duncker's claims for The Women's Press of 60 titles annually seems a misprint (see *SpareRib*, June, 1989, 202:29, for 60 as the total to date).

56. Carol Thurston, *The Romance Revolution*, 47.

57. Julia Llewelleyn Smith, "Model for a Woman of Substance," *Times of London* (3 January 1995).

58. Irene Coffey, "Lesbian Sleuths," *SpareRib*, 217:34-5; other signs of changing taste, *Erotica: An Anthology of Women's Writing*, Foreword by Jeanette Winterson; *More Serious Pleasures* (1990).

59. Jane Spencer, 25; 78-9; Katherine Sobba Green, 3.

60. Dale Spender, The Writing or the Sex?

61. Quoted in Figes, 24.

62. A. S. Byatt, "Choices: The Writing of *Possession*, 17.

63. This fate also befell such male writers as Machiavelli, Ibsen, and D.H. Lawrence. When Ibsen in 1900 suffered a stroke, for example, it was widely believed he had succumbed to the syphilitic fate of Oswald in *Ghosts* (1881).

64. These frictions are examined in a wider perspective by Virginia Held, "Mothering versus Contract," 287-304.

65. Elaine Showalter, *A Literature of Their Own*; *The New Feminist Criticism*, 260-1.

66. See "The *Gentleman's Magazine* and Its Women Contributors," chapt. 5 of Adburgham, *Women in Print*, 79-81.

67. Ruth Adam, *A Woman's Place, 1910-1975*, 199; 19-24.

68. Lillian Faderman, *Odd Girls and Twilight Lovers: A History of Lesbian Life in 20th Century America*. The term may have homosexual or heterosexual import depending on context; George Gissing's 1893 novel *The Odd Women* refers to feminists.

69. Lawrence Stone, *The Family, Sex, and Marriage in England 1500-1800*, 241-5.

70. As Sheila Jeffreys shows in *The Spinster and Her Enemies* not all spinsters were pining away for male companionship.

71. *The Third Miss Symons*, 46.

72. John Bayley, "The 'Irresponsibility' of Austen," 1-20.

73. Barbara Pym, *Jane and Prudence*, 6.

74. Hazel Holt and Hilary Pym, editors, *A Very Private Eye, An Autobiography of Barbara Pym in Diaries and Letters.*

75. John Sutherland, *Victorian Fiction*, 145-8.

76. Patricia Thomson, *The Victorian Heroine*, 114.

77. Laura L. Doan, "Pym's Singular Interest," *Old Maids to Radical Spinsters*, 141, 153.

78. Alice Thomas Ellis, *Unexplained Laughter.*

79. Wendy Cope, *Making Cocoa for Kingsley Amis.*

80. Candida Crewe, "Mad Don and English Man,"*The Times Saturday Review* (23 May 1992), 6.

5

Two Myths Concerning the Woman Writer:
the Anti-Matricentric Mode

Women can domineer and infantilize women just as
well as men can. They know exactly where to stick
the knife. Also, they do great ambushes. From
men you're expecting it.
—Margaret Atwood[1]

The first myth of the Woman Writer is that she exists as a
totality; the second myth is that she shares feminist concerns and
is championed in feminist criticism; whereas in both instances the
opposite more likely obtains.

In part these myths, like Shakespeare's oppressed sister, are
negative creations; just as the hypothetical eleven out of twelve
women prevented from writing in Tillie Olson's scenario or the
archetypal figure imagined by Gilbert and Gubar whom
patriarchy effectively handicapped, the Woman Writer exists less
in her own 'write' than as a Trojan horse to infiltrate the
fortifications of patriarchy.[2] The following constructions are
representative (italics added):

The "woman writer feels herself to be literally or
figuratively *crippled* by the debilitating alternatives her culture
offers" [i.e., to be a "passive angel or an active monster"].[3]

The "literary woman has always faced equally *degrading
options* when she has had to define her public presence in the
world."[4]

"Women setting out to write have been automatically
afflicted [with a] special consciousness of gender."[5]

"I consider women's literature as a specific category...
because it is, in a sense, the literature of the *colonized*."[6]

"Dependence, like a colony, is maintained through fear;
fear is a state of being and a central theme in women's novels."[7]

"The contradictions produced by this double positioning
[of women inside masculinist definitions and yet marginalized by
culture] *fracture* women's subjectivity as it is articulated in
women's writing."[8]

As signifier of oppression for feminist theory, the Woman
Writer, severely impaired as she is, does at least testify to her

condition; but French feminism more fully negates her because woman does not exist: "a woman cannot 'be'...cannot be represented" except negatively, according to Julia Kristeva, one of the spellbinding if often equivocating voices from which American feminists have only recently begun awakening.[9]

When the Woman Writer is not being negated in victim-feminism, other *idées reçues* construct her as a sisterly warrior whom a common enemy has muffled or driven underground; yet despite these (ms)constructions, women writers express a remarkable range of attitudes toward feminism, thereby championing their own agency while raising more elusive issues: Why do so many women authors part company with feminism? Is it primarily, as suggested earlier, to protect and preserve the free spaces of creativity? Why, on the other hand, do feminist critics disparage women writers? Or are such questions simply unfair? Aren't the critics, for example, really attacking writing conditions through the women writers? Not according to Margaret Atwood, who found that, having "bucked the odds, worked your little fingers to the bone and achieved some form of success, it was not overjoying to be labelled a 'token woman'....It wasn't any more fun being told you weren't a real woman because you weren't a lesbian."[10] Thus arises the uncomfortable inference that failed women writers are privileged over those who endanger the ideology by thriving either through the women's movement (like Atwood) or despite it (like Drabble).

To do justice, however, to the full register of attitudes Anglophone women authors have expressed toward feminism and to effectively demythologize the Woman Writer, one needs a scale of ten ranging from (-5) total rejection, strong misgivings, marked differences, clear distancing, to ambivalence, mild sympathy, warm interest, to fervent commitment (+5), with (0) registering ambivalence or neutrality.

(-5) Total rejection: For her unrelenting struggles against feminism, the enormously prolific and popular Victorian novelist Mrs. Humphry (Mary) Ward properly belongs in a class of her own. She made speeches against suffragism, founded, edited, and wrote for *The Anti-Suffrage Review*, and, in *Delia Blancheflower* (1915), satirized the "neurasthenic and fanatical suffragette who burns down a country home to dramatize her cause."[11]

Though Doris Lessing has since claimed that she could burst into tears at the question of her being antifeminist, her statements in 1982 stand as among the most critical: "What the feminists want of me is something they haven't examined because it comes from religion. They want me to bear witness. What they would really like me to say is, 'Ha, sisters, I stand with you side by side in your struggle toward the golden dawn where those beastly men are no more.' Do they really want people to make oversimplified statements about men and women? In fact, they do. I've come with great regret to this conclusion."[12]

Joan Didion depicted herself in 1972 as a writer "committed mainly to the exploration of moral distinctions and ambiguities" for whom "feminist analysis may have seemed a particularly narrow and cracked determinism." The "idea that fiction has certain irreducible ambiguities seemed never to occur to these women, nor should it, for fiction is in most ways hostile to ideology." Distinguishing an earlier form of feminism in "de Beauvoir's grave and awesome recognition of woman's role as 'the Other,'" she perceives the current women's liberation movement as artificial Marxism, an "aversion to adult sexual life," and a flight into revolutionary "romance."[13]

Noting she does "not believe in the all-men-are-swine programme," Anita Brookner vowed to "take on the feminists."[14]

(-4) Strong misgivings: Fay Weldon declared, "Ideological correctness always seems to me to be very dangerous, because there is no correct way—you have to be open and receptive rather than saying you know what you believe."[15] When asked directly about feminism, she replied: "I don't think that women are nicer than men. I think it has very little to do with gender; I think it has to do with power. If you put a woman in a man's position, she will be more efficient, but no more kind."[16]

In a similar vein, Edna O'Brien, who "would like women to have a better time" does not "see it happening, and for a very simple and primal reason: people are pretty savage towards each other, be they men or women." Finding herself no "darling of the feminists" who find her "too preoccupied with old-fashioned themes like love and longing," she "resents being lectured at" when she "has enough trouble keeping madness at bay."[17]

Opposing a left-wing polemics that pit "hierarchy against equality, theory against practice, intellect (cold) against feeling (warm)"—dualisms normally attributed to patriarchy—Susan Sontag sees "feminists" perpetuating the same "philistine characterizations." Hence, "feminist criticism... needs to be rethought" regarding "its demands for intellectual simplicity, advanced in the name of ethical solidarity."[18]

(-3) Marked Differences: Muriel Spark, whose suffragette grandmother marched with Mrs. Pankhurst, concurs with her mother that the battle is over, and now "women's lib, the movement, has defeated itself because more and more they tend to clump women together and I don't quite like that."[19]

(-2) Distancing: Gail Godwin, deeming herself a feminist, had second thoughts in responding to a feminist counterattack of a critical review, declared, "Yes, as a writer, I *do* resist being fitted into a tradition of writers solely on the basis of our being a woman. I prefer to choose my own gender-free tradition of writers who I see as being kindred spirits."[20]

Similarly, Iris Murdoch is "passionately in favor of women's lib, in the general, ordinary proper sense of women's having equal rights," but does not see "much difference between men and women, because the ordinary human condition still belongs more to a man than to a woman," and so is not "much interested in the female predicament."[21]

Margaret Drabble also speaks to distancing: when an interviewer mentioned her earlier "mother-centered" novels, she agreed she "wrote about the situation of being a woman" but was "not interested in women's issues at all."[22]

(-1) Marian Evans (George Eliot) ambivalently wrote that the "'Enfranchisement of Women' only makes creeping progress; and that is best, for woman does not yet deserve a much better lot than man gives her."[23]

(0) For articulate neutrality, Margaret Atwood's "growing involvement with human rights issues" leads her to these formulations: "one cannot deprive any part of humanity of the definition 'human' without grievous risk to one's soul. And for women to define themselves as powerless and men as all-powerful is to fall into an ancient trap, to shirk responsibility as well as to warp reality."[24] Her neutrality recently took a turn of political defiance in expressly writing about bad girls, only to be followed by an olive branch, claiming it's no longer likely that "anybody

who says 'boo' is a traitor" to the movement.[25]

Speaking of men and women, Nadine Gordimer remarked, "I don't really feel we're all that different." For her, there's an "over-riding humanity...to know hurt, pain, fear, discouragement, frustration, this is common to both sexes."[26]

(+1) Joyce Carol Oates' eschewing any distinctively female voice while describing herself as a "(woman) writer" and as a "feminist critic or sympathizer," seems to be a fair way of owning a desire to break out of her parentheses while keeping her options open.[27] But her misgivings would shift her to the minus scale when she insists that "by denying subtlety and humanity to roughly one-half the population, and by delineating Maleness in place of specific human beings who happen to be male, the writer with feminist interests severely jeopardizes her power to create imaginative literature."[28]

(+2) Erica Jong and Mary Gordon both portray their struggle to write in terms of overcoming male resistance and in prose that affirms a feminist edge.[29]

In addition to the obstacles in a sexist society, Alice Walker had to come to terms with how "white women feminists revealed themselves as incapable as white and black men of comprehending blackness and feminism in the same body, not to mention the same imagination." She coped by identifying herself as a "womanist," allied with an international women's movement. Audre Lord and other black feminists have raised similar issues over feminist publishing and bookfairs.[30]

(+3) While urging a women writer to have "a room of one's own," and to "think back through her mothers," Virginia Woolf, nonetheless, adapts male ideals of Impersonality (T.S. Eliot) and androgynous creativity (Coleridge).[31]

(+4) Angela Carter writes, "the women's movement has been of immense importance to me personally and I would regard myself as a feminist writer because I'm a feminist in everything else and one can't compartmentalize these things in one's life."[32]

(+5) For Sara Maitland, feminism was the fairy godmother who "transforms all the old stuff around Cinderella into new and useful equipment," so that the old stories could be "told through brand new shining feminist eyes." Set upon a quest to "become a Feminist Writer," she heads down a "narrow passage between two grinding rocks" of politics versus great writing, of gender versus imagination, of theory versus inspiration. At first "women-in-struggle were the goodies and men were the baddies," but as the quest continues, the "stories got darker." Finally, "when she wrote about women and wrote truly out of her own experience of herself as a woman she had to recognize the conniving, treacherous, unloving, unlovely things she did." But if "women choose madness and badness daily and mythologically... the Feminist Writer could not go on with her quest without telling these stories too."[33]   Zoë Fairbairns agrees, "you can acknowledge that women do let other women down and still be a feminist. We make bad choices and bad decisions sometimes. Stories come out of people's failings and falsities, and how they resolve them."[34] And so the quest continues....

That statements of women authors' attitudes toward feminism are only one of the three texts they produce goes without saying. In addition, there are their fictional texts and the texts of their lives, preserved in letters, memoirs, interviews, etc. And although one can appreciate the poststructuralist temptation to play the Author-Is-Dead card, to rely too heavily on biographical evidence, or to read the literary text as a transparent cultural document, it is clear that all three texts are potentially relevant. Thus to assert that Margaret Drabble is (+/-) feminist may imply that she has disavowed a commitment to the woman's cause in interviews (-), that she has marched for abortion rights (+), or that her texts display or disregard supposed feminist properties—both cases have been made (+/-). Fay Weldon's *Praxis* taken in isolation would reverse her (-4) into a (+4); but *Puffball* would bounce her back.

It all depends on the text of privilege, but even women writers' self-representations within a feminist-friendly mode differ from feminists' ideological constructions of them into unitary wholes. And should disruption threaten, as when both "Anita Brookner and her fictional mouthpieces break with feminism," a major rescue operation is summoned.[35] Having granted that "individual women characters do constitute the villains" and allowing a "procession of sisters, mothers, students, and acquaintances, all of them tirelessly manipulative and demanding, who rob the heroines of their opportunities for love or security," the literary feminist nevertheless believes "women as a class come off well," even though most feminists have shucked gender as class; but, whatever *class* may signify, women as a class do not cohere in Brookner's delicate and discerning novels, permeated as they are in bourgeois sensibility.[36]   Such 'msreadings' are not lacking in interest, yet to attribute feminist sympathy to writers who concentrate selectively on women's situations is misleading but not unusual.

Literary feminists' corrective efforts extends even to explicitly feminist fiction. After Patricia Duncker has stipulated the qualities of woman's writing as utopian/ oppositional/angry and situated between women/communal, she quotes Helen, a stand-in for Michele Roberts in her feminist texts, who is struggling with the demons of writer's block. Helen imagines a "gang" of adversaries "lining her up against a wall and firing injunctions at her: stop; you are boring, obscene, self-indulgent, peripheral, *wrong*."[37] This gang consists of "the outraged nun, the hurt relatives, the mocking male reviewer, the male militant, the correct feminist." The latter perplexes Duncker into innocently quipping "whoever she is," before admonishing the author to give up her solitary task of defining self/woman and to seek answers more closely "within the community of women."[38]

No wonder, with feminist critics' admonitions of orthodoxy and with academics' either/or binds, that creativity's anomalous freedoms are viewed with suspicion or reduced to monism. This is especially true now when theory has been valorized over its various others; for it must be acknowledged that a checkerboard clarity of limited, prescribed moves has a certain appeal over a seemingly random topography of dead-end lanes, broken signposts, and motley clusters of people in or around villages—it *is* nice to know where you're going, though also boring and often deceptive. Thus to read the text of Isak Dinesen's life, for example, is to find her endorsing then disavowing feminism; to read the text of her fictions, like "Babette's Feast," is to find feminist affirmations: so which is she?[39] The teller/tale dichotomy is then compounded by definitions of what comprises feminist fiction, by the real, and by authors' often oscillating statements. Confining the Woman Writer to feminist *manquée* or feminist *malgré-elle* falsifies issues, for not only does Woman Writer conceal many diverse women writers, but any *named* woman writer swims through the trawls of theory, defeating any project of labeling—Drabble as pro-/anti-/non-feminist.

Yet as the monomyth recedes and a multiplicity of attitudes—including dissonant messages—among women writers toward feminism emerges, it comes as no surprise that some feminist critics have launched counter-offensives. Privileging woman's cause over literary worth, these assaults sacrifice the straw figure of Woman Writer on the altar of polemics under the guise of sisterly sympathy. Though wishing to avoid a "'narrowly feminist' reading" of Iris Murdoch, Deborah Johnson is nonetheless disappointed when textual evidence compels her admission that Iris Murdoch "cannot ultimately be claimed as a feminist writer."[40] Such an outlook is similar to labour-party critics of D. H. Lawrence who found his promising working-class origins did not live up to their Marxist expectations, or to debate in the 1950s over whether Graham was a truly Catholic novelist. Sectarian critics, who seek reenforcement of their orthodoxy and are predictably disappointed when literature doesn't provide it, subtly undermine the writer's agency or simply miss it.

The first sustained rhetorical assault on women writers' agency occurs in *The Madwoman in the Attic*. There, the "female artist['s]... battle ...is not against her male precursor's reading of the world but against his reading of *her*.[41] This totalizing discourse is predicated not only on the monomyth of the "female artist" but on the unqualified power of her oppressive other. The case for patriarchy is so strong in fact that women are constructed virtually in terms of their oppression. "Woman's socially determined sense of her own biology," for example, minimizes her own personal history, her role in inscribing her identity, and her needs for caring, nurturing relationships foregrounded in feminist psychology. "In patriarchal society the woman writer does experience her gender as a painful obstacle, or even a debilitating inadequacy...she is victimized...alienated from male predecessors"; "her fear of the antagonism of male readers, her culturally conditioned timidity about self-dramatization, her dread of patriarchal authority of art, her anxiety about the impropriety of female invention" all set her apart from male writers and foreclose her hopes for producing quality work.[42] Moreover, "patriarchal socialization literally makes women sick, both physically and mentally," though what kept many of them relatively healthy along race/class lines is not explained.[43] Instead, her presumed failures are excused: "surrounded as she is by images of disease, by traditions of disease, and by invitations both to disease and to dis-ease, it is no wonder that the woman writer has held many mirrors up to the discomforts of her own nature."[44]

In these rationalizations of women's failure to compose healthy texts, the Woman Writer seems to be afflicted by nothing so much as a severe case of rhetorical overkill. But if the plight of the woman artist has been rendered hopeless, the artist as such, who "kills experience into art," doesn't fare much better.[45] One way or another, the Woman Writer is in for it, whether "sentenced" to male texts or allowed to break free and kill her own experience for the sake of female texts.[46]

Emerging from this double-bind is a two-natured theory of woman: a false nature imposed on her by patriarchal tyranny which has kept her in a state of bondage or captivity—unnaturally domesticated or tamed; a second, more authentic nature being liberated retroactively by current feminist criticism. But madness, which continually recurs in women's texts, is multiply determined; and an ideologically split woman seems to be the offspring of a bad marriage between patriarchal dominance and feminist theory at its most deterministic.

If the victimization model nulls the prospects of the Woman Writer, the subversion model voids the integrity of her texts—either the Woman Writer is split or her texts are. In these scenarios, women novelists are so devious that many have even "succeeded in hiding the covert or implicit feminism in their books from themselves," and these secrets have supposedly gone unnoticed for hundreds of years and by thousands of readers until the mid 1970's when North American feminist scholars suddenly discovered the key.[47] By uncanny good fortune, these long-buried secrets, once properly interpreted, coincided precisely with current feminist needs. Annis Pratt explains the writer's supposed subversive tactic by the "drowning theory," after a practice in black churches in which the congregation banged pots to drown out songs of freedom. In other words, women's prose in previous centuries was just so much banging to shield secret wishes—their texts not cohesive wholes. Instead, the writer becomes either a sort of Mata Hari whose message is hidden by "all kinds of feints, ploys, masks, and disguises," or else a prescient postmodernist shrewdly "deconstructing" male texts.[48] Predictably, the "message they [feminist critics] find behind women's narrative manipulations is always the same. Rage at patriarchal oppression is the 'truth' behind every woman's fiction and the feminist critic's job is to discover and uncover its strategies of concealment."[49]   The monomyth produces monotony.

Either as crippled victims or as closet revolutionaries, women writers are deprived of diversity as well as agency and collapsed into the Woman Writer where she ends hopelessly alienated, thwarted from creative realization, drilling out prescribed messages with ingenious encodings.[50] It is one thing for these ideological discourses to disregard historical records of numerous women writers publishing and at times outpublishing men, but another to stress the Woman Writer's congenital failure (albeit through no fault of her own) to measure up to today's standards of ideological orthodoxy.   "We must...not be too judgmental from an ideological feminist point of view," Pratt cautions her readers lest they feel too superior to the Brontes or George Eliot.[51] Underlying ideological discourses is another one binding the various strategies together—a discourse of lack.

In this more inner discourse women writers and/or their characters suffer a lack in proportion to the critics' evident needs for ideological feedback.   During the liberation period, for example, earlier women characters lacked "autonomy," as at other times they may lack empowerment, community, their own voice, body, or other means through which to write.[52] Sometimes lack is given a more positively spin, as in Virginia Woolf's "early declarations of literary identity repress a potential feminist awareness."[53] This is rare, however, and the lack-mode reaches its apex among French scholars like Hélène Cixous who doubt that "feminine writing" even exists.[54] The orthodox answer is that, like the Loch Ness monster of the gendered sentence, which many have sighted from afar but no one has yet captured, yes, the creature exists, but only hypothetically as *l'écriture feminine*—last sighted bobbing up in the *oeuvre* of Jean Genet who writes of boys masquerading as women.[55]   Not to be confused with the accumulated body of prose by actual women writers, whom it disregards and demeans, *l'écriture feminine* is the mythical style of the mythical Woman Writer.

In other respects, however, feminist criticism has proven enormously successful in decentering established readings of texts and in exposing an array of sexist biases passing as value-free. Indeed, feminism need not per se interfere with women's writing as abundant evidence reveals; what does set off alarms is when "moral distinctions and ambiguities" (Didion) or the evenhanded allocation of human nastiness (Weldon) that form the rich tapestry of human experience are replaced by the ideological checkerboard of prescribed or proscribed jumps: "If you can't say something nice" about women, keep quiet is Atwood's take on feminist silencing of women writers.[56] Yet the larger point is not that feminism may be good or bad for women writers, since it is so variously experienced, but that women writers cannot be contained by a feminist hegemony any better than by other political systems.

Of the two ideological stereotypes—victim/closet revolutionary—the one initiates a rhetoric of rejection; the other, one of disappointment. In both, women's writing (re)performs a Lacanian discourse of lack or castration, which ideological feminist readings attempt to redress by fetishizing a hypothetical *l'écriture feminine*. The woman writer is then retrospectively empowered as the victim or the revolutionary *manquée*. The fetishizing of the victim (who empowers those who champion her cause) emanates from a refusal to countenance any woman writer as self-empowered under the evil totality of patriarchy and consequently fails to evolve a positive theory of women's creative work, clinging instead to Harold Bloom's ill-suited theories of anxiety or reviving Freud's obsolete account of female development via Lacan.[57]

All women authors are thus forced onto the "Procrustean fainting-couch of a dis-eased tradition," as Gail Godwin finds to her dismay in reviewing a politically-correct anthology of women's literature; and it seems redundant to delve into the distant past to find women writers penned-down and hemmed-in by male hegemony when feminist critics have already pegged-in their own version.[58] Such ideological fervor can at least plead consistency; thus, in the 20th Century, women writers must expect to be "haunted" by the "most painful option" and still be handicapped by "affiliation" complexes, "masculinity complexes," even by a "bewildering multiplicity of stances toward the past."[59] How this apparent change for the better—yet still double-binding—should have come about under patriarchy, given its unyielding oppression and women's writers' ambivalence toward feminism, is not clearly addressed. The change, which is really no change, perpetuates the rejecting/fetishizing discourse which now handicaps women not by lack but by plenitude of choice.

It may be that any politicized reading of texts is fetishistic insofar as fig-leafs of ideological totality are superimposed on a presumed, present lack. So long as these readings impact at discrete points, subversive contextualizing strategies such as feminist, Marxist, or other ideological constructions may coexist, but insofar as they impose their own hegemonies, their energies fetishize. Consequently, literature in the postmodern is an unremitting struggle of competing ideologies, agendas, and utopias. Everything is contested; even psychoanalysis, which should serve as an instrument for dissolving fetishizing tendencies, may itself be applied in a totalizing fashion. Even the liberal-humanist position that seeks an ideological-free zone is just as apt to be co-opted by its own complacencies.

Essentialism, a reliable signifier of the fetishizing impulse, fosters another variety of feminist attack on women writers. The target at first glance seems an unlikely one. If the specter of the shrewdly ambitious George Eliot, who sized up the women's movement of her day and calculated it to be an unprofitable investment of time and energy, haunts the martyrology of ideological feminism, it is less clear why Margaret Drabble, who has long concerned herself with women's situation, should take such a drubbing. True, some feminists resented her being able to stay home and write novels while her husband supported her; but her offense, according to Showalter, issues from a desire to "lose the label of woman's writer" and to find a male protagonist for *The Ice Age* (1977). Her penalty is to have an important feminist message in her next novel, *The Middle Ground* (1980), excised in Showalter's insistently titled essay, "Women Who Write Are

Women," in order to twist the text into its opposite intent. The novel concerns Kate, a journalist with a feminist slant, who has been propelled into a midlife depression by aborting a defective fetus. Over lunch with an old friend, she says in irritation, "Look, Hugo, it's all very well for you, and I'm as bloody sick of bloody women as you are, I'm sick to death of them, I wish I'd never invented them, but they won't go away just because I've gotten tired of them. Will they?" In sum, she is drained after her abortion and played out from her efforts for women, but just because she feels down doesn't mean their problems can be wished away. She thus affirms the importance of the cause apart from her flagging commitment, and so to break off the quote after "I wish I'd never invented them" as Showalter does, elides the weary but firm feminism in the passage and misleads readers about the author's candor.[60]

Of course, women who write are women, but they may also resist labeling and prefer to think of themselves as South African, African-American, Marxists, Magical Realists, or simply as persons writing. The power of naming has been mishandled not only by men; moreover, privileging gender over class, race, and all other identifications objectifies women as notoriously as patriarchy allegedly did formerly and, in denying them their subjectivity, deprives them of the right to name themselves. Puzzled by this, Showalter runs through a distinguished list of women authors—Mary McCarthy, Cynthia Ozick, Iris Murdoch, Nadine Gordimer, and others—who have resisted totalizing by gender, but is convinced she knows better. Cynthia Ozick replied, "Sexuality is condition, not tradition....Biology is what we can't help; culture is what we can. Sex is given: civilization is what we give. Sexual identity is what we have; art is what we make."[61]

The historical record clearly shows that women writers have always made art out of a mixed tradition of all sorts of constructed genders and have every intention of continuing to do so. Therefore, instead of compelling all women writers to march lock-step under a gendered banner of sisterhood, a matricentric discourse of difference would acknowledge all points on the plus/minus scale. As essentialism is discredited by recognizing gender as created/constructed, men are divested of their innate evil, and if a new enemy is still required, let that be ideology itself. Ideology provides for the secular mind what miracles and visions had once provided for the religious mind. Always certain in its simple, confident affirmations, ideology, lacking a referent, reveals the righteousness of the subject.

Replacing reason, ideology can claim anything—even Freud's implication in Virginia Woolf's suicide. By asserting that her reading of Freud "contributed to her suicide," Louise DeSalvo revives the figure of the Victorian lady on her fainting-couch and treats Woolf's "writing in much the same way a doctor might treat a diseased patient's body: as a screen on which symptoms are manifest."[62]

With the woman writer so thoroughly victimized, colonized, retroactively fetishized or revolutionized, and finally pathologized, the mystery of her failure to write may seem solved. But the double-binds imposed on her better attests to unresolved contradictions within theory. The implicit syllogism reads that patriarchy oppresses women: the outstanding sign of which is the plight of the Woman Writer. But since the case for patriarchal malignancy is founded on the evidence of her own debility, women writers can be empowered only insofar as their voices inscribe their incapacity or oppose their oppression. The price for political allies, however, is the denial of agency.

All the same, by resisting classifications of women writers as victims, male-possessed, or foiled revolutionaries, and by avoiding the double-bind displacements (the attributions of lack uncannily resemble Karen Horney's analysis of men projecting castration-fears onto women), one is better able to encounter women's own unfolding matricentric dimensions, in their lives as well as in their writings. None of this is to exempt women's writing from cultural oppressions, but merely to refuse an ideology of oppression the final word.

Notes

1. "If You Can't Say Something Nice," 21.

2. As Angela Carter says about the mythic Shakespearean sister, "So what....The concept is meaningless" ("Notes from the Frontline," *On Gender and Writing*, 76); similarly, the fervor of Tillie Olson's prose in *Silences* does not compensate for lack of quantitative data nor alleviate doubts that she denies difference by privileging male models of creativity; if one could reason from an absence of data to positive conclusions as she does, anything would be possible.

3. Gilbert and Gubar, *The Madwoman in the Attic*, 57.

4. Gilbert and Gubar, 64.

5. Lynn Sukenick, "On Women and Fiction," 28.

6. Christiane Rochefort, "The Privilege of Consciousness," quoted in Showalter's *The New Feminist Criticism*, 259.

7. Jane Miller, *Women Writing About Men*, 18.

8. Sally Robinson, *Engendering the Subject*, 11; however, she also argues for women's writing being "multiple"—a case of multiple fractures, perhaps, 10.

9. Julia Kristeva, "La femme, ce n'est jamais ça," 137, *Interviews*, 98; for Kristeva's "lack of interest in women as agents," see Ann Rosalind Jones, "Julia Kristeva on Femininity." While Kristeva prefers to write on male authors (Mallarmé, Proust, Joyce), she has written on de Stael and Duras; and though her strategies of negativity can be off-putting, she does allow for a circumscribed female agency. Like many gifted women writers, however, she insists on writing in her own "personal name," rather than as a woman—a strategy of entitlement that alienated her from militant feminists

(*Interviews*, 124; *The Samurai*, 180-3). Thus her experience with ideological correctness dovetails with Margaret Atwood's.

10. Atwood, "If You Can't Say Something Nice," 20-21.

11. Janet Todd, editor, *British Women Writers*, 691; John Sutherland, *Mrs. Humphry Ward*, 300-09.

12. David Streitfeld, "Doris Lessing and the Madness of Our Times," 15; quoted from Lesley Hazelton's "Doris Lessing on Feminism, Communism, and 'Space Fiction,'" 21.

13. Joan Didion, "The Women's Movement," *The White Album*, 109-19.

14. John Haffenden, *Novelists in Interview*, 70-1; Margaret Diane Stetz takes these negatives as a positive challenge and strives to save Brookner from herself and make her writings safe for feminists, describing her first as an "unconscious feminist," then a "reluctant" one, and finally as a "woman-centered" feminist *malgré-elle* ("Anita Brookner: Woman Writer as Reluctant Feminist," 96-112).

15. Nicci Gerrard, "The Fay Weldon Academy of Laughter," 10-11. Elsewhere Weldon observed, "feminism is there if you wish to make it available to you," and admitted, "I am a feminist, but I would not describe myself as a feminist novelist." Then in an even-handed put-down, she declared, "women are probably incorrigible if they're allowed to be, and men are incorrigible because they're encouraged to be" (Haffenden, 312-3, 315).

16. Marjorie Williams, "Fay Weldon, Fancifully."

17. Edna O'Brien, *Writers at Work: Paris Review*, 251-2.

18. Susan Sontag, "Notes on Art, Sex, and Politics."

19. Lynn Barber, "The Elusive Magician."

20. Gail Godwin reviewed *The Norton Anthology of Literature by Women*, for the *NY Times Book Review* (28 April 1985) and responded to letters (26 May 1985).

21. Jack Biles, "An Interview with Iris Murdoch," 119.

22. First quote from Nancy Pollard, "Margaret Drabble: 'There Must Be a Lot of Women Like Me,'" 255-67; second from Joanne Creighton's "Interview with Margaret Drabble," 25.

23. Quoted (69) in "George Eliot and the Woman Question," *George Eliot*, 65-81) by Jennifer Uglow, who considers Eliot's attitude toward "organized feminism" to be "ambivalent," 70.

24. Margaret Atwood, *Selected Words*, 14, 428-9.

25. Sarah Hall, *New York Times* (23 November 1993).

26. Nadine Gordimer, "A Story for this Place and Time," Interview with Susan Gardner, *Kunapipi* 3:(Fall, 1981).

27. Joyce Carol Oates, "(Woman) Writer," in *First Person Singular*, 190-7; "'At Least I Have Made a Woman of Her,'" *The Profane Art*, 36.

28. Oates, *NY Times Book Review* (21 Nov 1976).

29. Janet Sterburg, *The Writer on Her Work*, 169-80; 27-32.

30. Alice Walker, "A Child of One's Own: A Meaningful Digression within the Work(s)" in Sternberg's *The Writer and Her Work*, 121-40; *SpareRib* (June, 1991), 224:29.

31. Marilyn R. Farwell, "Virginia Woolf and Androgyny," 433-51; Virginia Woolf, *A Room of One's Own*, 79; 108.

32. Angela Carter, "Notes from the Front Line," 69-77.

33. Sara Maitland, "A Feminist Writer's Progress," 17-23.

34. Zoë Fairbairns, *SpareRib* (February, 1991), 220:29.

35. Stetz, 98.

36. Stetz, 97.

37. Michele Roberts, *The Visitation*, 81.

38. Patricia Duncker, *Sisters and Strangers*, 18. In fact, Michele Roberts is involved with a community of London feminist writers, including Sara Maitland, Michelene Wandor, and others. The American writer, May Sarton, is also chastised by Duncker for "hysterically disdain[ing] the label 'Lesbian,'" 22.

39. Judith Thurman, *Isak Dinesen: The Life of a Story Teller*, 173; Marleen Barr, "Isak Dinesen's Female Artists as Precursors to Contemporary Feminist Fabulators," *Feminism, Utopia, and Narrative*, 23 (21-33).

40. Deborah Johnson, *Iris Murdoch*, xi, 112.

41. *Madwoman*, 49.

42. *Madwoman*, 50-1.

43. *Madwoman*, 53.

44. *Madwoman*, 57.

45. The quote is from Albert Gelpi, *Madwoman*, 14.

46. *Madwoman*, 91.

47. Annis V. Pratt, "The New Feminist Criticisms," 183.

48. Pratt, 183.; *Madwoman*, 119.

49. Ros Ballaster, *Seductive Forms*, 21.

50. Feminist-inspired critics occasionally differ: Dale Spender, for example, eloquently argues for female agency: "by the second half of the eighteenth century most of the women writers of serious fiction were concerned with ethical questions. They wanted to explore the human predicament and to understand human nature, and threaded through their novels are the issues of what is right and what is wrong, what can be improved and what cannot. They asked why human beings behaved in certain ways and whether they could behave differently. And they undertook all their explanations of character and judgment, of the individual and society without knowing anything of Sigmund Freud and his psychology....these women were asserting their identity in a society which did not grant them existence in their own right" (*Mothers of the Novel*, 2-3).

51. Pratt, 183. Understandably, it is hard to be humble when women were assured by Adrienne Rich, "We know more than Jane Austen or Shakespeare because we know more about the lives of women" (*"When We Dead Awaken*: Writing as Re-Vision," *College English*, 25); nor is it difficult to see why recent feminist readers feel superior to George Eliot when they judge her by their own liberationist standards. For these readers, *Middlemarch* is either a failure, instating a "closed world whose survival depends on the continuing life of values cherished by the author," preventing her "from arriving at a radical solution--to the problem of female energy the book proposes" and in this reading "condemns" (Lee R. Edwards, "Women, Energy, and *Middlemarch*" in the Norton Critical Edition of the text [1977], 683-93); or else it is a feminist melodrama in which the women are virtuous victims. In *Madwoman*, for example, Rosamond, whose narcissism Eliot signifies by referring to her preoccupations with her "hair of infantine fairness" (76) in

contrast to Dorothea's emergent capacity for sympathy as
signifying maturity, is reduced—or elevated, depending one's
point of view—to victim status. She and Dorothea are twinned
as "oppressed," "victims," and "imprisoned by" their marriages
(514-16). Thus does the rich tapestry of art become the plain
checkerboard of ideology.

52. In Sydney Janet Kaplan's *Feminine Consciousness in
the Modern British Novel*, lacking in the characters' "feminine
consciousness" is a "recognition of their own autonomy," 177.
Psychoanalytically, lack is predicated on two stages of early
loss: the caregiving relation during weaning and the separation/
identification process, which may be schematized as the loss of
the oral object, and the threatened loss of part of the libinized
self, schematized as the castration complex. No doubt
Lacanians would account for these frustrations by referring the
lack to phallic issues, but there may also be the loss of a need-
gratifiying object in feminist discourses of women authors'
lack. Thus Virginia Woolf's project of writing back through
one's mothers is fraught with lack—on some level.

53. Makiko Minow-Pinkney, *Virginia Woolf and the
Problem of the Subject*, 2.

54. Hélène Cixous, "The Laugh of the Medusa," *Signs*,
875-93.

55. Hélène Cixous (in, "Sorties," *New French Feminisms*,
98 refers to an "abundant, maternal, pederastic femininity" in
Genet's writing, which Nelly Furman construes as
"representative of 'feminine writing'" ("The Politics of
Language: Beyond the Gender Principle?" in *Making a
Difference*, 74. For Makiko Minow-Pinkney, "'feminine' writing
is an attempt to inscribe positions against or alternative to
those of the dominant male order"—a definition that would
include many men and exclude many women (*Virginia Woolf
and the Problem of the Subject*, 16).

56. Atwood, "If You Can't Say...", 15.

57. In the perverse scenario, according to Louise Kaplan, victimization is a form of empowerment which allows the fetishized victim to conceal her strategies of vengeance (*Female Perversions*, 257-8). A distinction should be made between women who are victims/survivors of actual violence and victimization discourse. As a legal strategy that complements the critical rhetoric being discussed, women in law are finding that the "victim status and special protection can backfire, perpetuating stereotypes of helpless womanhood"—and thus unable to be awarded custody of their children. For Brooklyn Law School professor Nan Hunter, "woman-as-victim is a cultural script that evokes sympathy without challenging the hierarchical structure....a kind of melodrama that doesn't lead to any change in the conditions that cause victimization" (Tamar Lewin, "Feminists Wonder If It Was Progress To Become 'Victims,'" *Washington Post* (10 May 1992).

58. Godwin, *New York Times*, 28 April 1985.

59. Gilbert and Gubar, *No Man's Land*,1: 184, 168, 170-1, 185. Though promising gender contests ("The Battle of the Sexes"), the book's not-so-hidden agenda is an exhaustive catalogue of fictional sexual abuse along strict gender lines—all violators being male, all violated being female. Margaret Atwood gives this sort of analysis-by-taking-down names a hilarious send-up in "Writing the Male Character," *Second Words: Selected Critical Prose*, 412-33). Moreover, the modern stage where the battle of the sexes was fought out with great vigor and intellectual bravura in the drama of Ibsen, Shaw, and Strindburg is disregarded. Similar selective strategies occur in the *Madwoman*, with its logical leaps, affinities for the subjunctive tense, forcing of diverse texts into a contrived colloquy, and anecdotal approach. Thus the text opens: "Is the pen a metaphorical penis? Gerald Manley Hopkins thought so." There follows a quote, which indeed indicates the poet once expressed such a view in a private letter, followed by the universal application: "Male sexuality, in other words, is not

just analogically but actually the essence of literary power" (3-4).

60. Elaine Showalter, "Women Who Write Are Women,
New York Times Book Review (6 Dec 1984),1 ; Margaret Drabble,
The Middle Ground, 4. For sympathetic readings of the novel,
see Gail Efrig, *"The Middle Ground"* in *Margaret Drabble: Golden
Dreams*, 178-85, and Flora Alexander, *Contemporary Women
Novelists*, 24-29. Ideology also deletes the facts in Virginia
Woolf's supposed account of being "locked out" of the famous
"Oxbridge" library, which Showalter uncritically repeats (*The
New Feminist Criticism*, 244); whereas Woolf's access was
contingent on being "accompanied by a Fellow of the College or
[being] furnished with a letter of introduction" (*A Room of
One's Own*, 7-8).

61. Letter to *NY Times Book Review* (6 Jan 1984. "Simply
to invoke anatomy risks a return to crude essentialism, the
phallic and ovarian theories of art, that oppressed women in
the past," writes Showalter the theorist against her own practice
(*The New Feminist Criticism*, 250).

62. Louise DeSalvo, *Virginia Woolf: The Impact of
Childhood Abuse on Her Life and Work*, 127; Peggy Phelan in a
review of DeSalvo's study, *Women's Review of Books* (March,
1990: 16). Other readings that foreground the mother's role in
Virginia Woolf's disturbances are elided (e.g., Betty Kushen,
Virginia Woolf and the Nature of Communion; Shirley Panken,
Virginia Woolf and the "Lust of Creation"; Alma Halbert Bond,
Who Killed Virginia Woolf?. Thus, DeSalvo not only overlooks
the mother's role in respect to issues of symbiosis but, in
finding Virginia's older sister Vanessa supportive, excludes the
sadomasochistic relationship examined by Bond and others.
The subject is examined in detail in "Who's Afraid of Who
Killed Virginia Woolf?" chapt. 10 of my psychohistorical study,
Enactments. Meanwhile, DeSalvo and other feminists have
alledged sexual abuse by Djuna Barnes' brothers, for which her
recent biographer found no evidence (see Phillip Herring's
letter, "Djuna and the Scholars," *NY Times*, 4 Feb 1996).

6

Sources of the Matricentric
and Searches for an Adequate Psychoanalytic Discourse
on Women

> Men and women may not be the same, but what we
> call masculine and feminine characteristics may be
> distributed   unpredictably, in varying degrees
> among them....If there are natural sex and gender
> differences, they exist and develop in the context
> of culture. Perhaps they are, in the end, what we
> make of them.
> —Wendy Kaminer[1]

> She's got the balls to tell you the truth. I do too.
> —Rosanne Barr[2]

I

Are women more conservative than men? If Teiresias was
blinded for improperly answering who enjoyed sex more (women),
what might be the consequences for posing such a manifestly
fatuous, sexist, question-begging question? One consequence is
that once asked, it cannot be unasked, even if, like the legendary
Ship of Fools, it is unmoored to drift to its proper banks before
it infects sane discourse with such progeny as: what is
conservative? How is it to be measured *vis à vis* men and women?
Is it drawn from anecdotal data that suggest whereas men appear
more disruptive, rebellious, and prone to violence, women tend to
be more *pre*servative? What are, in any case, its essentialist
implications?

Asked but unanswerable, the initial question was
implicitly posed during a crucial shift along the axis of
difference in the women's movement around 1976-78. Up until
then the dominant liberationist pitch minimized difference by
privileging androgyny /equality as a solution to oppressive
stereotypes affecting both sexes; separatists held that roles as far
as men were concerned were innate, deliberate, or conspiratorial.
But in the late seventies a new woman-centered emphasis
foregrounded woman's special capacities as either salvageable

from patriarchal hegemony as in Adrienne Rich's *Of Woman Born: Motherhood as Experience and Institution* (1976) or as still intact as in Carol Gilligan's *In a Different Voice* (1982).[3] The strongly felt need to upgrade mothering which Rich tapped into, necessarily meant upgrading mothers, a task made exceeding arduous by a demeaning maternal discourse in previous feminist writing. Shulamith Firestone, for example, held that the girl, sensing her mother's rejection for whatever reason, "produces an insecurity about her identity in general, creating a lifelong need for approval."[4] Phyllis Chesler had gone on record as maintaining that "most women are glassed into infancy...by an unmet need for maternal nurturance."[5] However, sixteen years later in *The Sacred Bond*, she endows biological motherhood with a magical aura. But that was in the long run; in the short run feminist readers were encountering Nancy Friday's conflictual *My Mother, My Self*. But then as angry daughters shifted their gaze to their own beloved children, the tables began turning (though abortion issues kept the old battle lines alive).[6] As many feminists began having children, they were drawn into mainstream politics to negotiate "high-quality, affordable day care."[7]

Ever since Chodorow's momentous opening line in 1978: "Women mother," the privileging of motherhood over sisterhood has fostered a conflict-free, mono-gender model of female development insofar as feminist ideology bars any positive role for fathers.[8] Whether it was the sacred bond of Chesler's revisions, the frayed bond in Chernin's focus on eating disorders as the girl's flawed attempts to separate and individuate, or Chodorow's pattern of regression and repetition, the maternal dyad spanned to absorb the girl's later psychosexual phases of triangulated conflicts in an oedipal period *sans* father.[9] In sum, while motherhood overcame sisterhood, fatherhood, remaining too highly charged to be theorized, was relegated to personal memoirs of doomed quests like Germaine Greer's, *Daddy, We Hardly Knew You.*

This elision of fatherhood also meant that motherhood, no longer viewed as imposed condition, could be scrutinized for its internal ambivalences. Yet research suggested that most women are relieved when their last child flees the nest;[10] some mothers, notably Doris Lessing and Frieda Lawrence, don't wait for the nest to empty—they leave first.[11] Maternal bonding itself was soon being questioned.[12] If not biologically bound, mothering is still powerfully experienced: "shattering, ridiculous, earthbound, deeply warm, rich, profound."[13] Culturally framed, "to be a mother is to take on one of the most emotionally and intellectually demanding, exasperating, strenuous, anxiety-arousing, and deeply satisfying tasks that any human being can undertake."[14] For this anthropologist, motherhood is represented matricentrically: not just as having a baby, but as a "transformation into womanhood."[15] Thus the apparent gain for women's finding a positive procreative identity, rooted in a matricentric maternal dyad, may, in its score-settling marginalizing of fathers, reenforce emotional bonds based on conserving the original connection.[16]

In contrast, the liberationist stance had featured woman's capacities for doing anything a man could do and maybe better, while its corollary downgraded those things that fell exclusively to women's lot—housework, breeding children. Tee-shirts *du temps* proclaimed "A Woman Needs A Man Like A Fish Needs A Bicycle" and "Woman's Place Is in the House and the Senate." Then the woman-centered stance featured the very things women had always been saddled with, raised to a higher level. "Sisterhood is Powerful" was upstaged by an "ethics of caring," by "ongoing attachments... sustaining a web of connection," and by a concern with generational continuity.[17] In the new order of the day, the rallying cry was the quality of woman rather than her equality with man. Feminist criticism responded to the spirit of the times with a gynecritics that discovered women as producing positive meaning.[18]

But long before its removal from *SpareRib*'s masthead in 1990, Liberationism had succumbed to the *zeitgeist*; radical feminists who turned to anti-pornography causes made strange bedmates with right-wing zealots; while woman-centered approaches found compatibilities with separatists on difference—up to a point. However, since all of these factions are, one way or another, essentialist, their respective fortunes may be less successive than alternate strategies always available on ad hoc bases; and in contrast to gender constructivism, their premises if not their goals are closely aligned to an intellectual fundamentalism, purification agendas, categorical thinking, innate natures, etc., that either reinstate conservative agendas or simply provide a "rationale for the status quo."[19]   Yet the farreaching effects of the woman-centered vision are not only conservative in their essentialism but also in the historical context where questions arise about the depths and extent of women's oppression if they are able to find a measure of fulfillment in their traditionally separate spheres or through such self-help agencies as, for example, promoted in Gloria Steinem's treatise on self-esteem.[20]

     Thus the question about women being more conservative than men can be posed more restrictively: have most women, over extended historical periods, been more politically conservative than men, and, if true, are most women still so today with their expanded choices?   Do the rebellious energies aroused by the pressure-cooker of oppression decline when the steam is released (as seems the case for other activist groups)? Recent American and British political history is suggestive because at the polling-booth women can express their preferences with impunity. Yet Reagan had been elected in 1980 on a platform opposed to both abortion rights and the Equal Rights Amendment; in 1984, with Geraldine Ferraro on Walter Mondale's presidential ticket, American women had an opportunity for the first time to vote a woman with feminist values into national office. Indeed, Anne Wexler remarked to the news media that women would pick the next president, and when Reagan emerged from the landslide, she was compelled to admit that women's choices were clear. (Ferraro insisted that rather than harming the ticket, having a woman boosted the vote, according to her calculation, by 1/15%.)

     Was the debacle because, while women want a candidate who will promote family values, they also want one who will protect them with a strong defense policy? Or do they, as some suggested, mistrust their own sex? The pattern repeated itself in the 1988 election with a liberal democrat and a woman campaign manager going down to defeat against Bush's anti-abortion stand and exploitation of racial fears (his promises of a family-care package were vetoed). By this time, the ERA had long since died and its prospects of revival minuscule. In assessing the various causes that led to its defeat, Berry notes that while "75% of the female legislators in states that did not ratify, as opposed to 45%

of the men, supported the ERA," the formidable, grass-roots conservatism of Phyllis Schafly's movement took credit for the defeat.[21] Berry construes the defeat as a paradoxical victory for difference: "many people did not want women to be equal to men. In some cases they wanted women to be better off—more advantaged than men and in other ways subordinated."[22] But the kind of difference that triumphed was remarkably traditional.

Writing of Thatcherism, a "movement rooted in an unashamed glorification of the bourgeois values of individualism and self-sufficiency," Nicky Hart concludes, "what seems clear is that it was through women rather than men that the Conservative Party was handed the reins of governmental power" and effectively dismantled the welfare state.[23] In her view, the "conservatism of women stems from domestic isolation and insulation from alternate sources of political organization"; in particular privatization is credited with encouraging wage earners to invest more in their "conjugal household" than in themselves.[24] However construed, security has played a decisive role in women's voting preferences in both countries. Post-Thatcher polling in England examined three categories that might be expected to divide along gender lines, but neither in (1) *women's issues* ("abortion, child care, domestic violence, maternity leave, equal pay, equal opportunities, care of the elderly") nor in (2) *domestic agenda* (education, welfare, pensions) were there differences; only in (3) *foreign policy* were women "significantly more pacific and green."[25] In the U.S., spurred by outrage over the Anita Hill testimony, 1992 became the Year of the Woman, but despite the emergence of strong women candidates for Congress, "fewer than a third" of women polled "said they wanted to see one presidential candidate name a woman; 57% said it did not matter much to them."[26] In the popular vote for president in 1992, women joined men in slightly larger numbers to elect Bill Clinton in a campaign dominated by economic issues; but in light of Bush's all-out attacks on women—single-parents, abortion-counselling, abortion, maternity-leave—one might have expected women to reject him overwhelmingly at the polls.[27] In 1994's watershed vote that saw the House and Senate go Republican, media hype about white-male backlash belied the meager turnout

of 39%: women either stayed away or went Republican.[28] Only
two years after the Year of the Woman, the conservative
Concerned Women of America claimed a membership of 600,000
to NOW's 250,000.[29] In 1996, Women came to Clinton's rescue,
providing him with the victory, but did not affect the balance in
other races.[30]

Beyond the political context, the question expands from
whether women often make conservative choices to: if so, why:
innate or conditions? Yet the former sounds prejudiced, and the
latter has not been documented. And while U. S. feminists have
been energized by Naomi Wolf and Susan Faludi, in England
Rosaland Coward, rejecting *Backlash*'s media-manipulation
excuses, found many women's ambitions and commitments being
traded in for the domestic fulfilments of childrearing.[31]
Catherine Hakim, a feminist don publishing similar findings in
the *British Journal of Sociology* (1996), provoked an outcry.

More discomfiting is women's historical involvement in
right-wing extremism. In modern Germany the "new freedoms,
which had exhilarated a few during the flapper era of the 1920's,
unsettled the majority of women, for whom new opportunities
meant loss of protection." Following suffrage and in reaction to
feminist organizations, "during the 1920's a formidable force of
anti-feminists had coalesced."[32] According to Claudia Koonz,
"wives wanted not emancipation from their families but leverage
over their husbands. They supported family protection because
they believed the family supported them." They "seized upon the
rhetoric of rights, but twisted its meaning to mean the 'right' of
women to remain protected in their domestic sphere." Their slogan
"Emancipation from Emancipation" was taken up by the Nazi
ideologue Alfred Rosenberg; their demands for a domestic
"*Lebensraum*" dovetailed with Hitler's imperial agenda. Their
"inchoate longings" for "authoritarian rule" prepared "them to
welcome the Nazi state."[33] The consequences: "busily
administering welfare services, educational programs, leisure
activities, ideological indoctrination, and consumer organizations
—Nazi women mended while Nazi men marched."[34]

In America in the 1920s, upwards of a half-million "white
Protestant women joined the Ku Klux Klan, where their "poison
squads" that spread "rumor and slander" and their "organized

boycotts" complemented male terrorism and proved them "major actors...responsible for some of its most vicious, destructive results."[35] Ideals of pure white womanhood and gender equality enticed women into normalizing the Klan not only by their activities but by indoctrinating their children. "Support for gender equality," Blee concludes from a review of the larger social context, has "complex" dimensions, and "bears an uneasy relation to other progressive political beliefs."[36] Moving into the present, Kathy Dobie's investigative piece on women among the skinheads offers a sad account of victims reproducing—in various ways—other victims.[37]

Add to these examples the racial purity campaigns in nineteenth-century U.S. feminism, the Imperialist jingoism of Victorian women travel writers, the anti-communist/Hitler-friendly "Mothers' Movement" against Roosevelt and the allies,[38] and it can be concluded that women who may be liberal on gender-based issues of rights, education, and health turn increasingly conservative once family, race, and class are factored in.[39] If you "examine a not-in-my backyard movement over halfway houses or homeless shelters, you'll find a woman leading the charge," writes Cathy Young, citing Louise Day Hicks, "who led the nasty anti-busing crusade in Boston in the early 1970s."[40] In fact, up to the 1980s, according to Hester Eisenstein, women's voting patterns in the U.S. "split, as did men's, along lines of class, ethnicity, region, and political conviction"—a pattern persisting in recent national elections.[41] Not factoring in the gender-bending influence of power fueling the climb up the slippery slope of politics, Eisenstein and others are at a loss to explain why ideological sisterhood should take a drubbing in the 1992 New York Senatorial primary when Elizabeth's Holtzman's personal assaults on frontrunner Geraldine Ferraro secured victory for a right-wing male.[42]

Meanwhile, cultural studies are interrogating the many *idées reçues* of sexual oppression. In England, a more moderate but comparably conservative image has been replacing the Victorian stereotype of the middle-class housewife as the Angel in the House. Langland portrays her instead as the domestic "adjunct to a man's business endeavors."[43] No upwardly mobile servants marry their masters as in previous times: the wife "performs the ideological work of managing the class question and displaying the signs of the family's social status"—guardian angel of the status quo.

Following the upheavals in East Europe, many women who had worked under oppressive conditions began saying the "goal should be to create an economy where women do not have to work—a view that dovetails with the rising emphasis on the importance of traditional values, large families and religion."[44] (It is a view that also dovetails with resurgent nationalism, ethnic pride, and antisemitism.) Closer to home in El Salvador, the right-wing demagogue behind the death squads, Roberto D'Aubuisson, enjoyed great popularity among women for his good looks and macho style.

When women rule (Guida Jackson lists 700) the results have been mixed.[45] In the Medieval world, a "female member of an economically or politically powerful family often enjoyed considerable authority and freedom of movement in what we today would consider the 'public sphere'"; some women inherited fiefs, counties, and even kingdoms, but may have encountered problems in ruling in their own right.[46] Although there had been a few precedents, the sixteenth-century witnessed a remarkable upsurge of female empowerment as women occupied the thrones of France, Spain, England, and Scotland. Moreover, despite compromises and constraints, many of the women who ruled exercised real power over their subjects, but collectively do not present evidence for gender-inflected difference.[47]

These precedents have held up. Mrs. Thatcher's militarism along with her decimation of health services, education, and the arts are painfully recorded. Mrs. Ghandi, herself the embodiment of strong feminist convictions, achieved little success in regulating population growth and less in abolishing the brutal practices of bride-burning.[48] Mrs. Aquino made progress in redistributing the country's land among the poor. Mrs. Bhutto was removed from office over charges of corruption and nepotism, only to be returned and removed again, discredited among the populace for practicing her father's brand of autocratic vengeance and squandering her energies on plans to immortalize him in costly monuments.[49] In many instances, women in power are still beholden to entrenched patriarchal systems as Mrs. Chamorro is to the Sandinistas; but ultimately, like any other politician, they must be judged on what they accomplished, not on what they may want to see accomplished. Irene Pivetti, the Speaker of the Italian Parliament, who has shown herself to be anti-*maschilismo* as well as anti-abortion, claims she "has never thought whether to be a feminist or not."[50]

In addition, a feminism "which seemed to drape an aura of innocence and suffering around every woman" had produced its own double-binds for women seeking power.[51] The personal-is-political slogan, which Elizabeth Fox-Genovese and husband Eugene trace to Italian fascism, came to haunt Geraldine Ferraro in 1984 as she dodged questions about family finances by claiming "certain things are personal."[52] Under an all-enveloping mantle of blame, Jeane Kirkpatrick could complain of Reagan's "classical male sexists" without seeing any "connection between the obstacles she had faced and the administration's policies."[53] And whether having a woman on the U.S. Supreme Court will favor women depends entirely on the women in question and the question.

Wives of men in power have often behaved as co-dependents, fueling their husbands' greed like Rosane Malta Collor of Brazil, Imelda Marcos of the Phillipines, and Elena Ceausescu of Roumania, or fostering their cruelty like East Germany's Mrs. Honecker with her forced adoption policies.[54] When women do become politically active, they may behave like stereotypical males, becoming bitterly divided among themselves as in the case of the ERA; better organized as in Denmark and Australia around women's concerns; or as in the U.S. galvanised by single issues like abortion rights or sexual harassment.[55] Indeed, the cause for reproductive freedom as well as the equally fervent devotion to fetal-rights and the heroic protests of Argentinean women against their disappeared sons, daughters, and spouses suggest that women are most aroused over matricentric concerns, i.e., issues that immediately affect their sense of identity as women, and that in areas of environment, world peace, human or civil rights they remain indistinguishable from male counterparts.[56] In fact, after comparing U.S. women's voting patterns in light of a new-leadership/different-voice rhetoric, Cathy Young found a widespread but ill-considered essentialism and wonders whether there is "such a thing as a 'women's agenda'?"[57] In the 1996 Presidential election, however, Clinton's bridge-to-the-future slogan resonated more strongly with women's concern for generational continuity than his opponent's divisive agenda.

Feminism as lifestyle encourages anti-intellectualism, according to Karen DeCrow, who is "appalled when feminists don't read anything. They're into Tarot cards; they stay away from science because they say 'it's male.' Someone has cancer and they sit in a circle and chant for you...if you mention Simone de Beauvoir, they think it's a wine."[58] Carol Sternhell reports on walking out when a directors' meeting of the fall 1991 National Women's Studies Meeting Association closed with a "healing circle."[59] She goes on to describe the sessions she attended as "devoted to testimonials of pain. In every session women oppressed accused other women differently oppressed of oppressing them. Fine. Feminism taught us to begin with our own pain—the personal is political, after all. But no one ever moved beyond the stories, beyond pure feeling, beyond victimology."[60] According to Wendy Kaminer, the above attitudes promote a retrograde protectionism: "competition isn't 'sisterly,' and it isn't as selfless as women are supposed to be," although Sternhell's account depicts a veiled reentry of competition over being the most oppressed.[61] Susan Haack, professor of philosophy at the University of Miami, identifies "preposterism" in claims that "feminism has radical consequences for this or that area," which "often turn out to be trivial, or obviously derivative from some male philosopher, or manifestly false."[62] There is no question that women are victimized in numerous ways, but false and misleading statistics cited by advocacy groups and militants inflate the image of woman-as-victim to Holocaust proportions, and when Sommers corrects the number of deaths from eating eating disorders from 150,000 to 150-300, it is not reassuring to see her personally attacked or her work appropriated for conservative agendas.[63] Drawing on conclusions from various advocacy groups, President Clinton asserted that 700,000 rapes and 4 million assaults on women occur annually, but when these estimates were analyzed the hard data were halved.[64] The actual numbers are serious enough: enhancing them only reenforces an ideology of the victim. Neither adoption of Foucault's ideas of power as relative and dispersed nor accounts of complicity have made much headway over this powerful legitimizing ideology—even men's groups are finding the appeal of oppression irresistible.[65]

Corrective data may alter an ideologically-skewed polarity of sexual difference based on essentialism and allow more nuanced inquiries. In spheres of power and politics, for example, while women in the 1980s voted for conservative governments in the U.S. and England, they often did so for different priorities and motives from men. The fact that it may come down to the same thing in *real politik* need not detract from its also highlighting matricentric priorities.

Through all its myriad forms, the matricentric focuses those enduring aspects of women's lives, whether construed in a rhetoric of essentialism, discourses of difference or of rights, or in conservative causes. In general, the kinds of fiction women write, often to the discomfiture of their feminist sisters, matches up with the matricentric concerns women have historically displayed. Three groups of narrative stand out: (1) Traditional women's narratives tend to be matri-monial, less because women credit men with undue powers of fulfillment, than because marriage was the socially accepted form through which she entered patriarchy's Symbolic Order where her own matri-centric needs would presumably be protected and realized. Matricentric realization through a freely-chosen marriage between equals may well be women's counterpart to Enlightenment narratives of human liberation (that favored men).[66] Whether romances reinforce women's oppression or serve as an agent for social change by preserving feminine spaces of emotion or incorporating feminist notions, their overwhelming success is undeniable: by 1984, one in four American women were reading over a romance a week, estimates Carol Thurston, who attempts a positive spin on her data.[67] (2) Narratives centering on woman's situation or feminine consciousness respond to needs for gender-reinforcement and self-identity often unavailable in society. Hence, these over time may become utopian, lesbian, erotic, etc. (3) Feminist narratives interrogated prevailing male as well as matricentric models while constructing new matricentric modes on them (e.g., Marilyn French's *The Women's Room* unravels the marriage plot). In all three, the matricentric anchors the experiences and modulates the voices of women's writing just as their fictions also modulated male voices.[68]

Three additional considerations may be brought to bear: 1—Cutting through the above groups is a re-visionary *praxis* which feminists have cited as implicitly subversive and which feminist authors have occasionally adopted. But as soon as one gets down to cases, complications arise: women's writing often effects a toning down of the re-visionary model; for examples:

(1) Susan Hill's *I'm King of the Castle* (1970) is a toning down of William Golding's *Lord of the Flies* (1954);

(2) Maureen Duffy is an accomplished writer, but her *Capital* (1975) which takes its cues from *Ulysses* (1922), suffers in comparison;

(3) Margaret Atwood's *Surfacing* (1970) is a downscaling of D.H. Lawrence's *St. Mawr* (1924);

(4) Angela Carter's *The Passion of New Eve* (1977) rewrites Philip Roth's *The Breast* (1972) along with porno-narratives like deSade and *The Monk* but manages neither to transcend nor trash them;

(5) Zoë Fairbairns' *Benefits* (1979) and Margaret Atwood's *The Handmaid's Tale* (1987) settle for a narrower range than George Orwell's *1984* (1948);

(6) Anita Brookner's *A Friend from England* (1987) reads well but adds nothing to James's *The Ambassadors* (1903); in fact, Edith Wharton took over the novel of Jamesian sensibility without substantially transforming it, and Brookner has succeeded mainly in freeze-drying the tradition; moreover, the working-class women marginalized in Wharton were foregrounded in contemporaneous fiction by Crane and Norris;

(7) Anne Tyler's *Breathing Lessons* (1988) draws on the same themes of family betrayal in the same Mid-Atlantic, midcult mode as John Updike's Rabbit novels (1962-90);

(8) Jeanette Winterson's *Sexing the Cherry* (1989) evokes Peter Ackroyd's more gothically perverse *Hawkmoor* (1985);

(9) For all its pleasures, A.S. Byatt's *Possession* (1990) draws on John Fowles' *The French Lieutenant's Woman* (1969) and David Lodge's *Small World* (1984), whose next fiction, being a playful rewrite of Elizabeth Gaskell's *North and South* (1855), illustrates the free-masonry of re-visionism and the gender-free ease to transgression;

(10) Maureen Moore's *The Illumination of Alice Mallory* (1993) plays off the unsatisfactory sexual exchanges of her working-class heroine in Vancouver, B.C., against D. H. Lawrence's hero in *Sons and Lovers* to great comic effect, but since it contains little that Lawrence doesn't encompass, chances are he would have enjoyed it immensely.

Such examples suggest that a radical re-vision of male texts is more honored in theory than in *praxis*, although a gendered priority in the reader's response inevitably subjects such comparisons to subjectivity. For example, how significant is it that D. H. Lawrence's Lou Witt will work out her renewal within the New Mexican wilderness, while Atwood's heroine, after a few days camping out in Quebec, acts ready to return to the same sterile society both authors had rejected? Whereas Orwell's *1984* plunges deeper into the implications of his ideas, Atwood's *The Handmaid's Tale* subsides into the staples of the thriller, and the ideas never get frighteningly grounded in character. If Edith Wharton was marginalized in her society as a woman, her own texts marginalize members of other races and lower classes; accordingly, Stephen Crane's *Maggie of the Streets* renders him a feminist writer. But these are arguably personal readings.[69] Perhaps A. S. Byatt is not tamer than but different from her male precursors, Fowles and Lodge.[70] Perhaps Drabble's *The Waterfall* does not so much abridge *Lady Chatterly's Lover* as re-situate it. Anxiety of influence, intertextuality, re-visioning—all rely on evidence far too tenuous for any intellectual court of law; but indisputable is Byatt's matricentric swerve away from male models in her textual commitment to matching-up, picking up the pieces, and generational continuity—*voilà la différence*.

2—In light of the new freedoms and rich diversity of British women's writing in recent decades, how would it fare in terms of creative adventurousness with such male counterparts as David Lodge, Malcolm Bradbury, Peter Ackroyd, Bruce Chatwin, Graham Swift, Julian Barnes, and Martin Amis? Adding to the problem, women authors often receive mixed messages from their female critics today as they once did from male critics. Having been conditioned by generations of women's domesticated writings, some feminist scholars have privileged the "little things in women's lives...the small nurturing things that women do"; and after having supped full on a feminist anthology of "female experiences of creation and procreation, marriage and maternity," Gail Godwin "longs to flee the echo chamber and seek refreshment on the seas of Joseph Conrad or the prairies of Willa Cather."[71]

     3—Despite the many innovations in 20th Century women's fiction, the tenacity of the marriage plot, bolstered by the ever booming business in romances, has to be addressed in its own right. If women were once constrained by its conventions, it is hardly true today, nor has it been the case for sometime. In "The Art of Fiction" (1888), Henry James attacked the "happy ending" that distributed "prizes, pensions, husbands, wives, babies," and in "The Future of the Novel" (1899), he mocked its "ready-made and sadly the worst for wear" conventions. Finding "its plasticity, its elasticity" to be "infinite," he called for the novel's inclusion of "whole categories of manners, whole corpuscular classes and provinces, museums of character and condition" as yet unvisited. More to the point, he welcomed the "revolution taking place in the position and outlook of women" and anticipated the day when "by the play of the pen" women writers would "smash with final resonance the window all this time most superstitiously closed."[72] How far James was heeded may be debated, but that a woman writer could have smashed the stifling window of the past as early as 1911 is born out in Gertrude Colmore's militantly penned *Suffragette Sally*.[73] A swan doesn't make a summer, and as Nicola Beauman's study shows, most of early 20th century writing serviced women's more traditional needs (as romances continue to do, despite efforts to politically-correct them).[74]

     Transmogrified again, the question of women's conservatism may now be phrased more narrowly to why *should* women's writing be matricentric? This question spans into three areas: biological, cultural, psychological.

     Sociobiologists like Donald Symons would have little difficulty with the issue.[75] For them, *homo sapiens*, like all other species have a powerful investment in genetic transmission as the best means so far devised by nature to insure future survival of one's own species. Sexual dimorphism represents a long-evolved division of reproductive strategies within a species. For males (mammal, primate, human), there are advantages in spreading one's genes around in the widest possible field in order to secure a percentage of offspring surviving; for females, offspring survival is enhanced by a monogamous pair-bond and quality care given to relatively few. In the best of all animal and human worlds, accommodations and allowances lead to some sort of successful compromise. In their view, utopian feminists who privilege a primordial bond with an abiding maternal earth have neglected the actual evolutionary processes. To the liberationist cry, 'I don't mate in captivity!' the sociobiologist replies, 'Fine, but you'd better mate in domesticity, for it is only through home-basing, birth-spacing, maximum maternal care for a few offspring in a stable environment that you stand any chance to succeed in the genetic sweepstakes for which evolution has carefully fitted you over several million years.' Lest this be rejected as male-scientist bias, Helen Fisher's evolutionary gloss lets woman too enjoy variety and be as sexually aggressive as men; but her "two alternative strategies"—monogamy, promiscuity—coincide with what otherwise have been construed as male-generated stereotypes of "the madonna or the whore."[76] Thus, whatever culture may construct actually arises from a biological base—so runs the sociobiological scenario, and on whatever level one confronts it, human evolution remains the one grand-narrative that underwrites all the others and can't be theorized away.

Accordingly, if women's fictions mix suitable mating, the value of relatedness, the sweeteners of romance, if they stir in equal-opportunity, and add the yeast of generational-continuity, such writings are replications of their biological fittedness.[77] Presumably men would be inscribing their genetic codes in Don Juanism and Restoration-style comedies where libertine males practice "random copulations" and only reluctantly bargain their way into more lasting, pleasurable unions with pair-bonding female wits.[78] It is in the end a question of biological-based drives reifying into cultural feedback patterns and sex-traits: males favored for dominance/aggression, females for receptivity/nurturance. But however far one accepts these extrapolations, it must be admitted that, despite all the inter/tra species variety, without a biocentric base no discourse on women's writing could begin, even though biology is more container than definer of gender's maddening mixes.[79]

Other evolutionists like Stephen Jay Gould query

sociobiology's unmediated incursion into culture, which they envision as an entirely new enterprise requiring *homo sapiens* to don a second *sapiens*.[80]   Thereafter, biology proposes, culture disposes; male reproductive models may subside into male myths. And once cultural studies examine gender construction as performative or imposed, as masquerade or self-fashioning, as oppressive or transgressive, biocentrism has long since been supplanted. Now all is mediated in sign-systems of historically produced   gender-representations.   If   women   still   seem conservative, it's only because they have internalized cultural encodings for survival under patriarchy (competitive and disruptive among themselves, men are conservative in their possessiveness toward women). If their texts favor matching-up over leaving lives in disarray, it's only because they have been conditioned to good-housekeeping standards of tidying-up, and so forth.   For if culture is humanity's medium, it is also a hierarchical   power-broker,   and   hence,   this   argument   runs, inherently ideological.[81]   In Western societies the dominant discourse is patriarchal, rationalist, capitalist, and imperialist. The body is culturally defined and reproduced; sex succumbs to sexuality and gender, constituted in accord with the masculine ideology, transformed, and deployed by power discourses (*à la* Foucault). The system may be oppressive, but presumably what has   been   constructed   can   be   deconstructed,   and   dominant ideologies   can   be   deconstructed,   transgressed,   or   otherwise undone: the variously colonized can be uncolonized. And insofar as the matricentric serves a conservative construction, it too presumably can be deconstructed, but the process may also begin yielding more elusive structures. At this point, just as gender's biocentric base is transformed by culture, for the sake of adequate discourse a third dimension beyond cultural autocracy must be factored in.

Any quest for an adequate psychoanalytic discourse, however, is complicated in the postmodern because psychoanalysis has been subserviently joined to cultural studies. No longer is there the old modernist, motive-hunting psychoanalytic mode, with its metanarrative of universals that excited debates over the Oedipus complex among Trobriand Islanders, but instead a postmodern relativizing mode for historicized subjects who wield their Freud to deconstruct the rule of the father. This was the appeal of Lacanian analysis during the exciting May of 1968, which delivered it from the clinic and seminar-room to the streets and cafes and left many confused, not the least of whom being Lacan himself.[82]   Ever since, postmodernism has consulted psychoanalysis on the historically constituted subject (which largely replaced the Freudian psyche's ideosyncratic personal history). But neither this elevation through cultural politics nor the prior foundation in universals lies the psychoanalytic zone of competence; rather it is with how male/female children engage common and special developmental conflicts to become infinite varieties of men/women. In short, not with products but with processes, not with a transhistorical self (or ego), but with an internal dynamic system (or psyche), not with a culturally constituted subject or with "surface phenomena" of traits or cultural variants but with transference phenomena, not with a theorized, non-existent mirror-stage but with the actualities of maternal mirroring.[83] Between an individual's unawareness of his/her cultural encodings and the dynamic unconscious in which adherence to "ideals and values figure in a scheme of repression" are differences of kind not of degree.[84]

Theoretically   bridging   the   two   spheres,   Lacan's developmental schemata, which privilege phallus/castration as pivots of desire, have been welcomed for providing insights into the patriarchal hegemony he names the Symbolic Order and for discourses of subjectivity derived from sexual difference. But a subjectivity in the subject reinstates questions of transhistorical self-constructs and the plausibility of a similar subjectivity in children predating sexual difference, which, especially for Lacanians, puts girls on a path of lack and phallic masquerade, boys on one of castration fears and symbolic mastery. Though the folly of the Lacanian law that "the woman has to undergo no more or less castration than the man" has gone largely uncontested among French feminists and analysts, retained by Julia Kristeva, for example, as "symbolic castration," such archaisms along with a female castration complex, have long since been relinquished by American analysts.[85]

An initially shared subjectivity in early childhood is firmly grounded, however, in Margaret Mahler's accounts of the separation/individuation process as well as in mainline Freud and

Melanie Klein, where subjectivity arises when the infant negates the hallucinated, absent breast and, by initiating defenses against its threats, demarcates the unconscious from the conscious. Rather than a totalizing process of distorted identification via Lacan's mirror-stage, psychoanalytic advances include conflict within a larger scheme of relatively healthy development. "As infant and mother come to form a stable interactional system, the organizing influence of that system gives psychological meaning to innate physiological functions," and these "interactions lend gender-specificity to the emerging sense of self."[86]

Gendered features of an emerging self accrue through the girl's genital sensations and like-mommy identificatory affects, which, according to Sherkow and others, antedate observation of genital difference. The girl's struggle to mentally represent her sense of a vagina as an incorporative organ is conflicted not primarily due to penis envy but because the vagina, unlike other organs that interface with the environment, has no sphincter and thus cannot be controlled. In responding to the anxiety thus aroused, the girl may "repress awareness of the organ altogether," writes Sherkow. Herein resides the girl's first act of gendered agency, a truly psychoanalytic act stemming from intrapsychic danger signals.

Ubiquitous but not decisive, penis envy, the real or imaginary missing organ, is overdetermined by the girl's own subjectivity, representing, for example, her feeling of missing out on mother's abundant love; ultimately, organ envy figures as a developmental task the girl negotiates in establishing a "narcissistically valued view of her own female body."[87] The "father's role in the girl's development is an important influence on her growing sense of femininity," especially as a "protector against the threat of maternal engulfment."[88] Subjectivity is structured through identifications with both parents; it is heightened, intensified, and enriched by the child's engagement with the primal scene, involving exposures to or fantasies about parental intercourse or adult sexuality, which excite such powerful identifications with the sexual partners as to implicate the child ever after in sexual perplexities.[89]

These more complete developmental schemata refute current notions of a dominant "male economy" of castration/fetishizing truncating the girls' subjectivity, for it is now understood as beginning earlier than awareness of sexual difference and as subsisting thereafter in its own right.[90] Following the child's discovery of difference, a psychodynamics of drive-derivatives and compromise-formations, of desire and identification, lays the groundwork for transcultural, transhistorical psychoanalytic discourses, which take into account an array of culturally prescribed gender-role options.

Just as the pair-bond favors female reproductive success, so is marriage woman's traditional mode of accessing the so-called Symbolic Order, which, however circumscribed, transports female desire beyond Lacanian strictures. Lacan's developmental schemata are at best rudimentary: weighed down with portentous declarations, they falter from lack of clinical underpinning and, while stimulating to philosophers and linguists, are severely limited, if not merely tangential, to child development.[91] His mirror-stage, for example, in which a reflected ideal-I is introjected while an unintegrated, segmented body is denied, initiates a foredoomed personal narrative of splitting and alienation for all genders. The process Lacan cites stems from mimickry and imitation among animals rather than identification in the psychoanalytic sense; his notions of desire prompted by the mother's wish for a phallus through her child who tries to realize his/her desire by embodying the mother's desire continues his defensive discourse at the expense of drives—in Lacan's closed system, mother is a signifier of deficit, man is a castrated woman, and paranoia prevails.[92]

Undoubtedly, Freud is less clever than Lacan, but if one follows the latter's advice instead of his practice and returns to the former, a different problematic emerges. Freud's grand narrative succinctly proclaims, "Where id was there ego shall be." But he also construed oedipal narratives of male development as metanarratives of human development, and his discourse on female development may now be read as an only partly successful struggle to transcend androcentric positions.[93] To his credit, he welcomed women into his movement and did many remarkable things for his female patients, not the least revolutionary being to listen; but when he formulated a narrative of female desire, a phallic priority brought about a major derailment instead of a minor detour.[94] The girl's desire for the penis/phallus is seen as a primary fallout of her castration complex, and the inevitable frustration leads her to seek a penis-baby from father in compensation. Karen Horney caught the phallocentric fallacies in the scenario and proposed that the "desire to have a child (from the father)" predates the "desire for a penis," though her inclination to innate femininity removed her from the playing field.[95]

Although Freud's essays on female psychology retain a historical interest, they have long since lost their standing in the field; yet they continue to exercise great influence on British Lacanians and literary feminists generally.[96] Thus Kristeva construes family dynamics as "power relations," with the father as "possessor of the mother [and] dispenser of gender identity"; while Rose and Mitchell construe psychoanalysis not as a theory about how "little girls become 'feminine,'" but about how they "never become women."[97] Why these writers would strive to out-Freud Freud at his most unreliable is perplexing. Freud himself belatedly acknowledged the girl's preoedipal ties to mother as equivalent to encountering the Minoan-Mycenean civilization, but opted to remain, so to speak, with the Greeks.

Psychoanalytic theory, however, continued to evolve, and by the 1970s offered more cogent accounts of female development. Perhaps the most striking innovation was that the "girl's manifest wish to have her own baby" begins appearing after the first year with displays of an interest (initially shared with boys) "in live babies and dolls."[98] Moreover, this wish is the "result of an identification" with the primary caregiver and assumes the "quality of a drive, of an inborn gender characteristic" not found in boys (the wish to conceive from father comprises a later oedipal form).[99] In other words, the traditional clinical view (always on shaky ground at best) that the girl's wish for a child was a defensive response to castration issues is now amended by infant observation studies which allocate a primacy of the wish "to nurture a baby" in the girl, associated with the earliest sense of gender-identity modeled on the procreative mother: "wishful fantasies of being a mother with a baby in a dyadic relationship then form the core of her female gender role as well as her ego ideal."[100]

Thus, when the girl later engages the perplexity of sexual difference, she need not discover her subjectivity through envy for a missing organ and can re-access earlier maternal ties or her "core gender-identity" for support rather than feel compelled to deal with father or other males at a disadvantage.[101] No longer defined by difference, she can pursue a developmental route which is not potholed with deficits, but yet which differs, insofar as it is fueled by drives, conflicts, and compromise-formations, from similar-sounding scenarios of Chodorow and meliorists like Gilligan who selectively cite psychoanalytic texts to abridge them.[102] The difference is that as psychoanalysis portrays development as conflict for both sexes, Chodorow on the one hand presents narratives of identification as a conflict-free zone without overdetermined desires or drive conflicts, while Gilligan on the other gives accounts of moral development without concurrent drive development—of love *sans* libido. For the most part, such intended improvements do in fact support an attenuated matricentric position, but only by reverting to a corrective psychology or one of traits bereft of intrapsychic conflict.[103]

To more firmly situate the matricentric, a genuinely psychoanalytic account means that the girl's wish to mother, however represented in the primitive psyche (e.g., to fuse with, replace, or identify with the primary caregiver), will undergo all the overdeterminisms, displacements, sublimations, and vicissitudes that Freud articulated for the instinctual drives and their derivatives. It may include: I want to be strong, powerful, (re-)productive; I want to nurture myself, I want to feel close to/replace mommy; I want father's praise, brother's envy; I want to be a nurse, a doctor, or an artist and create new forms, etc. Thus, springing from a host of nuclear wishes, such identificatory, libidinal, and reparative narratives can nourish a girl's development into the kind of woman she aspires to become and initiate the matricentric directions of her writing. The psychoanalytic dimension of the matricentric then signifies gender-inflection without restriction to any alledged gender-based traits as inwardness, intuition, caring/sharing, and innate or constructed conservatism, though all three contributors— psyche/bio/cultural—can work in various reenforcing ways toward an end product which grants the cultural highest visibility.

Once overdeterminism and intrapsychic needs are

included, however, it grows clear that if there are some ways in which one cannot return to Freud, there are other ways in which one can. If the privileging of desire as *jouissance* in Lacanian feminist discourses exempts it from personal history, detaches it from erogenous zones, and awards it the autonomy of a Jungian libido, genuine psychoanalytic narratives of desire would in one way or other deconstruct each of these. Psychoanalysis impacts on desire when it confronts desire's own anxieties over realization, i.e., when desire's projects are jeopardized by aggressions or inherent contradictions, signified by the oedipal impasses and the castration complexes, where loss would negate gain. The fact that girls may enter this arena with an added leverage of core gender-identity does not immunize them from painful conflict and psychic restructuring beyond the maternal dyad. For both sexes, the impossible desire for either parent (not soothing wishes for ongoing attachment, but a powerful jealous passion for possession and interaction) leads either to humiliating defeat due to inequities of size, capacity, and knowledge, to persisting dilemmas over lack, or to counter desires aimed at breaking free of the parental hegemony—otherwise best mediated through identification. In such ways is Freud's grand-narrative of instinctual emancipation founded on a gender-blind conflict model.[104]

In this model, the child may transform or displace his/her angry frustrations into attitudes of oppression stemming from the inherent and seemingly autocratic powers of the parents as every child's original other. That these feelings may be replicated by oppressive social conditions implies neither that the conditions are imaginary nor that the original feelings are insignificant. It does imply that early developmental conflicts are continued through personal narratives and relationships via displacement and overdeterminism. Accordingly, the girl's manifest wish for a child may be activated by a conflict over separation, loss, envy, or feelings of helplessness, any of which might stimulate identification both with the aggressor (in Anna Freud's historic discourse on defense) as well as less defensive identifications with a positive source of nurture and well-being as emphasized in meliorist feminist versions.

But regardless, such a *manifest* wish-cluster will soon form a nucleus of desire with latent content and, mingling with other desires and conflicts, assume the *latent* content of otherwise unrelated manifest wishes as the girl struggles through her developmental phases. During adolescence, for example, doing sex (manifest rebellious wish) may distract her from conceiving like mommy (latent positive wish), but the inordinately high number of unwanted, "accidental," yet easily preventable pregnancies among teenagers speaks to the overdeterminism of wishes. Just as problematically, child-bearing may comprise parental acceptance, validation of self-worth, or authentic membership in communities (like the Spain of Lorca's *Blood Wedding*) where women are poised on a narrow fulcrum of fertility/barrenness. In the creative sphere, the reconstituted (sublimated) form of this procreative core of desire may resolve sexual conflicts as when Virginia Woolf draws the nuptial curtains in the darkness of her imagination to invite a "collaboration" between the "woman and the man" in order to accomplish the "act of creation."[105] In the primal scene of creativity, the internalized parents contribute to self-transmutations via creative renewal.[106]

The contrast then between theories of gender in culture studies or trait-psychology and in psychoanalysis is profound. In the former, gender is externally constructed, that is, stamped on passive subjects to encode a cultural power-system; in the latter, gender is created out of a limited range of family-transmitted, cultural-sanctioned options by the child's active as well as anxious desires leading to internal structures of identification that blend the defensive with the adaptive. In the former, gender as encoded stereotypes, may be transgressed by crossdressing or other offbeat lifestyles; in the latter, such strategies may be undermined by the agent's internal representations of sexual dualisms which promote perverse scenarios or defend against painful awareness of the primal scene.[107] In the former, victims are summoned to indict oppressive systems; in the latter, avenues of agency open. In the former, literary applications seek in vain a cluster of fixed traits discernible in a subversive politics or a linguistic stylistics: the feminine sentence, the female voice, an authentic feminine consciousness, or in a current version a "female form" as the "circular return, a pattern wherein episodes set in the past alternate with episodes set in the present and are completed when past becomes present"—a standard description also of numerous male narratives from Oedipus to *Ulysses* but only of a select few female narratives.[108]   Currently, while some Anglo-American feminist scholars entertain a French-based cluster of traits— disrupture, multiplicity, heterogeneity, *jouissance*—others find that French feminists muddle essentialist and socially constructed views of women.[109]   In any case, traits transformed into styles prove notoriously mercurial and migrate capriciously across gender lines. In the latter, the emphasis falls not on *what* traits, but on *how* women's writings affirm historically/culturally psychologically modulated senses of themselves in a designated matricentric process.

The two psychic agencies that mediate a child's quest for suitable gender-identity are joined in the figure of the Roman doorway god Janus. The one glance turns inward toward early family identifications which are strongly flavored with prescriptions and prohibitions (call this agency the superego); the other glance looks outward toward peers, the community, the culture at large for models of aspiration (call this one the ego-ideal, though it draws on primary narcissism or, in Kohutian terms, grandiose self-images).   Development-as-conflict thus means, to a greater or lesser degree depending on how open or closed is one's social environment, that the individual struggles to mediate among external constraints, internalized demands, and highly-charged inner aspirations.[110]   Obviously, the split between superego and ego-ideal, which is always experienced as widening or narrowing, is not bound to be simply between (negative) family and (positive) culture (or vice versa), since either may range from insidiously oppressive to humanely supportive.   Psychoanalysis is not there to sharpen conflicts between self and surround, but to delineate an elusive terrain of inner conflicts (e.g., how individuals struggle to accommodate inner wishes with internalized demands, aspirations, and caveats).

Thus to rely on monocausal gender-constructions of cultural oppression is to succumb to binary banalities with the frustrated child constructing his/her-self not as adult man or woman but as subject (i.e., child/victim), for insofar as all ideologies are alien to the child who is nonetheless at their mercy, all discourses of oppression lead to a deadend splitting of victims/victimizers. Thus to depict gender conflicts as a dialectics between oppressing constructions of woman from male desire and liberating ones from women's multiplicity is to operate horizontally on a we/them axis at the expense of psychoanalytic verticality.[111] These elisions of the child's experiences of subjection along with agency and his/her personal narratives of desire and complicity mark a crucial lapse in cultural studies' otherwise valuable contributions. A biocentric reading of homo sapiens takes into account the prematurity of human birth; psychodynamic readings cite the child's acquiescence in omniscient protective deities as a response to the primordial condition of human helplessness; Margaret Mahler's developmental narratives note a human hatching-out from maternal symbiosis in the second year of life. Lest cultural studies replace the child's fantasies of benevolent deities with oppressing ones, any discourse on gender aspiring to adequacy must take into account all three elements in which our human species thrives: biological, psychodynamic, cultural.

To do so is not only to foster a genuine postmodern spirit of diversity and multiplicity, but also to recognize that ideology/culture equations do not exhaust gender discourses. Once factored in, psychoanalysis is profoundly implicating on many levels. For just as Freud's structural hypothesis of ego, id, and superego as interacting psychic systems has radically subverted and transformed dualisms of mind/body and male/female, so does psychoanalytic discourse probe ways in which the one is also the other (especially as the creation of one's own projections). With Freud's structural hypothesis thus included along with the psychodynamics of overdeterminism and the economics of drive/defense, one enters a more adequate but also a more perilous psychoanalytic mode.

Regardless how matricentric concerns shape women's narratives of traditional matching-up as well as those of resistance to male definitions of origins, a psychodynamic theory of women's writing presumes the overdeterminism of all mental processes, including the imagination (which vanished from theory-laden postmodern cultural discourse to reappear dressed-down as culture-work). To rephrase the initiating question whether matricentric inscribes a conservatism in women's writing is to acknowledge these new problematics. The minimal etymological content assigned at the outset to the matricentric for purposes of organizing a gender-focused discussion of women's writing can now yield to a deeper inquiry into sources. Due to its minimal detonative and maximal connotative capacities, matricentric is not a reified quality, a trait, or a culturally constructed component of gender, but a signifier of dynamic processes stemming from a nucleus of early wishes, identifications, sublimations, and goal-directed activity discernible, for present purposes, in the cultural sphere—namely, writing. Therefore, one could also consider matricentric writing as a distinctive way of controlling these dynamic processes.

On the level of essentialism, one could safely say men are not matricentric, even though they draw on early maternal ties in the creative process and invoke a tropic lexicon of conception, gestation, and birth.[112]   At the very least, then, as a gender signifier, matricentric is a source of difference and a means by which the conservative can be further interrogated (e.g., as control).   Neither simply affirming nor negating biology, matricentric legitimizes inquiry into the variables through which the girl negotiates her early equations of being female as being like mother, consolidates her identifications, and creates her sense of gender. Thus construed, the matricentric encompasses a more balanced and hence more adequate discourse on women's writing than either ideological feminism or cultural and gender studies allow.

Because gender permeates cultural life and so impacts on writing at various levels and with varying force, it is always tempting to read gender as permeated by culture. But if all women's writing were thus permeated, there would only be gradations within the red band, the red would be read as oppression, and there would be no true purple; but because other forces also impact on writing—imagination, inner conflict, empathy, technical skills, tradition, material culture—writing is also freed-up to exceed as well as to affirm gender. Although the matricentric varieties that pivot on courtship/matching, self-origins, and social ex/inclusion foreground gendered aspects of women's creative work, women's autobiography proves a fruitful field for discerning how a sense of personal gender is actively created through whatever prevailing cultural mode—religious, sentimental, gothic, feminist—as one descends down the centuries. Citing Lucy Hutchinson, the biographer of her husband during the English civil wars, Margaret George writes, "simply, or rather consciously, seriously, she created *herself* in the men's world and with the material handed her," so that "in reproducing in her own terms the hardening definition of the female role she embellished and strengthened it."[113] In other words, she was given a role but made of herself more than the given role.

Another discernible way in which gender impacts on writing stems from the development-as-conflict model at the point where the glimmerings of sexual difference first arise. The particular psychic consequences of anatomical differences noted by Freud as the onset of the castration complex and point of divergence for male/female development has since factored in primary (but very rudimentary) feminine identity which diminishes the force of castration fear. His error stemmed at least in part from misapplied aesthetics as well as misperceived development, for he satisfied himself with an elegant formula of sexual complementarity: the castration complex forecloses the boy's oedipal agenda as it initiates the girl's.[114] Her envy over lack either spiraled off into a "masculinity complex," or spurred her desire to receive a substitute (penis/baby) from father.[115] The prospect of castration goads the boy to relinquish his untenable ties to mother and, following a heterosexual route, to introject the paternal function, enabling him in due course to direct his gaze toward a more suitable libidinal object. Thus, after a briefly shared bisexual (or symbiotic) past, the boy's and the girl's developmental routes diverge according to differing phase-specific needs, and cultural influences reenforce difference to such an extent that they misleadingly appear to have constructed gender in total.

Psychoanalytic revisions offer complementarity of a kind. Allowing for hypothetical bisexual endowments, both sexes experience a primary identification with the original caregiver (mother, most often) during a symbiotic phase in which, through mirroring and good-enough early nurture, a core-human self awakens. Thereafter, the boy disidentifies with mother while forming his first libidinal object from her image, and when prospects along this line are disrupted by castration fears he yields up the object but not the gender of his desire as he embarks on a protracted quest to consolidate a masculine sense of identity.[116] Thus, his identification is a two-step process while his prevailing desire is singular. The girl retains and extends her original identification with mother, while her desire becomes a two-step process in her shifting libidinal interest from mother to father.[117]

Even without adding homosexual variations to these narratives of heterosexual development, there is abundant space for variety and conflict. Far more than formulas of culture-work can encompass, creativity may be enlisted to undo traumas along these developmental trajectories, to master conflicts, to fill gaps, or to fuel desires for representation in public media. The gendered differences in developmental schema seep into fictional narratives in various contrasting ways. Heroic struggles with an array of mythical monsters, dragons, medusas, sphinxes, gorgons, and so forth have often been interpreted—since the hero is consistently male and the monster usually female—as the boy's need to overcome his attachments to mother and disidentify by separating out the slayer from the slain. To a lesser degree, heroines in fairy tales find fiendishly ingenious ways of ridding themselves of evil step-mothers, witches, and what-not, but the underlying conflicts here seem to focus on splitting or ambivalence; and whereas the hero's exploits lead to manhood, the heroine's usually aim to gain a prince (perhaps as signifier of womanhood). Moreover, the male need to disidentify is depicted as a mortal combat, after which he is wounded and healed by an Iseult or made whole and empowered by an Excalibur.

But if his need to disidentify is inscribed as the primal crime (against mother), he is soon perpetrating an equally grave oedipal crime (against father).[118] No wonder so much of literature signed by men is marked by violence, generational revolt, ruptures in relationships, and dislocating turbulence; when women figure in this struggle, they are more often emblems of dangerous regression than prospects for mutual affection. In epics, adventure stories, and countless novels there runs a protracted quest by the hero for some saving (re)generative power which precedes libidinal enterprises. These quests become *bildungsromanen*, picaresques, encyclopaedic extravaganzas with open-ended structures that among other things open a patrilinear line for the novel stemming from Cervantes, Diderot, Balzac, and hence a European tradition separate from the somewhat insular English origins theory with its feminine accent, domestic syntax, marital punctuation, and paternity/maternity disputes over origins.[119]

In sum, literary narratives that accent sexual difference do so in accord with developmental schema. Disidentified from mother and divested of her strength, the boy faces on the one side the monstrous fears of his archaic past and on the other the yawning abyss of castration. Vaguely, he sights in the remote distance prospects of acquiring a self-identity through engagement with superior males, solitary travels over deserts, ship-wrecks on sea-journeys, jungle-quests, high-noon shootouts—all holding out the promise of eventual libidinal success.

"Childe Harold to the ruined tower came," writes Browning, anticipating T.S. Eliot; but Childe Harold is always coming to the same ruined tower destroyed by his impossible desires and collisions with castration that one way or another stir up the psychic realities to be fought, repeated, mastered, and absorbed. If the gift or prize of masculinity can be won, it can also be lost. The male quest is nothing if not driven by fears of desolation, annihilation, loss, and despair. It has little to do with facile stereotypes of "dominant discourse," cited only to be glibly dismissed in postmodern discourse; and perhaps in a study devoted to the slighted interests of women's writing, a pause to contemplate the literature of the other's other is not out of order.

Since the girl's gendered self draws more directly on sustained maternal identifications, her imagination need not be as charged up to fuel protracted and perilous quests for what is already nearly hers, or for that matter to begrudge the other gender its imaginary and real adventures in quest of masculine selfhood. Neither does it mean that she should roll over and play horn-of-plenty to the errant—in various respects—knight. Nor finally does it mean that wholeness or personal womanhood is an easily accomplished goal. It does mean that women will not duplicate the male quest (which their texts may critically deconstruct, creatively re-vision, disrupt, or modify through love) and that insofar as they are unaccommodated in male narratives they will prefer to find other creative forms for their quests. In fact one reading of the female hero suggests that the quest for healing, ostensibly of the ailing fisher king, amounts to an androgynous desire for wholeness; but other literary feminists discredit androgyny as amounting to a mere abstract personhood unworthy of social or literary goals.[120]

Obviously, to speak of gender-fueled narratives is not to reduce them to their gender base or to settle for an essentialism of traits, types, archetypes, or prescribed patterns. Nor is it to expect an unbridgeable gulf between matricentric narratives and a counterpart in a problematic patricentric mode (hitherto deemed normative). More modestly, it is to locate a powerful source of difference in those matricentric or self-(en)gendering processes as they flourish in women's myriad creative endeavors.

Notes

1. Wendy Kaminer, *A Fearful Freedom*, 9.

2. Rosanne Barr referring to her friend Bonnie Sheridan in *People* Magazine (13 April 1992).

3. Hester Eisenstein, *Contemporary Feminist Thought*, 70.

4. Shulamith Firestone, *The Dialectics of Sex*, 147.

5. Phyllis Chesler, *Women and Madness*, 18.

6. Kristin Luker, *Abortion and the Politics of Motherhood*.

7. Shari L. Thurer, *The Myths of Motherhood*, 290.

8. Nancy Chodorow, *The Reproduction of Mothering*.

9. Kim Chernin, *The Hungry Self*.

10. Sandy Rovner, "Debunking the 'Empty Nest' Syndrome," 14.

11. Rosemary Jackson, *Mothers Who Leave*.

12. Diane E. Eyer, *Mother-Infant Bonding: A Scientific Fiction*; Nancy Scheper-Hughes, *Death Without Weeping*.

13. Louise Erdrich, Introduction to *The Blue Jay's Dance*.

14. Sheila Kitzinger, *Ourselves as Mothers*, ix.

15. Kitzinger, ix; patricentric versions of woman's transformation into womanhood would of course center on her sexual initiation, and the matricentric would in any case encompass more than literal pregancy and birth: both Lawrence and Drabble depict heterosexuality as deliverance.

16. In *Reading from the Heart*, Suzanne Juhasz applies
preoedipal-based, object-relations theory to account for
"why...so many women read (and write) love stories" (Prologue).
She frames the inquiry by picturing herself as a girl reading "in
a square green upholstered chair. I curled my legs up under me
or hung them over the chair's broad arms. Beside me on the
end table was a pile of crackers. The living room was shadowy,
its soft carpets and long curtains in half-light....There I could be
found most afternoons, with...my nose in a book" (1). This
"merging of self and book," noted in E.M. Broner's review, aptly
captures the regressive, symbiotic quality of this memory
("Loving to Read, Reading to Love," *Women's Review of Books*
[May, 1995], 18). While revealing the pleasures of a certain
kind of reading and writing, the book as the maternal good-
breast also exposes the limits of certain matricentric
experiences.

17. Carol Gilligan, *In a Different Voice*, 74, 62.

18. Elaine Showalter, *The New Feminist Criticism.*

19. Katha Pollitt, "Are Women Morally Superior to Men?"
The Nation (28 December 1992), 804.

20. Gloria Steinem, *Revolution from Within.*

21. Mary Frances Berry, *Why ERA Failed*, 82. Mrs.
Schlafly is one of the victim's in Andrea Dworkin's account of
women "controlled and manipulated" by the Right (*Right-Wing
Women*, 34.

22. Berry, 83.

23. Nicky Hart, "Gender and the Rise and Fall of Class
Politics," 21-3.

24. Hart, 28.

25. Joni Lovenduski and Pippa Norris, "Why Can't a Woman Be More Like a Man?" 12-13.

26. Robin Toner, "Bush and Clinton Sag in Survey," *New York Times* (23 June 1992; In the end, history was made by four women elected to the U.S. Senate, while two other women candidates were defeated by incompetence (Penn.) and infighting (NY).

27. In the popular vote, which Clinton won by 43% to 38% for Bush and 19% for Perot, the women's vote split 46% to 37% to 17% respectively. With the Bush vote about the same for men and women, the real difference emerges in fewer women (17%) and more men (21%) voting for Perot, although he had come out as pro-choice. A further breakdown of women's voting preferences by race, class, and religion also skews the results. Black women voted 86% for Clinton, 9% for Bush, and 5% for Perot (*NY Times*, 5 Nov 1993).

28. Ann Devroy, *Washington Post* (11 April 1995).

29. Suzanne Fields, "Feminism and the New Congress," *Los Angeles Times* (13 April 1995).

30. Ellen Goodman, "Victory at the Gender Gap," *Washington Post* (16 November 1996).

31. Rosalind Coward, *Our Treacherous Hearts: Why Women Let Men Get Their Way.*

32. Claudia Koonz, *Mothers in the Fatherland*, 13, 104.

33. Koonz, 13, 105-7. Freud may have over-generalized when he wrote in 1930 that "[Man's] constant association with men, and his dependence on his relations with them, even estrange him from his duties as a husband and father. Thus the woman finds herself forced into the background by the claims of civilization and she adopts a hostile attitude towards it" (*Civilization and Its Discontents*, 103). But such views assimilate

perfectly to Koonz's account of German women.

34. Koonz, xxxiii; in "A Response to Eve Rosenhaft," she sharpens her conclusions about the recasting of memory into "gendered terms that bifurcate Nazi active/masculine/evil—and non-Nazi passive/feminine/good" (*Radical History Review*, 43 [1989] :84). "The complicated story of Italian feminism's accommodation to fascism" has been told by Victoria De Grazia in *How Fascism Ruled Women, Italy, 1922-1945*, 238.

35. Kathleen M. Blee, *Women of the Klan: Racism and Gender in the 1920s*, 2-3.

36. Blee, 178-80.

37. Kathy Dobie, "Long Day's Journey into White," 22-32.

38. Glen Jeansonne, *Women of the Far Right: The Mothers' Movement and World War II*.

39. Paula Giddings, *Where and When I Enter: The Impact of Black Women on Race and Sex in America*.

40. Cathy Young, "Female Trouble."

41. Hester Eisenstein, "Scholars in Women's Studies Can Help Put This Fall's Election into Perspective," *Chronicle of Higher Education* (23 Sept 1992), B-2.

42. Alison Mitchell, "For Feminists, It Wasn't What They Had in Mind," *NY Times* (17 Sept 1992).

43. Elizabeth Langland, "Nobody's Angels: Domestic Ideology and Middle-Class Women in the Victorian Novel," 291.

44. Celestine Bohlen, "East Europe's Struggle with New Rules, and Old Ones," *NY Times* (25 Nov 1990).

45. Guida Jackson, *Women Who Ruled.*

46. Lois Honeycutt, "Female Succession and the Language of Power in the Writings of Twelfth-Century Churchmen," 190, 201.

47. Lisa Hopkins, *Women Who Would Be Kings: Female Rulers of the Sixteenth Century.*

48. Pranay Gupte, *Mother India*, 442-5.

49. Stanley Wolpert, "History's Hold on Bakistan," *New York Times* (12 November 1996); Barbara Crossette, "Enthralled by Asia'a Ruling Women? Look Again," *New York Times* (10 November 1996).

50. John Phillips, "Saint Irene Sweeps Clean," *London Times* (24 Feb 1995).

51. Ellen Hawkes, *Feminism on Trial*, 391.

52. Christopher Hitchens, "Radical Pique," *Vanity Fair* (February, 1994), 35; Hawkes, 390; "If the personal is political, then, by an implacable logic, the private must be public," Fox-Genovese wrote in *Feminism Without Illusions*, 99. What is public, of course, can be policed.

53. Hawkes, 392.

54. James Brooke, "For 'Cinderella' First Lady of Brazil, Midnight's Toll Is Scandal and Wrath," *NY Times* (4 Oct 1992).

55. Hawkes depicts American feminism in the eighties as fraught with "internal jealousies and power plays, ideological confusion, even plain exhaustion" (8 and Epilogue).

56. Ann Snitow reports on a research group that asks, "Under what circumstances do women decide to band together as women, break out of domestic space, and publicly protest?"

Her answer was that "Almost all the women we have been studying present themselves to the world as mothers (hence 'motherists') acting for the survival of their children" ("Pages from a Gender Diary," 210). Nazism succeeded in part by adapting to motherist issues. The fact that women define matricentric issues in radically different ways is the central argument of Kristen Luker's *Abortion and the Politics of Motherhood* where both pro-choice and pro-life advocates polarize the issues by differently defining woman's basic identity.

57. Cathy Young, "Female Trouble."

58. Karen DeCrow, quoted by Hawkes, 404.

59. Carol Sternhell, "Sic Transit Gloria," 5-6.

60. Sternhell, 6.

61. Kaminer, *A Fearful Freedom*, 8.

62. Report on the "Committe for the Scientific Investigation of Claims of the Paranormal," *NY Times* (7 July 1996).

63. Christina Hoff Sommers, *Who Stole Feminism?* 11-12; Naomi Wolf corrected later editions of *The Beauty Myth.*

64. John Schwartz, "Statistics on Crime Against Women Are Engulfed By Political Fog," *Washington Post* (27 March 1995).

65. Kay Leigh Hagan, *Women Respond to the Men's Movement.*

66. For Enlightenment thinkers, women and family were beyond the perimeters of the social contract. According to Virginia Held, Rousseau argued that "within the household, the man must rule and the woman must submit to this rule"

("Mothering versus Contract," in *Beyond Self-Interest*, 291.

67. Carol Thurston, *The Romance Revolution*, vii.

68. Eagleton terms this the "feminization of discourse," *The Rape of Clarissa*, 13.

69. There is also in *The Handmaid's Tale* an unprocessed girl's oedipal fantasy in its traditional Jane-Eyre-governess form, inhibiting the serious issues from being more fully probed.

70. In an interview with Kate Greenaway, Byatt cites *The French Lieutenant's Woman* as having "partly provoked" her novel (*Observer*, 16 Sept 1990).

71. The first quote comes from Lynda Bundtzen, chair of women's studies at Williams College, in an essay by Cathy Young, "Women in the Nineties"; the second from Gail Godwin quoting from the Preface of *The Norton Anthology of Literature by Women*, followed by her own review in the *NY Times* (28 April 1985).

72. Though elided from DuPlessis's text, James was urging the spirit of her study: *Writing Beyond the Ending*, which is of course impossible within her "proposition that narrative structures and subjects are like working apparatuses of ideology"—yet it happened (3). See "The Art of Fiction," 294-5; *The Future of the Novel*, 40-41; Joseph A. Boone, "Modernist Maneuvering in the Marriage Plot: Breaking Ideologies of Gender and Genre in James's *The Golden Bowl*," 374-88.

73. This remarkably forthright and committed novel has been reissued as *Suffragettes: A Story of Three Women* (London: Pandora, 1984); for the larger picture, see Angela Ingram and Daphne Patai, *Rediscovering Forgotten Radicals: British Women Writers, 1889-1939*. In *The Victorian Heroine: A Changing Ideal, 1837-73*, Patricia Thomson finds a progressive change in the latitude and legitimacy of the heroine's motives for choosing or

rejecting marriage. The traditional feminine reason for
marrying to acquire a "comfortable home and a wealth of love"
is balanced against a quasi-feminist goal of "equality,
community of interest, likeness of intellect," while the socially-
unacceptable alternatives of old maidenhood or prostitution
yield to a more positive definition of chastity congenial to the
"feminist dream" of "honourable spinsterhood" (113-9). On the
other hand, Patricia Stubbs is inclined to view the novel as
"retrograde in its depicting of women confined to a private
domestic world" (*Women and Fiction: Feminism and the Novel,
1880-1920*, x); a view also pursued by Carolyn Heilbrun in
"Marriage Perceived: English Literature 1873-1941, *What Manner
of Woman*, 160-83.

74. Nicola Beauman, *A Very Great Profession.* Women
writers' contribution to Modernism emerge from obscurity in
Benstock's *Women of the Left Bank*, Hanscombe's and Smyers'
Writing for Their Lives, and Marek's *Women Editing Modernism.*
Writing explores a group of writers (H.D., Bryher, Dorothy
Richardson, Gertrude Stein, Djuna Barnes, Harriet Monroe,
Amy Lowell, and others) who shared neither Bloomsbury's
glamour nor the suffragettes' militancy, but in their
bohemianism, rejection of heterosexual bonding, and recourse
to networking, comprised an "implicit" sort of "cultural
feminism." Ardis makes a strong case as well for the disruptive
emergence of the New Woman in early modern fiction by
women as well as by men (*New Women, New Novels.* The debate
on romances continues with *Dangerous Men and Adventurous
Women*, edited by Jayne Ann Krentz.

75. Donald Symons, *The Evolution of Human Sexuality.*

76. Helen E. Fisher, *Anatomy of Love*, 94.

77. "Romances are fundamentally about mate selection,"
conclude Bruce Ellis and Donald Symons, and while offering
lip-service to changing roles, these narratives are virtually
unchanging and transcultural. Contrary to the emphasis on
variety of partners and activities in male pornography, "in a

romance novel, the hero discovers in the heroine a fulfilling focus for his passions, which ensures his future sexual fidelity"; as he becomes dependent on her, sex scenes serve as models of female sexual control. Thus in this context biology enters culture as sexual fantasies reinforce sexual dimorphism and ensuing reproductive strategies ("Sex Differences in Sexual Fantasy: an Evolutionary Psychological approach," 544-5]). Although the authors synthesize previous studies in conjunction with their own tests of unscreened undergraduates, I do not detect any allowances made for non-heterosexual responses. But their mate-selection thesis is confirmed in a report on the new romance hero: "a man for whom children and family come first," who apologizes, "makes us soup when we're sick, and picks up kids from soccer" (Donna Abu-Nasr, "They cook. They Clean. And They Sell," AP [5 Nov 1995]). Gadpaille bridges the sociobiology of reproductive strategies and psychological functioning in "Innate Masculine/Feminine Traits: Their Contributions to Conflict," 401-24.

78. Quote from Ellis and Symons, 533; Norman Holland, *The First Modern Comedies.*

79. Susan Sperling's "Baboons with Briefcases: Feminism, Functionalism, Sociobiology in the Evolution of Primate Gender" questions the sexist assumptions of sociobiology along with the feminist revisions, and the postmodernists' treatment of all "epistemologies in evolutionary science" as "equally mythic social constructions," 26.

80. Stephen Jay Gould, "Genes on the Brain," 5-9.

81. Helen Fisher agrees with the proposition that "men are neuro-endocrinologically wired...to attain positions of rank, authority, and power," *Anatomy of Love*, 286.

82. Sherry Turkle, *Psychoanalytic Politics*, 69-93; Elisabeth Roudinesco, *Jacques Lacan & Co.*, 454-6.

83. Donald Kaplan, "Some Theoretical and Technical Aspects of Gender and Social Reality," 4.

84. Donald Kaplan, 9.

85. Jacques Lacan, "Seminar of 21 January 1975," in *Feminine Sexuality*, edited by Juliet Mitchell and Jacqueline Rose, 169; Julia Kristeva, *New Maladies of the Soul*, 87-102; for current views among American psychonalysts, see Susan Sherkow, "The Role of Vaginal Awareness in Female Development," and Wendy Olesker, "Female Genital Anxieties," paper delivered at the (1996) Meeting of the American Psychoanalytic Association.

86. Phyllis and Robert Tyson, *Psychoanalytic Theories of Development*, 32-32.

87. Tysons, 265.

88. Tysons, 263.

89. See P. Ikonen and E. Rechardt, "On the Universal Nature of Primal Scene Fantasies," and my *Creativity and Culture.* Here in this powerful nucleus of infantile life is situated one reason for the inadequacy of both Lacan's linguistic unconscious and of culture studies to advance an adequate discourse on human beings.

90. Sally Robinson, "Misappropriations of the 'Feminine,'" 50.

91. For a critique of Lacan by a practicing feminist psychoanalyst, see Jane Flax, *Thinking Fragments: Psychoanalysis, Feminism, and Postmodernism*, 89-97.

92. Dervin, "Lacan and the Fate of Transference."

93. Marianne Hirsch, "Prelude: Origins and Paradigms," in *The Mother / Daughter Plot*, 28-39.

94. Psychoanalysis "with its emphasis on the baneful effects of sexual repression," according to Betty Yorburg, "provided the ideology for the sexual revolution" of the 1920s ("Psychoanalysis and Women's Liberation," 76); Nancy Chodorow in "Freud on Women," is more circumspect.

95. Karen Horney, "Genesis of the Castration Complex in Women," 46. Despite her promising, independent line of inquiry into early female development, Louise Kaplan questions the essentialist assumption of an "innate femininity" in *Female Perversions*, 187-8; other analysts, like Shirley Panken, assess Horney more generously; for a sample of recent thinking among women analysts, see Lucy LaFarge, "The Early Determinants of Penis Envy."

96. Juliet Mitchell and Jacqueline Rose, *Feminine Sexuality*; Mary Jacobus, *Leading Women*, 18-21.

97. Ann Rosalind Jones, " Julia Kristeva on Femininity"; Angela Weir and Elizabeth Wilson, "The British Women's Movement."

98. Henri Parens, "On the Girl's Entry into the Oedipus Complex," in Blum *Female Psychology*, 82.

99. Parens, Ibid; see also Robert Stoller's voluminous work on primary femininity, e.g., *Sex and Gender*; Herman Roiphe and Eleanor Galenson, *Infantile Origins of Sexual Identity*; Dale Mendell, editor, *Early Female Development*; Irene Fast *Gender Identity*; Tysons, *Psychoanalytic Theories of Development*.

100. Tysons, 266.

101. Robert Stoller, "Primary Femininity," in Blum's *Female Psychology*, 61; H. Roiphe and E. Galenson, *Infantile Origins of Sexual Identity*.

102. For libido's mollification into love, see Carol Gilligan and Eve Stern, "The Riddle of Femininity and the Psychology of Love," 101-114.

103. On a Meet-the-Author Panel at the Winter, 1992, meeting of the American Psychoanalytic Association, Chodorow, who had just completed her own analytic training, admitted to the many conflictual areas of mother/daughter relationships, but had nevertheless opted in her writings for a constructive, i.e., corrective approach, one that had generated as much enthusiasm among her feminist colleagues as it now elcited skepticism among her fellow analysts. Drawing on intrapsychic conflict models, another woman analyst, Elizabeth Lloyd Mayer, expanded on two organizing concepts—primary femininity and castration fantasies—as contributing to female gender identity. Thus girls are concerned not to envy what they don't have but to deal with what they do have, to discover what they are as well as what they are not ("Contemporary Theories of Female Sexuality," Panel at the American Psychoanalytic Association, Winter, 1991); see also Lucy LaFarge, "The Early Determinants of Penis Envy."

104. Freudian drive theory affirms as well as transcends gender, for in specifying that the instincts are inherently conservative by reason of their seeking homeostasis as a return to an earlier state (which led Freud in turn to speculations about a death instinct), he delineated a theoretical common-ground for the sexes.

105. Virginia Woolf, *A Room of One's Own*, 108.

106. Susan Stanford Friedman ("Creativity and the Childbirth Metaphor: Gender Difference in Literary Discourse," 49-82) explores women's ambivalence over this metaphor and the gender distinctions in its uses; Susan Kavaler-Adler's *The Compulsion to Create: a Psychoanalytic Study of Women Artists* examines early conflicts affecting women's creativity.

107. Such are the implications of Louise Kaplan's *Female Perversions*, 61, 96.

108. Gayle Greene, *Changing the Story: Feminist Fiction and the Tradition*, 14; later the author explains her focus is restricted to something called "feminist metafiction," so apparently there is no "female form" after all, 25.

109. Rachel Blau DuPlessis, *Writing Beyond the Ending*, 1-19; Sally Robinson, "The 'Anti-Logos Weapon': Multiplicity in Women's Texts," 115; "multiplicty and heterogeneity" really owe more to Bakhtin's carnivalesque and dialogic than to French feminism.

110. In "Heiress to an Empty Throne: Ego-Ideal Problems of Contemporary Women," Sederer and Seidenberg discuss the conflicts between traditional maternal roles and new opportunities wrought by feminism.

111. It is also to deny the complex role of fathers in the development of women writers, from Frances Burney on. As an example of the Woman/women approach, see the Introduction to Sally Robinson's *Engendering the Subject*, 1-18.

112. Susan Stanford Friedman, "Creativity and the Childbirth Metaphor." Among psychoanalytic texts, see Daniel S. Jaffe, "The Masculine Envy of Woman's Procreative Function"; Ruth and Theodore Lidz, "Male Menstruation: A Ritual Alternative to the Oedipal Transition"; Robert Stoller and Gilbert Herdt, "The Development of Masculinity: A Cross Cultural Contribution."

113. Margaret George, *Women in the First Capitalist Society*, 6.

114. The quest for analogy in the boy's and girl's development led Jung in 1912-13 to propose the ill-fated "Electra complex," which Freud rejected by 1921; thereafter the concept disappeared from psychoanalysis, enjoyed a marginal

existence in Jung's analytical psychology, but underwent a
strange recussitation in academic psychology where it was
misattributed to Freud and discussed in textbooks (for more see
my "The Electra Complex: Academic Psychology's Phantom
Limb," adapted with Christopher Kilmartin to "Inaccurate
Representations of the Electra Complex").

115. It is this discredited formulation that Gilbert and
Gubar resurrect in order "to understand the ways in which a
number of twentieth-century women artists have sought to gain
aesthetic potency through forms of male mimicry" (*No Man's
Land*, 185); even as a rough analogy between unconscious
processes and literary strategies, levels of discourse get
hopelessly confused.

116. Ralph Greenson, "Dis-identifying from Mother: Its
Special Importance for the Boy"; since a positive line of male
development is elided from feminist psychology, one may
consider Lillian Rubin's account of how the boy "must
relinquish his earliest bond with the mother" ("On Men and
Friendships"; of course early nurturing experiences are
continued among boys in the transitional sphere of play (as
designated by D.W. Winnicott) through soothing activities and
mastery games with dolls and toys. It is here that children's
creative drives come to the fore.

117. These complicated processes obviously entail a great
deal, e.g.: "psychological femininity always includes some
degree of identification with the femininity of the father (and
the father's mother *and* father) and some degree of
identification with the masculinity of the mother (and the
mother's father *and* mother)," Louise Kaplan, *Female
Perversions*, 189.

118. Martin Grotjahn, "The Primal Crime and the
Unconscious," 306-14.

119. Milan Kundera, *The Art of the Novel*; James Tatum,
editor, *The Search for the Ancient Novel*.

120. Carol Pearson & Katherine Pope, Chapter One, *The Female Hero*; Carol McMillan, *Women, Reason, and Nature*.

Afterword

Return to the Three Planets

We are, perhaps, *trapped* in theory....
—Kurt Spellmeyer[1]

But in order to write about life as I intended to do,
I felt I had first to live.... With an idea developing
in my head, a pen in my hand and a notebook
before before me I was in bliss.
—Muriel Spark[2]

Women write. They write to express something of
themselves or of their world; they write for pleasure, for profit,
and to be read. They may write anxiously, modestly,
triumphantly, transgressively, opportunistically, as well as in a
variety of modes, manners, genres, subgenres, styles, and attitudes.
They write relatively fluently from mixed traditions where
previous writers of various genders have learned from, been
influenced by, put up resistance to, struggled with, loved, hated,
or disregarded other writers of various gender mixes. From the
perspective of gender-purity, literary traditions are hopelessly
muddled; from that of the gendered writer, they are infinitely
rich, often dangerous, and rarely resistible.

Women write through a culture which traditionally
restricts and oppresses along lines of gender, class, race, and
ethnicity; they write through a biology which has historically
been misdefined and misappropriated,[3] and through gendered
psyches which bear the marks of these impositions while being
fueled by their own distinctive blends of creative energy and
purpose. Such blendings can never be fully contained by any
given approach, matricentric included.

Women write with relative agency that factors in adversity
along with privilege, conflict along with conflict-mastery, and
aims along with effects. Writing from a hand of whichever
gender plays over a psychoanalytic spectrum: at one point is
conflict-fixation, a static circularity, but conceivably also one of
extremity, intensity, and uncompromising tenacity; at the other
point is a version of the conflict-free sphere of American ego-
psychology (an adaptational model).[4] Between the gravity of

repetition-compulsion and the freer atmosphere of creative facility, most writing ranges. In these regions, conflicts may be mastered or at least ameliorated through language and representation, through displacement onto narrative sequences and plausibly interconnecting lives. Though adaptive, writing creatively displays transitional functioning (à la Winnicott) in a cultural medium which, in balancing subjective and objective perceptions (or pleasure and reality principles à la Freud), discovers an often expanded, hence adaptive role for illusion in emotional and mental life.[5] Thus art contributes to the shared illusions that constitute culture—embracing some, discrediting others.

Put more clinically, agency enters writing as compromise-formation, i.e., as an ideosyncratically suitable accommodation that enables writers, whether they are doing creative work, practicing criticism, or expounding theory, to engage a medium of expression that blends desire and defense into new wholes. The fact that the pleasures of writing offer only indirect gratification—the murders or *jouissant* mergings, the blissful copulations or exchanges of vows, being always only symbolic—attests to writing as mediated, post early-repression, and overdetermined (or multi-functional). Certain subjective aspects of writing—the sense that a writer exists principally when he or she is realizing illusions through writing, that language writes the texts from previous texts, and so forth—have been overstated in postmodern death-of-the-author tenets.

Although creative work is more imagenic and narrational while critical discourse more conceptual, all writing is prone to latent/manifest contents, to subtexts/hidden agendas, and in general to a structure of tiered significations or meanings, received and recreated by readers with similarly tiered psychic systems. Insofar as postmodernism implies that the author's death did not follow from natural causes but was a prerequisite for self-authorisation of the critical theorist, a psychoanalysis of writing implicates the theoretician, the critic, the ideologue along with the creative writer. Academics in general who view themselves as deep interpreters or deconstructors of the literary text—in effect practicing a peculiar variant of psychoanalysis without a psyche—are especially prone to the peculiar distorting evasions, idealizations, and projections of countertransference equivalents.[6]

In this context, a recurring idealization in feminist discourses is writing-the-body. The phrase may imply the preoedipal pleasures of conflict-free merging in the maternal dyad (Julia Kristeva's semiotics locating a slighted *jouissance* within the Lacanian Imaginary), be represented as the act of giving birth (Jane Gallop), or take the form of lesbian sexual fantasies (Monique Wittig). Because Lacan's Symbolic Order is defined along lines of male-oedipal/patriarchal-socialization formulae, the girl's preoedipal ties to mother presumably escape oppressive symbolic bindings and are assigned a near literal immediacy. Psychoanalysis may be summoned to validate this bodily zone as in "psychoanalytically oriented feminist criticism" keyed to the "female psyche or self, shaped by the body, by the development of language, and by sex-role socialization."[7] But if this sounds psychoanalytic, it isn't; true, the emergent psyche is affected by bodily sensations and organizied around orifices but mainly insofar as they engage early drives, wishes, fantasies, and defenses, which combine with family relationships to form one's personal history and sense of identity. While it is also true that writing may overcome repression—or more likely may dodge certain repressive barriers while bowing to others—the body enters psychoanalytic discourse as a cluster of psychic representations, making itself felt through needs, affects, prohibitions, and often expressed via an archaic mode of primary-process mentation.[8]

Insofar as writing operates through both the psychic apparatus and the central nervous system, the body is always mediated by language and never achieves its distinctive immediacy of touch; hence, the body can never be written directly, only equivalently. Writers may seem to be writing the drives insofar as the drive zones are mentally and linguistically represented, but writing also entails writing the defenses and the inhering conflicts bound up with these drives, so that the desire-in-the-text experienced by readers does not violate their reality sense but imparts a sense of shared agency. Phyllis Tyson's strictures on Melanie Klein also apply to later feminist uses of object-relations theory as well as to French psychoanalysis: "Kleinian theory is primarily topographical rather than based on

Freud's later structural theory...with none of the self-regulating functions" of the later model. "Fantasy to her is the concrete expression of a drive, not a compromise between impulse and defense derived from ego functioning, in the course of which reality is taken into account."[9] In other words the viability of the 1915 topographical model ended a decade later when Freud introduced the structural hypothesis in *The Ego and the Id*; yet the vast majority of Lacanians and cultural theorists revert to the older, rudimentary structure which tends to weld the id to culture with the ego's distortions but without its mediations and reality-testings; thus agency is elided and replaced by discourses of victims/oppressor.

Rather than the female body's anchoring women's writing, a filtering through the matricentric self as encompassing body and psyche, gender-inflected self/object-representations, personal history, and cultural traditions, seems more promising. Such a self would also include psychic representations of gender-specific functions (menstruation, giving birth, nurturing, etc.), psychosexual stages and psychodynamic representations of gendered fantasies and actions, plus all of those derivatives of psychic energy that fuel the imagination and enter the creative sphere.

Through a lessening of repression, creativity may invite free play with stereotypes, their subversion and dissolution, and their replacement with more promising versions. But even when creativity sanctions regression to earlier developmental stages or entertains a return of the repressed, it is always under modified conditions, about which the author may consciously know little and others probably even less. Psychoanalytic reconstruction within the clinic setting is always jerry-built and tenuous; outside the clinic it is even more haphazard.[10] Any psychoanalytically-derived certitudes claimed by cultural studies are likely to prove wishful thinking.

The various deconstructions and reconstructions performed on literary texts by the third planet of theory may be insightful or—just as plausibly—well-intended but corrective measures dictated by prevailing cultural ideologies. Trust the tale not the teller, as D.H. Lawrence famously remarked, but postmodernism makes that difficult when the teller has long since been terminated and all texts are suspects at large to be taken into custody and interrogated under the white hot gaze of prevailing theory. Confessions extracted under such conditions may reflect the interrogators' deepest conspiratorial fears or fondest utopian dreams. While texts proliferate, truth is de-authorized, cast as an *aporia*, enemy agent, or end-game to neverending language games. But if 'truth' had sometimes been applied autocratically, oppressively, and fetishistically, its abandonment has fostered a borderline mode of critical consciousness that distrusts quality, levels individual differences in the name of cultural diversity, restricts causality to victimizers, and seeks scapegoats for an impoverished present.

If theory finds texts suspect, while others find theory suspect; if agency is subverted by agents with dubious agendas, there are finally only the options of proposing hypotheses and continuing to listen: to the texts, to their interpreters, and to their authors. Women's voices alone may not reclaim agency or embody truth, but they are there on the second planet, and worth attending to. Rarely confirming cultural agendas or gender theories about writing—and so rarely heard—they nonetheless confirm their own diverse agency.

Women writers reflecting on their own writing processes seldom address theory directly, but they often traverse critical terrain and contribute obliquely to the discourse. As noted, Virginia Woolf seems to be evoking a female literary tradition when she remarks that "a woman writing thinks back through her mothers," but in defining creative processes she actually thinks back to Coleridge's assertion that a "great mind is androgynous," draws on Jungian animus/anima archetypes to espouse a "fusion" that "fully fertilises" the mind through the "woman having intercourse with the man in her" brain and vice versa; her exemplary model of the "man-womanly mind" is not Jane Austen but William Shakespeare.[11] More consistently androgynous, Michele Roberts believes that the "writer should struggle to be bisexual and learn from the father as well as the mother," and then gives the prospect a matricentric spin: "You have to start with your femaleness, *not* with writing like a man, and grow and expand from there, find your masculine part too."[12] Other writers with feminist interests like Fay Weldon find it more difficult to access their inner male: "I feel at liberty to invent women, as I'm female. I merely describe men."[13]

Just as writers entertain a sort of primal scene of sexual polarity in their imagination, so does the mingling of the sexes extend over literary tradition to such an extent that one can never safely tell who is inside whom—thinking back through mothers leads to fathers—so that ultimately no one exists apart from countless generations of couplings. What survives in "Virginia Woolf," Joyce Carol Oates argues is not the woman writer or her personality, but a "bodiless" mimesis, an "artful assemblage of words, because writers "aspire to invisibility," to "refine themselves out of existence" (as Joyce's Stephen Dedalus had proposed).[14] Bracketing herself as a "(woman) writer," Oates, though aligned with feminist goals, downplays the woman writer's inscribing her gender along with the female body. Similarly, Edna O'Brien dismisses a specifically feminine anxiety in writing. When asked by Philip Roth, "Does the job fundamentally come down to the same difficulties then, regardless of gender?" she replied: "Absolutely. There is no difference at all; you, like me, are trying to make something out of nothing and the anxiety is extreme."[15] In this light, writing (like subjectivity) does not arise out of sexual difference, but following the primal repression's self-generating act of negation: the hallucinated breast must be renounced in order for its substitute to be found in reality. To the extent that writing continues this quest it is overdetermined *ab initio*.

Although gender never fully dissolves into a writer's identity, many women writers affirm the generative power of writing to forge identity. "Being a writer before I am a woman," conveyed Elizabeth Bowen's sense of herself, and Rosamond Lehmann phrased her career as destiny: "I was bound to write. I never considered anything else as a possibility for my future."[16] Among British women writers I interviewed, Sara Maitland stands out for claiming she writes as a woman and feminist (likewise Angela Carter, Michelene Wandor, Zoë Fairbairns, and Michele Roberts[17]); others answered as follows: "I write as a person" (Margaret Drabble); "I write as a novelist" (Elizabeth Jane Howard); and with a gesture of impatience: "Look, I'm a storyteller: I polish my prose for style not for politics" (Lynn Reid

Banks). Of course, the control women rightfully claim over what they make into prose does not extend to what will be made of it thereafter.

Notes

1. His "way out lies in...the domain of the 'arts,' understood not as the cunning lies told by an elite, nor as the proerty of specialists whose goal is technical virtuosity, but as traditions of attunement with the world, available to everyone everywhere but also now diligently suppressed" (*College English* 58:8 (1966): 893, 911.

2. Muriel Spark, *Curriculum Vitae*, 103, 192.

3. Thomas Lacqueur, *Making Sex.*

4. Susan Kavaler-Adler, *The Compulsion to Create: A Psychoanalytic Study of Women Artists.*

5. Simon A. Grolnick, *et als,* editors, *Between Reality and Fantasy.*

6. See Teresa Ebert's Marxist critique of the idealized body in ludic feminism ("For a Red Pedagogy").

7. Elaine Showalter, "Feminist Criticism in the Wilderness," 256.

8. See, for example, the inner world of Sabina Spielrein in John Kerr's *A Most Dangerous Method*, 19-20.

9. Phyllis and Robert Tyson, *Psychoanalytic Theories of Development*, 73.

10. See Donald Kaplan on "boundary problems," in "The Psychoanalysis of Art: Some Ends, Some Means."

11. Virginia Woolf, *A Room of One's Own*, 101-2.

12. Olga Kenyon, editor, " *Women Writers Talk*, 172.

13. Kenyon, 206; Jane Miller, *Women Writing About Men*, 13.

14. Joyce Carol Oates, "(Woman) Writer," 193.

15. *NY Times Book Review* (18 Nov 1984), 40.

16. Victoria Glendinning, *Elizabeth Bowen*, 90; "Rosamond Lehmann," *Writing Lives*, 151.

17. "Michele Roberts," *Women Writers Talk*, 165.

Appendix A: Feminism: What's in a Word?

The simple answer is 'a great deal,' but there is in fact no simple answer. Any one of the following components can foreground feminism and serve as a whole. As a movement, women's *cause* revolves around *slogans* (personal is political, sisterhood is powerful), and *issues* (reproductive freedom, comparable pay, women in combat) function as entry points. Thus as a *praxis* it may privilege the fast-track of careerism or the domestic sphere of children, depending on whether one resides in a Western democracy or in Central Europe. But if global, feminism has no global *agenda*. In shifting from a liberationist stance to one of diversity, *SpareRib*'s editors wrote, "the recognition of the existence of gender subordination and the need to break down its structures has often led to the wrong conclusions—that it engenders monolithic and universal issues, strategies and methods, applicapble to all women in all societies in all times."[1] *Cases* ("Baby M") dramatize but also complicate issues by returning partisians to the human arena where privileging the surrogate mother's rights overshadows those of the child and the adoptive parents. In order to weld past to present and action to purpose, *theories* are developed; these are greatly shaped by identity politics within any preexisting culture. Thus British feminism is collectivist and socialist (their exponents complain of a peculiarly American brand of celebrity feminism); French feminism favors the metaphysical and speculative; American feminism divides variously among radical forms (utopian/separatist) and liberal forms (mainstream, accomodationist, keyed to strategies of empowerment).[2] Amidst these impulses, an Anglo-French focus on gender as constructed and on feminine pleasures as distinctive *jouissance* puts in sharp relief the mostly North American liberationist movement as essentialist or biocentric (at least until *jouissance* is probed for its essentialist assumptions).[3] American feminists' views dispersed to the negative and positive poles of woman's presumed nature, with Susan Brownmiller, Andrea Dworkin, Catherine Mackinnon, *et al*, emphasizing her rapability by exposing male lust/agression, and with Carol Gilligan *et al* foregrounding her generativity through her relatedness, her special ways of knowing and forming ethical decisions.[4] A fierce *rhetoric* of oppression/victmization on the one hand and a gentle one of

innate superiority on the other fueled these theoretical positions
and fostered divergent discourses. Partly shielding their
incompatabilities and disclaimers notwithstanding has been an
overarching *ideology* of male dominance in a global patriarchal
system and a *mythology* embracing sisterhood buoyed by a
primordial matriarchy.[5] Filtered through all these divisions is an
ethics that distributes virtue and vice along gender lines.[6] In
sum, every aspect of feminism has become so overdetermined and
so highly contexualized as to qualify as a floating signifier of
indeterminant meanings.

　　　This discursive *mélange* was instanced in the summer of
1989 when the U.S. Supreme Court handed down a decision
restricting women's access to abortion. The effect of this *case*,
which clearly set back the women's *cause*, was construed by Molly
Yard, President of NOW, as evidence of a "a war on women".[7]
Was it? In effect, an *ideology* of male hegemony, fueled by an
essentialist rhetoric and legitimized by a totalizing *ethics*, shifted
the debate from a real-world setting—where a moderately
conservative woman sat on the court with at least a few moderate
to liberal collegues, where the anti-abortion campaign is "manned"
by as many women as men, and where freedom-of-choice'ers
likewise included a gender mix—to a purely *mythological* realm of
archetypal gender combat.

　　　Does this imply that, despite allegiance to cultural
diversity and the qualifying force of class, race, and ethnic
considerations, feminism will react under fire with a totalizing
essentialism? Not necessarily. In repudiating liberationist
totality, the *SpareRib* editors also recognized "no one enemy":
patriarchy is a "main component," but only "one part" of the "web
of oppression."[8] Is it then possible to support the cause without
acceding to the polarizing rhetoric, the psychological splitting, or
the transhistorical ideology? So one hopes; certainly there are
signs of sporadic resistance to "ideological policing."[9]

　　　In "Cultural Feminism Versus Post-Structuralism: The
Identity Crisis in Feminist Theory," Linda Alcoff addresses the
underlying problem of defining woman; but, following Alice
Echols, her assigning the term "cultural feminism" to the radical
or essentialist positions of Adrienne Rich and Mary Daly gets
confused with the kind of postmodern cultural feminism arising

from postmodern cultural studies instanced by the radical politics of Teresa Ebert, who vehemently denounces postmodern, ludic feminism. In "Pages from Gender Diary," Ann Snitow also follows Echols in exploring the "central feminist divide" between the "need to build the identity 'woman' and give it a solid meaning and the need to tear down the very category 'woman' and dismantle its all-too-solid history." In noting that opposing definitions stem from academic theorists versus social activists, she explores such oppositions as Radical Feminists and Cultural Feminists, Essentialists and Social Constructionist, Motherists and Feminists. In the end, she expects the divisions to be resolved not through thought but through historical processes. In her chapter, "The Construction of 'Woman,'" Carol Lee Bacchi believes that the category of *women* might be retrieved as a "political identity," but for support she reverts to sex-linked traits like childcare and peaceableness.[10] For Wendy Kaminer, feminism is torn between egalitarian/protectionist impulses (*A Fearful Freedom*). For Nicci Gerrard, feminism is "so fragmented and dispersed that it is hard to perceive any exclusive directions: socialist, separatist, and cultural, with a host of splinter factions."[11]

In similar fashion, Elaine Showalter locates four models (biological, linguistic, psychoanalytic, and cultural) of feminist criticism, which can be seen either as signifying a healthy pluralism or as the proverbial wisemen sizing up the elephant from their respective positions.[12] Noting that "one is bound to feel that feminism as theory has pulled the rug from under feminism as politics," Kate Soper addresses the dilemma as "heterogeneous" discourse and feminism as community in "Feminism, Humanism, and Postmodernism."[13] With no intended offense, what might be called the pasta-approach of feminism as the all-purpose additive to serve with such main dishes as existentialism/psychoanalysis/marxism/ postmodern etc. is taken in Rosemary Tong's *Feminist Thought*. Studies purporting to provide "the feminist perspective on this or that" have been skewered by Susan Haack as a species of "preposterism."[14]

Outside the pasta range are the conservative feminism of women who want free choice along with traditional family values, the capitalist feminism of Madonna, and the patriarchal feminism of Camille Paglia, who, it is said, has alone unified all academic feminists against her; although in focusing on her content, they overlook her formal role as trickster whose mocking of insiders' latest intellectual fashions concedes feminism's new establishment status.[15]   Of course, many serious-minded feminists would not credit this triad as feminist at all, thereby marginalizing other women and reinstating hierarchies of orthodoxy.

So many branches have tended to conceal if not replace the trunk. If a radical branch posits a feminism without men, a constructivist branch uneasily affirms, as a recent title worries, *Feminism Without Women* by Tania Modleski. Both, however, are predicated on patriarchy as a dominant other since the essentialism of the one inevitably essentializes the other. But as Diana Fuss concedes in *Essentially Speaking*, the two diverging branches are best seen as ad hoc strategies, either one being evoked subject to time, place, and circumstances; and, as Modleski's discourse inadvertently demonstrates, academic theorists are diehard essentialists in respect to their reliance on categories; thus she posits "the lesbian perspective," innocent of the multiplicity of lesbian writings and their politically-incorrect positions on s/m; and even more innocently she summons the evil specter of "the nuclear family."[16]   One recalls in this context, Harry Truman's wish for a one-handed economist, since all his economic advisers would tell him "on the one hand, but then on the other hand.... Here one wishes not for a one-handed feminist discourse (of which there are many) but for a multi-handed one that can accommodate differences within as well as outside feminism. It *is* true that on the one hand the nuclear family has been the site of oppressive roles and domestic violence, but on a relative scale the nuclear family is hardly dominant; and, as it declines, even less desirable conditions result: single households correlate with poverty, fatherless families correlate with delinquent behavior.[17]   Picture a white academic preaching the evils of the nuclear family on any inner city street-corner, and the absurdity is clear: the Boyz N de Hood want dads.

If feminist discourses display division among as well as within cultures and between theory and practice, there is also running through these texts various binary opposites. Most basic assumptions and strategies stem from either biocentric or constructivist positions and reinforce attitudes of either complicity or victimization. Formerly, the one led to separatist agendas, the other to mainstreaming; more recently, the dichotomy has been rephrased as "difference feminism" versus "equality feminism" by Katha Pollitt, who proceeds to deconstruct the positions of Chodorow and Gilligan as changing the +/- signs of stereotyping while retaining its modus operandi.[18] Pollitt's back-to-square-one analysis suggests that feminism is more about questions than about answers and thus encourages everyone to rethink the whole subject afresh.

This is salutary, but in the current, highly-conflicted context, what does it mean to say one is pro-feminist, or anti-feminist? Apart from unregenerate misogyny or generalized support, it is virtually impossible to privilege a feminist text that does not exclude other feminist texts, not to mention other non-feminist data. Yet the term must be employed, somehow.

"The basis of feminist theory and organizing was and is the idea that women do have something in common as women," writes one theorist, and however "their experience may differ according to their different access to racial and class privileges, and their differences in cultural backgrounds, women share an oppression as women."[19] Yet "all women are oppressed as women."[20] Again: "What makes something a feminine point of view should be explained in terms of oppression of a particularly fundamental kind....Women are oppressed because that which gives them their identity as women is an oppressive concept."[21] Also articulating this position are Andrea Dworkin, Catherine MacKinnon, Marilyn French, Mary Daly, and many others. It should never be denied that women have objectively been victimized, mostly by men, over long periods of times and among diverse cultures, and yet to build a movement or to construct an ideology on victimization has often resulted in reinforcing helplessness, producing resentment or rage without remedying the condition. As woman defines the victim, victim defines woman. Victimhood both empowers and negates. Women are thus put in a double bind which, however apparent to others or unfair to them, is best addressed and resolved by women. Otherwise, the prevailing situation of new solutions being proposed every few years—androgyny, equality, separatism, *jouissance*—and the proliferation of factionalism, mixed messages, and internal conflicts will persist. The backlash/war-on-women/beauty-myth conspiracy rhetoric both addresses truths and conducts its own war on complexity; it also disproves the claim that women's history is passing beyond victimology to resistance, a thesis advanced in *Hidden from History*.

Women continue to be raped, abused, and harassed by men and should be free to speak out about it in ways to be heard and effect change—and be supported in doing so—but postmodernism situates the real outside discourse and tends to transform victims into rhetorical discourse: hence, in feminist writing the paradigm of the victim should either be explicit so that everyone knows where they stand or else not be implied to discredit dissent. If this sounds ungracious and unduly touchy, readers may recall Deborah Tannen's finding in *You Just Don't Understand* that women experience lack of men's support for their feelings as an attack.[22] If this sounds extreme, consider an occasion when five women panelists (including Susan Faludi and Catherine Mackinnon) "backed the view that rape, far from being a pathology, reflects the norm in male-female relations in our society. As proof, Mackinnon asserted that 47% of all American women have been sexually assaulted and 25% raped. When a male panelist questioned these numbers she retorted, "That means you don't believe women."[23] What occurs in exchanges is the sliding of *most*: thus from the uncontestable 'most assaults on women come from men' emerges 'most men assault women.' Turning from rhetoric of rape to research on rape, one discovers recent "findings confirm that most men are not ordinarily aroused by depictions of sexual violence."[24] When rhetoric and research, facts and ideology, do not inhabit discrete domains, the latter are often driven by the former. Thus Naomi Wolfe's claim of 150,000 annual deaths due to eating disorder had to be corrected downward to approximately 300; widely publicized claims about 9 million women killed as witches in early modern Europe have been overestimated by a "factor of 200," according to Robin Briggs, who cites "between 40,000 and 50,000 executions, of which 20 to 25% were of men.[25] If men are unwelcome in these areas, even feminists who critique feminist theories have been accused of "trashing."[26]

Through all these disputes and discourses lurks relativism. In one or more of its manifestations, feminism is adopted by women and personally adapted to their own needs, wishes, deficits, aspirations, and agendas. Feminism as personal vehicle constitutes the final reason for difficulties in definition, but it is plausibly the most important way in which the term operates experientially. Unfortunately, when women's subjectivity is textually addressed, a prior investment in theory or polemics distances most discourses. Eve Kosofsky Sedgwick in "Jane Austen and the Masturbating Girl," for example, has been concerned to subvert sexual identities and roles by disconnecting sexual practice from gender, but in disregarding the role of conscious or unconscious fantasy tied to a sexualized other, she opts for run-of-the-mill behaviorism, the least informative model of human sexuality; as Louise Kaplan remarks, "unlike other animals, we are creatures whose sexual lives are governed almost entirely by fantasy."[27] Kaplan and others have found that cross-dressing and perverse sexual fantasies don't signify a kinky liberation from gender-role dominance but rather the rigid expression of hate or "reenactments of childhood traumas."[28]

In "Sexuality in Human Evolution: What Is 'Natural' in Sex?" Mina Davis Caulfield employs a blend of Marxism and feminism to critique the sociobiological equation of natural with androcentric reproductive strategies; and while she argues for human sexuality as self-created and culturally mediated, her not factoring in any psychoanalytic contribution invites utopian speculations. Obviously, while evolutionary processes like sexual dimorphism cannot be ignored, they should not support a Panglossian teleology of whatever exists is the best of all possible adaptations, but what does exist cannot by dismissed simply due to an apparently arbitrary or male-skewed adaptive process.

If woman's subjectivity has been colonized, appropriated, and generally constituted by men (which to a degree it has),[29] there is a tendency in feminist psychological revisionism to head off her subjectivity at the pass—less a science than a strategy to equip her psychology with feminist capacity. For example, although Chodorow's chapter, "Beyond Drive Theory" is mostly taken up with the theories of Norman O. Brown and Herbert Marcuse, whose provocative cultural applications remain peripheral to psychoanalysis, she attributes a singularity to

classical drive theory that takes her perilously close to inferring
that drives are something males have, object-relations what
women have. "The drive-repression dynamic," she writes, "by
contrast, is an Oedipal theory—a theory of generation and
potentially of relationship to be sure—but a theory of the father.
It does not require women other than as Oedipal object of
cathexis."[30] While analysts might see this as the oldest form of
resistance to Freudian theory or, as the title of Rusell Jacoby's
Social Amnesia implies, a return to "conformist psychology," it is
not to argue for the correctness of Freud (especially in respect to
his theories of female development) but for the kind of adequate
discourse that would endow women with a drive development
appropriate to their gender. And while recent work by such
women analysts as Margaret Mahler, Judith Kestenberg, Phyllis
Tyson, and Eleanor Galenson *appear* to be included, their
contributions to female drive-theory are not. The result is a
reinstateing of the driven-male/related-female stereotype, and the
oppressive chestnut that men desire, women love is roasted again.
It is good sexual politics, but not good psychology. All the same,
it goes without saying that Chodorow has every right to formulate
theories of women according to her own lights and any theories
she prefers; one examines her psychoanalytic cards only because
that is the game she has chosen to play—increasingly so since she
has joined the analytic community. But it does seem unfortunate
that, once deprived of a phallus in classical Freudian/Lacan
theories, woman now finds herself deprived of a dynamic
unconscious in Gilligan/Chodorow theories. The lack-habit seems
extremely hard to kick.

The tendencies of Chodorow to appropriate psychoanalysis
to her home discipline of social science, as Gilligan's to align
psychoanalysis with educational psychology, may form part of a
larger resistance to psychoanalysis as a discourse of radical
alterity. As Teresa Brennan writes, psychoanalysis is a "theory of
how differnce and desire are created," not of "how a socially
constructed gender is internalized."[31] Within feminism,
psychoanalytic revisions began in 1949 with Simone deBeauvoir's
strategy to make Freud into an existential philosopher and then
to critique him as a bad existentialist. Consequently, as Juliet
Mitchell points out, "the Freud the feminists have inheirited is a

long way off-center."[32]

Of the various revisionist strategies is the feminist reversal of man into the second sex initiated by Mary Jane Sherfey's account of embryology in which "All mammalian embryos, male and female, are anatomically female during the early stages of fetal life."[33] Chodorow, whose inquiry into mothering factors in the matricentric drive in women's writing, nonetheless relies on normative concepts when she claims that "women as mothers (and men as not-mothers) produce sons whose nurturant capacities and needs have been systematically curtailed and repressed." The equation of parenting with mothering-as-nurturing and the elision of the father appears again in the formulation, "men are socially and psychologically reproduced by women, but women are reproduced (or not) largely by themselves."[34] Likewise, Gilligan, whose formulae on girls' moral development that attribute an ethics of care and concern for generational continuity over men's allegedly arid allegiance to principles, also underpins matricentric dimensions despite their reliance on a normative trait psychology. While these reversals may offer a welcome tonic if not lasting effect, more circumspect inquiries continue.[35]

Notes

1. *SpareRib*, 197 (January, 1989), 5-7.

2. All of these groupings are fluid and overlapping. Zillah Eisenstein, for example, in "Specifying US Feminism: The Problem of Naming," considers, in light of recent democratic movements, a "Post(?)-Socialist Feminism," 45-56. Scholars in the 1990s began scrutinizing a problematic White feminism, and Teresa Ebert distinguishes between ludic and Red feminisms.

3. As a Marxist, cultural feminist, Teresa Ebert opposes both patriarchy and "most [Anglo-American] feminist practices," for each "*naturalizes* sexual identity" in reifying the phallus ("Romance of Patriarchy," 25, 19).

4. In *Toward a Feminist Theory of the State*, MacKinnon writes, "To be rapable, a condition that is social, not biological, defines what a woman is" (178), but it can only be social if it is first biological (a point argued by Melinda Vagas in *The Women's Review of Books*, [February, 1990], 5-6; and, in the interest of accuracy, it should be added that men are also raped. Carol Gilligan, *In A Different Voice*; Mary Field Belensky *et al*, *Women's Way of Knowing*; and Deborah Tannen, *You Just Don't Understand.*

5. According to Tivka Frymer-Kensky, the oldest deities available to scholars were the Sumerian "two-gendered Pantheon which mirrors the duality of nature," derived from a rigid sexual dimorphism (*In the Wake of the Goddesses*, 12).

6. Most of the bad things done to women stem from men. It follows that men being sexist, women are the victims of sexism; thus if patriarchy is the problem, feminism is the solution. Simplistic as this syllogism sounds, it forms the kernel of countless arguments and texts—and why not, if true?

7. "IT'S WAR" was *Ms.*- Magazine's follow-through of the totalizing rhetoric on its August cover, and inside Gloria Steinem put the ideological icing on the cake by interpreting the decision as the results of one group living under the decisions of another, "in this case, a very old system called patriarchy" ("A Basic Human Right," 38-42). The "war on women" trope then expanded in various directions, becoming, for example, the titles of Marilyn French's 1992 study and of Susan Faludi's *Backlash: The Undeclared War Against Women* (1992).

8. *SpareRib*, 197: 5-7.

9. Daphne Patai, "The Struggle for Feminist Purity Threatens the Goals of Feminism"; Ann Snitow had also warned against the "premature unity" resulting from a we/them mentality over women's reaction to pornography ("Retrenchment versus Transformation: The Politics of the Antipornography Movement," in *Women Against Pornography*, 113). But while Erica Jong may opine that "some radical feminists are declaring every erection a potential rape," many other feminist writers continue to run on the we/them track (*NY Times* [23 June 1991], B-4).

10. Carol Lee Bacchi, *Same Difference*, 253-4.

11. Nicci Gerrard, *Into the Mainstream*, 5-7.

12. Elaine Showalter, *New Feminist Criticism*, 249.

13. Soper, "Feminism, Humanism, and Postmodernism," 11-12.

14. "A Gathering of Skeptics," *NY Times* (7 July 1996).

15. A conversative voice is heard in Katherine Kersten's "What Do Women Want?" *Policy Review*, 4-15.

16. On lesbian s/m, see Paulina Palmer, *Contemporary Lesbian Writing*, 25-27.

17. David Blankenhorn, *Fatherless America*.

18. Katha Pollitt, "Are Women Morally Superior to Men?" 799-807.

19. Sheila Jeffreys, *AntiClimax*, 282.

20. Patricia Duncker, *Sisters and Strangers*, 3.

21. Ismay Barwell, "Feminist Perspectives and Narrative Points of View," 67-68.

22. Deborah Tannen, *You Just Don't Understand*, 61.

23. Cathy Young, "Women, Sex, and Rape."

24. Daniel Goleman, "New Studies Map the Mind of the Rapist."

25. Robin Briggs, *Witches and Neighbors*, 8.

26. Teresa Ebert, "Red Pedagogy," 807.

27. Louise Kaplan, *Female Perversions*, 40.

28. Daniel Goleman, "New View of Fantasy: Much Is Found Perverse."

29. Thomas Lacqueur, *Making Sex*.

30. Nancy Chodorow, *Feminism and Psychoanalytic Theory*, 152.

31. Teresa Brennan, *A Reader in Feminist Knowledge*, 127.

32. Juliet Mitchell, *Psychoanalysis and Feminism*, 301.

33. Jane Sherfey, *The Nature and Evolution of Female Sexuality*, 141.

34. Nancy Chodorow, *The Reproduction of Mothering*, 7, 36.

35. Nancy Chodorow, "Freud on Women,"; Daphne de Marneffe, "Looking and Listening: The Construction of Clinical Knowledge in Charcot and Freud."

Appendix B: Interview with Margaret Drabble

DD: I was struck by what happened in the *Millstone* when the baby chews on the manuscript and improves the whole writing process and I think you mentioned that it wasn't quite by accident that the baby got into the room, the door was left opened; but you could look at it in the opposite way and say, well, men writers don't have babies chewing on their manuscripts, so is it a way of addressing the inclusion of the procreative process into the creative process for women writers?

Drabble: Yes, It is a possible way of looking at it. I thought it was meant to suggest many things...that if you are a woman working at home, your books are likely to get chewed up by a baby...that is literally true. Maybe when Rosamund lets the baby into the room she's not necessarily deliberately doing it but she is perhaps feeling at the same time that what her friend Lydia is doing is parasitic on her and the baby, and that she wishes to destroy what she sees as a parasitic process, which writing is, by allowing life to pick up the writing, so there's a conflict between the analytic parasitic process and the real life of the baby.

DD: Life is getting a little bit of its own back?

Drabble: Yes. Rosamund has the place to herself and she is using the baby as an instrument, I suppose.

DD: She is a rather unsympathetic character.

Drabble: She is probably unempathetic but I suppose rather than confronting the conflict that always comes into sharing a flat with anybody, she allows this. She set up this friendship with Lydia for her own convenience and perhaps had decided it was time it was brought to an end.

DD: As you say, there are several different ways of looking at it.

Drabble: I also would say that I thought it was quite funny in that it is a comic sequence and it's true that when I was writing *The Millstone* I had two small children and the third on the way and there always was the risk of losing your manuscript in any house with children ...of losing your papers or destroying your papers, feeling that it was very hard to keep all things in order, I suppose.

DD: Is it a way of talking about a conflict of roles that women are struggling to integrate?

Drabble: Well, that's a rather grand way of saying it but it talks about the conflict of time. You can't keep things under control, you can't do two things at once, you can't leave your house top-tidy while you are trying to look after your baby and write a book at the same time. I think it is back to the role of conflict but it also is a purely practical conflict...that's why I'm quite pleased with its being a completely practical instance. It illustrates not a deep-seated ill feeling between one childless woman who is creative artistically and one woman with a child who is not creative artistically, but it's just a perfectly ordinary situation in which women who tend to work at home have different kinds of practical and domestic problems, simply because they are working at home.

DD: Then in *The Waterfall* there seems to be a more ambitious treatment of relationships and more consciousness of literary tradition, and I wonder in naming your character Jane, if your Jane is re-writing the world of Jane Austen or Jane Eyre by her own lived experience?

Drabble: She's much closer to Jane Eyre than to Jane Austen.
                I know she had very little in common with Jane
                Austen.   There's quite a shot of thunder in the
                book. It's also true that her (second) married name
                is Jane Gray who is the victim who had her head
                cut off, so she did think that as soon as she got
                married, she was in for trouble and that her
                marriage was sort of an execution.

DD: There seemed to be some hostilities entered in Jane
                Austen as perhaps an expectable model from her
                parents generation or something that is passed on
                to her that she seem to be.

Drabble: There are a lot of things one can like or dislike in
                Jane Austen and one of the things is that she
                thinks marriage is a happy ending and that a
                socially acceptable marriage will somehow be all
                right in the long run.   That is what one can take
                her novels as meaning, and I think that Jane in
                The Waterfall knows that sex is more important
                than either marriage or acceptability and that she
                has been deceived, not by her parents generation
                only, but from the whole recorded convention that
                sexuality isn't the only thing.   I think she said
                something about Mr. Knightly and Emma and the
                implausibility of that plot which in turn I rather
                agree with Jane on that point...that is a rather
                implausible plot...that Jane Austen has a plot that
                is satisfactory at a certain number of levels but
                there's a level missing.

DD: Also the sense that marriage is the final stage of
                the plot?

Drabble: Yes, that marriage is the end of the plot and Jane
                does say that in the modern age, we drown in the
                first chapter, that most of the plot comes after
                marriage and we can no longer see marriage as a

happy solution and neither could Jane Austen, so it seems rather odd that all her plots were concerned with leading people to the altar, which is embedded in the plot, while so many are unhappy, married couples and there are hardly any happy, married couples.

DD: Yes, that's the other side. And then *Jane Eyre* also put that kind of conflict...the reason why 'I married him,' that's something that would be in the same line.

Drabble: Well, Jane Eyre is much closer to what Jane Doe feels because it is from a very deep deceptual novel and is saying that however impossible, unsuitable, reprehensible the man, emotion justifies action. The plot doesn't overtly say that but subvertly says it, and that the drive of passion will in fact force the plot right (or almost right but not quite right); it's just a commonplace of the romantic plot that you either die or you're badly damaged, one or the other. It is a price for adultery, well a price for passion. It wouldn't even be adultery...Romeo and Juliet weren't even adulterous, they were just passionate, that's all.

DD: So there's a revision of that scenario.

Drabble: Yes.

DD: And you're saying that you see Jane Eyre more as accepting the romantic convention—?

Drabble: Well I think Charlotte Brontë certainly accepted it. She had a deeply romantic imagination and in her later novel, *Villette*, she tried to control her own romantic fantasizing; her erotic fantasies came up in a much more plausible sequence of events than she felt in *Jane Eyre*, but still there is a very violent emotional strain which I didn't find in Jane Austen.

DD: In a way you are modernizing a literary tradition in your work?

Drabble: I wouldn't say modernizing. I would say it's a permanent aspect of human nature, that it is a combination of sex and death. I am not so much modernizing as doing another version of it. It has been done since the beginning of literature and it's a theme that goes on and on and on. And I suppose when I use the theme, I use it with Freudian hindsight. Charlotte Brontë didn't have Freudian foresight, in fact, not at all. She would have been horrified I think, to have been told what some of her plots appeared to mean, whereas I and Jane Gray know perfectly well what the plots mean. I wouldn't say that I was modernizing...I would say it was an archetypical plot/theme and as such I am referring to it but I wouldn't say the story is a literary story. I would say that Jane Gray seeks in literature and in myth and in psychoanalytic interpretation for some explanation of her own rather bizarre behavior; so it has connections not only with literary novels.

DD: So it's a more complete account perhaps of the same material that has been handled in other traditional ways?

Drabble: I don't think it is more complete...it is simply more...I don't think that it's more complete, I think, as I say with *Freudian hindsight* as anything written from the 1920s on. And it's referring to certain literary novels, yes.

DD: In a way what Freudian hindsight offers is a clearer or a more detailed picture—more conclusive picture—of our passionate selves, the unconscious, and so forth.

Drabble: I don't know if it offers a clearer picture...it offers a truer picture, not clearer.

DD: Incidentally, when I was visiting some friends in Leeds we hiked out on the North Yorkshire Moors to the Goredale Scar, and it was right around New Years, a glorious sunny day, and I wasn't aware I was looking at a literary landmark at the time.

Drabble: It's a wonderful, wonderful place, in fact it's a painter's place, it is one of the most painted landscape and I didn't think of it in literature, in people's journals and dairies; I don't think I have ever seen it in a novel but it's very much a painter's scene.

DD: So much of England's natural landscape has become literary. But it's the kind of male literary territory...for the most part... there were very few female points of reference.

Drabble: Well the Goredale Scar isn't very far from the Brontes and that's certainly a female point of reference...there are some female points of reference.

DD: I enjoyed a great deal *The Middle Ground* with the midlife crisis of Kate. Towards the end, it's interesting because it introduced various conflicts and problems and reasons for not going on. And what one would expect from a more traditional novel some kind of climatic moment and then a resolution of one kind of another but I had the feeling that it was more like a change in the weather and the storm clouds sort of dissipated and then you go on but everything else is still there, all the complexities are still there. Is that along the lines of what you had in mind?

Drabble: Yes, nothing happens in the book and at various points I toyed with the idea of making things happen, but it didn't seem right that they should. It's very much on the level of just being in the middle of things and nothing is being resolved at all.

DD: And instead of solutions, there is more of a kind of acceptance of self—?

Drabble: Yes, getting on with things—

DD: And that made it interesting. Maybe there is something in the male novel that requires more definitive endings although you can find so many exceptions.

Drabble: Yes, there are some exceptions—

DD: You know the sort of Newtonian sense that we have, we expect cause-effect, action/reaction, although the Novel tends to violate that.

Drabble: But I have a feeling as you speak...I think D. H. Lawrence has a lot of very inconclusive novels. Nothing is really resolved. You think the next thing might happen next, but you don't actually know...he only pretended to tell you what's going to happen or bring it to a falsely neat conclusion. He usually ends in the middle of something. Yes, I like that. Virginia Woolf does it too. She doesn't always do it but sometimes does it.

DD: She's a little bit more tempted to suggest something more final, sometimes.

Drabble:	Sometimes, but not always. *Mrs. Dalloway* is very much an open-ended novel...you don't always know when things are about to begin and you find yourself in the middle of something that was influenced by Mrs. Dalloway, so that kind of open-endness is a quality of Virginia Woolf.
DD:	Some of the earliest materials on you suggested the important influence of Doris Lessing among contemporaries. What male authors would you say figured in your development and understanding of writing?
Drabble:	So many really. I didn't read Lessing until I had written four novels, but I remember reading *The Golden Notebook* after I had already published, around the mid to late 60s.
DD:	Would you assign her a major role?
Drabble:	I would, but not on my early work because I hadn't read her. Similarly Virginia Woolf who I hadn't read until after I had read Doris Lessing actually. I certainly had written at least three novels before I read either of them seriously. But as to novelists, I read when I was younger...I think I was influenced by everything that I read, but more particularly by Angus Wilson, very conspicuously; Saul Bellow; D. H. Lawrence; Henry James probably, certainly; Arnold Bennett a little, in certain and more specific ways, and many, many others and it's very hard to to say who one's infuenced by. I am a great admirer of Stendahl.
DD:	What women writers would you have been reading very early when you were studying to write?
Drabble:	I had read the Brontës; I had read Jane Austen, George Eliot of course, Iris Murdoch...That's about

it, really.

DD: What about the kind of middle class women writers
               like Rosamond Lehmann?

Drabble: Well, I had read *Dusty Answer* when I was at school.

DD: And Elizabeth Bowen?

Drabble: I didn't read her. I have read her now but don't
               think I read her at that age. I may have read *Death
               of the Heart* quite early. I read the heavy stuff at
               Cambridge and did the Great Tradition and I was
               under the Leavis influence and they weren't in it
               certainly. That's why I miss Virginia Woolf of
               course because she wasn't on the syllabus and she
               wasn't considered at all and so I didn't have to read
               her, whereas I had to read Henry James, George
               Eliot, Conrad, who I didn't respond to at all.
               Conrad has been an absolute negative influence
               whereas Henry James, I did respond to a great deal
               and Dickens, I enjoy far more now than I did then
               but I think that's very common.

DD: Was there a model woman writer who implied, if
               she's able to do this, I could too?

Drabble: George Eliot was the greatest English novelist that
               there ever was. That was what we were taught and
               I certainly believed that and in a sense, I still
               believe it. Yes, there was a strong sense that she
               was the greatest 19th Century novelist and
               therefore, the greatest novelist because she was
               writing at the height of the greatness of the
               English novel. And *Middlemarch* was presented to
               us; I read it when I was fifteen and I thought it
               was absolutely wonderful and I knew it was okay
               to think, it wasn't like it was an historical romance,
               I heard it was a respectable novel, and I went on to

Cambridge where it was considered the great novel and it is indeed considered to be a great novelist so there was certainly a sense that a woman had written a great novel so there was no reason why women shouldn't write great novels. Yes, I think I was conscous of that.

DD: Was there anyone closer to your own time that you would turn to?

Drabble: No. I guess it was Iris Murdoch, I suppose, who had a great reputation in the late 50s when I was at the university but I identified more closely with Angus Wilson than with Iris Murdoch; I discovered his work myself when I was at the University. We didn't do anything contemporary at all and the latest that we did was Lawrence so I discovered Angus Wilson for myself. I know I was under 21 when I read everything he had written and I thought it was absolutely wonderful and I don't think I had come across Doris Lessing, or else it didn't mean the same kind of thing to me.

DD: Was there a sense that as a woman you were prohibited or barred from pursuing this vocation?

Drabble: None whatsoever.

DD: And did you encounter obstacles as a woman?

Drabble: None at all.

DD: Have you since?

Drabble: None at all. I have had every book that I have ever written accepted and published; you can't get less obstacles than that and no one has ever tried to stop me from writing.

DD: Do you expect to be read by male readers to the

same extent as by women?

Drabble: Really, I don't expect to be because I suspect
              women read more novels than men. I think in
              academic circles, I expect to be read by men as
              much as women, but in a wider readership, a non-
              university readership, then I expect more female
              readers.

DD: Even including your later work which seems to be
              equally about men and women?

Drabble: I think still that there are more women reading
              novels. Or certainly more women read the kind of
              novels I write and I think that in terms of genre,
              more women read contemporary fiction. More men
              read the genre of thrillers, Frederick Forsyth, I'm
              sure I must be right about that. I think more
              women read not only me but Anthony Powell, Iris
              Murdoch; it is a sort of bigger female readership.

DD: Powell?

Drabble: I threw him in because he's a male writer. I am
              sure he has a lot of male readers as well, but
              sensitive women read an infinitely greater number
              of novels than men, unless they are more
              professionally interested in English literature...then
              there would not be quite so many.

DD: Why do you think women need to read novels more
              than men?

Drabble: That's a very difficult question to answer. I think
              that quite often men's work involves a lot of
              reading or moving their eyes over papers which
              makes them slightly less anxious to spend their
              spare time reading. I think women at home during
              the day have a lot of odd half hours in between
              children and collecting people from school, the sort

of pattern of life that permits one to read for the
odd half hour more than it does for men.

DD: Is it feeding emotional needs as well for women?

Drabble: I think it is. But I think a lot of it is the practical
               shape of life. I think it does feed emotional needs
               and that women are more interested in and have
               more time to be interested in, and are generally
               more interested in people, the general interaction
               of people, and social life and the stuff of
               contemporary fiction.

DD: Do you think women's fiction plays a more
               particular role in keeping women in touch with
               their own feelings as women or also in touch with
               basic human realities that their environment may
               tend to downgrade?

Drabble: Yes, I do feel that, that people look to fiction as
               some illumination about their own lives or a sense
               of some people in the same predicament that they
               are in. A lot of women are very isolated;
               particularly I had a strong sense of this with early
               novels, when I had a large readership amongst
               housebound housewives with small children, who
               do read a great deal and who are isolated, who
               can't talk to their friends whenever they want to
               because of the baby routine, and I think they have
               very strong emotional needs that can be met by
               novels and they identify with predicaments and
               the emotional patent in the book.

DD: In an earlier interview, you mentioned that you
               were more interested in the situation of women
               than women's cause. Is that still a fair description
               of—?

Drabble: Yes, I suppose it is. I am not a politician on any
               front. I am more interested in how things are

rather than integrating my life to putting them
right. I am not an activist. I have campaigned on
specific issues with women's groups
sometimes...depending on what the issue is. I
certainly campaigned on the abortion front with
the pro-abortion campaign but that's because that
was an instance in which I could see specific
legislation making a specific difference. For other
issues I am less clear in my own mind; I am,
therefore, more interested in perhaps showing the
complexity of the situation in a novel rather than
saying, we must change the language of the hymn
book or we must change the language of the Bible.
I find that these are rather simplistic responses to
an immensely complicated historical process.

DD: How would it be fair to describe your sense of
               writing: as a happy wife, as a woman, as a feminist,
               or some other sense of yourself as a writer?

Drabble: I write as a person. I don't think of myself as
               being a woman or a man, or a feminist. I write as
               a person. I am occasionally conscious when writing
               that I must make an extra effort to present the
               masculine point of view which requires from me a
               certain amount of work. It's easier for me to write
               about my immediate circles so to move after that
               requires extra effort and work but I feel I ought to
               make that effort. So in that sense, I suppose I feel
               I should try not to write for the middle-class
               women all the time.

DD: I was noticing in some of your recent interviews
               that strong sense of yourself as a member of the
               English tradition of writers, or an interest in
               England as such, your commitment to your
               country... would that be something that's emerging
               more recently in your writing?

Drabble: I don't think that it's emerging. It's just that it becomes more defined. The more one's exposed to other countries which, naturally as a young person, I wasn't...I think one becomes more conscious of one's feelings about one's country as one gets to know people from other nations, as one gets to meet Americans and Europeans, Australians, etc., and then one gets to define by contrast what is specifically British.

DD: Wasn't *The Ice Age* more of an ambitious attempt to depict larger social problems?

Drabble: Yes, I am very interested in that.

DD: Affecting England per se. At least the earlier ones more concerned with the women's experiences, though the same is true of *The Middle Ground*. It still seems that you have extended the range of your focus, so that if you are fairly identifiable with the English tradition of fiction but not more so in terms of the women writers of earlier periods than of the mixed tradition.

Drabble: I would think the mixed tradition, yes.

DD: Do you feel the tradition has been available to you...that you can enjoy male artists equally with female artists?

Drabble: Yes, I certainly feel that.

DD: Are there any in particular that put you off?

Drabble: Male writers. I don't particularly enjoy spy fiction, war fiction. I could never get through Norman Mailer's *The Naked and the Dead*, for example, but I have enjoyed his other work because I do not understand that world. I find it distant and unpleasant. As far as war and peace, it's another matter, because the focus is so much broader than that.

DD: And *The Naked and the Dead* is an entirely male world.

Drabble: Entire male world with no point of reference.

DD: Were you at all interested in redressing any imbalance in *The Oxford Companion to English Literature, vis-à-vis* male/female writers. Did you include more women than perhaps were there before?

Drabble: I certainly did include more women writers but I think that was just what anybody would have done because of the change of attitude. I think it was interesting that the original *Oxford Companion* had fairly short pieces even on Jane Austen and the Brontës. I was certain that it would get big entries from any male editor today and I didn't think I was being unusual in that.

DD: Did you sort of drop a few males and then add—?

Drabble: I didn't drop any men at all. I simply added women. I dropped a lot of stuff that had nothing to do with literature to make room. I may have dropped one or two 19th Century clerics possibly who waren't really authors at all, but I didn't drop anyone who was recognized as an author.

DD: Is there in any sense, any longer, of a literary establishment?

Drabble: No, I never really knew what a literally establishment was or if there ever was one. I honestly don't know. Charlotte Brontë never belonged to anything...I suppose Thackerey did...

D. H. Lawrence never belonged to a literary establishment; Arnold Bennett, I don't think did either. Edmond Gosse was...I mean there were some critics in the world of literary establishment, and I suppose to that extent, we still have critics with some weight, or do we? I don't know.

DD: I put this to Elizabeth Jane Howard this summer and she said if there was one, it died out with Cyril Connolly. I read a biography of Elizabeth Bowen and it seemed in the 40s and 50s, there was a sense of literary assembly.

Drabble: I agree that this may occur with the passage of time, you see. It could be within 30 years, people will look back and identify with Angus Wilson and myself and Doris Lessing, all are people who know each other, when we don't really. Some of us know some of the others of us. Cyril Connolly was an interesting dividing point; I think it is true that he did represent some kind of focus.

DD: Is there a literary community or a community of women writers?

Drabble: What would I know, maybe; I know of some women writers who know each other very well. Elaine Feinstein, Beryl Bainbridge, Fay Weldon—they all know each other but I can't remember which of them are close friends, and of course, I know all of them but I don't think it's a community.

DD: Do you send your manuscripts around to many or is that unfair?

Drabble: No, I wouldn't do that, no.

DD: Some women do. Some women feminists have a kind of circle...they had one in the 70s where they looked at one another's work in progress, made comments, and actually now, they are reviewing one another's work.

Drabble: No, I wouldn't do that. I don't like to show things while they are in progress.

DD: Are you now free in a position to turn to fiction again?

Drabble: Yes, I am more or less. Literature is quite nice.

DD: You did no fiction writing at all while working on the *Companion*?

Drabble: No, There wasn't time.

DD: Did you come out of that work with a sense of a fresher awareness or new energy?

Drabble: Yes, I think I did.

DD: And you are planning to start another novel?

Drabble: Yes, that's right. I am toying with lots of ideas and sticking them together. I don't know what they will turn into.

Bibliography

Abel, Elizabeth, *The Voyage In: Fictions of Female Development.*
Hanover: UP of New England, 1983.

Adam, Ruth. *I'm not Complaining.* London: Virago, 1983.

_____. *A Woman's Place, 1910-1975.* London: Chatto &
Windus, 1977.

Adburgham, Alison. *Woman in Print.* London: Allen & Unwin,
1972.

Ahmad, Rukhsana. "What's Happening to the Women's Presses?"
SpareRib 223 (May 1991): 12.

_____. "Feminist Book Fortnight '91." *SpareRib* 224 (June
1991): 29.

Alcoff, Linda. "Cultural Feminism Versus Post-Structuralism."
Signs 13 (1988): 437-53.

Alexander, Flora. *Contemporary Women Novelists.* London: Hodder
& Stoughton, 1989.

Alther, Lisa. *Kinflicks.* NY: New America Library, 1976.

Althusser, Louis. *For Marx.* London: New Left Books, 1977.

_____. *Philosophy and the Spontaneous Philosophy of the
Scientists.* NY: Routledge, 1990.

Appignanesi, Lisa. *Femininity and the Creative Imagination: A
Study of Henry James, Robert Musil, and and Marcel Proust.*
London: Vision Press, 1973.

Ardill, Susan and Sue O'Sullivan. "Upsetting the Applecart:
Difference, Desire and Lesbian Sadomasochism," *Feminist
Review* 23 (1986): 31-58.

Ardis, Ann. *New Women, New Novels.* New Brunswick: Rutgers UP,
1990.

Armstrong, Nancy. *Desire and Domestic Fiction* NY: Oxford UP,
1987.

_____. "The Nineteenth-Century Jane Austen: A Turning
Point in the History of Fear," *Genre* 23 (1990): 227-46.

Atwood, Margaret. *The Edible Woman.* NY: Warner Books, 1969.

_____. "If You Can't Say Something Nice, Don't Say
Anything At All." *Language in Her Eye: Views on Writing
and Gender by Canadian Women Writing in English.* Edited
by Libby Sheier, Sarah Sheard, and Eleanor Wachtal.
Toronto: Coach House Press, 1990.

_____. *The Handmaid's Tale.* NY: Simon & Schuster, 1987.

_____. "Writing the Male Character." *Second Words: Selected*

Critical Prose. Toronto: Anansi, 1982.

_____. *Surfacing*. NY: Popular Library, 1972.

Auerbach, Judy, *et. al.* "Commentary." *Feminist Studies* 11 (1985): 150-161.

Bacchi, Carol Lee. *Same Difference: Feminism and Sexual Difference*. London: Allen & Unwin, 1990.

Ballaster, Ros. *Seductive Forms: Women's Amatory Fiction from 1684 to 1740*. Oxford: Clarendon Press, 1992.

Banks, Lynn Reid. *The L-Shaped Room*. NY: Simon & Schuster, 1960.

_____. *Two Is Lonely*. London: Penguin, 1974.

Bacchi, Carol Lee. *Same Difference: Feminism and Sexual Difference*. London: Allen & Unwin, 1990.

Barbach, Lonnie. *Pleasures*. London: Futura, 1986.

Barker, Pat. *Blow Your House Down*. London: Virago, 1984.

Barnstone, Alika. "Women and the Garden: Andrew Marvell, Emilia Lanier, and Emily Dickenson," *Men by Women*. Edited by Janet Todd. NY: Holmes & Meier, 1981.

Barr, Maureen. "Isak Dinesen's Female Artists as Precursors to Contemporary Feminist Fabulators." *Feminism, Utopia, and Narrative*. Edited by Libby Falk Jones and Sarah Webster Godwin. Knoxville: Tennessee UP, 1990.

Barwell, Ismay. "Feminine Perspectives and Narrative Points of View." *Hypatia* 5 (1990): 63-75.

Bayley, John. "The 'Irresponsibility' of Jane Austen." *Critical Essays on Jane Austen*. Edited by B.C Southam. NY: Barnes & Noble, 1968.

Beauman, Nicola. *A Very Great Profession*. London: Virago, 1983.

Behn, Aphra. *The Rover*. London: Methuen, 1987.

Belenkey, Mary Feld. Editor. *Women's Way of Knowing*. NY: Basic Books, 1986.

Bell, Quentin. *Virginia Woolf: A Biography*. NY: Harcourt, Brace, Jovanovich, 1972.

_____, and Marcus, Jane. Exchange. *Critical Inquiry* 11 (1985): 486-5-1.

Bell, Susan Groag and Karen Offen. *Introductions to Women, the Family, and Freedman: The Debate in Documents*. Stanford: Stanford UP, 1983.

Bennett, Tony. *Popular Fiction*. NY: Routledge, 1990.

Benstock, Shari. *Women of the Left Bank*. Austin: UP Texas, 1986.

Berry, Mary Frances. *Why ERA Failed*. Bloomington: Indiana UP, 1986.

Biles, Jack. "An Interview with Iris Murdoch." *Studies in the Literary Imagination*. 11 (1978: 115-26.

Blake, Kathleen. *Love and the Woman Question in Victorian Literature*. Brighton: Harvester, 1983.

Blakey, Dorothy. *The Minerva Press, 1790 -1820*. London: Oxford UP, 1939.

Blankenhorn, David. *Fatherless America:Confronting Our Most Urgent Social Problem*. NY: Basic Books, 1995.

Blee, Kathleen M. *Women of the Klan: Racism and Gender in the 1920s*. Berkeley: California UP, 1991.

Bleich, David. *Utopia: The Psychology of a Cultural Fantasy*. Ann Arbor, MI: UMI Research Press, 1984.

Bloom, Harold. *The Anxiety of Influence*. NY: Oxford UP, 1973.

Blum, Harold. Editor. *Female Psychology: Contemporary Psychoanalytic Views*. NY: International UP, 1977.

Bond, Alma Halbert. *Who Killed Virginia Woolf?* NY: Human Sciences Press, 1989.

Boone, Joseph A. "Modernist Maneuvering in the Marriage Plot: Breaking Ideologies of Gender and Genre in James's *The Golden Bowl*." *PMLA* 101 (1986): 374-88.

Bordo, Susan. "The Cartesian Masculinization of Thought." *Signs* 11 (1986): 439-56.

Bradley, David. "On Alice Walker: "Telling the Black Woman Story." *New York Times Magazine* (8 January 1984).

Braudy, Susan. Interview with Joan Didion. *Ms* 65 (February 1977).

Brendlin, Bonnie Hoover. "New Directions in the Contemporary *Bildungsroman*: Lisa Althers' *Kinflicks*." *Gender and Literary Voice*. Edited by Janet Todd. NY: Holmes and Meier, 1980.

Brenner, Johanna and Ramas, Maria. "Rethinking Women's Oppression." *New Left Review* 144 (1984): 33-73.

Briggs, Robin. *Witches and Neighbors*. NY: Viking, 1996.

Brown, Nathaniel. "The 'Double Soul': Virginia Woolf, Shelley, and Androgyny," *Keats-Shelley Journal* 33 (1984): 182-204.

Brown, Rita Mae. *Rubyfruit Jungle*. Plainfield, VT: Daughters,

Inc., 1973.

Brownstein, Rachel M. *Becoming A Heroine: Reading About Women in Novels*. NY: Viking, 1982.

Burke, Carolyn. "Supposed Persons: Modernist Poetry and the Female Subject." *Feminist Studies* 11 (1985): 131-47.

Burstyn, Varda Editor. *Women Against Censorship*. Scranton: Salem House, 1985.

Butler, Marilyn. *Jane Austen and the War of Ideas*. Oxford: Clarendon Press, 1975.

_____. "Inventive Mothers." *Women's Review* 10 (1986).

Byatt, Antonia. *Possession*. NY: Random House, 1990.

_____. "Choices: The Writing of *Possession*. *Threepenny Review*. 16:3 (1995): 17.

Cabot, Tracy. *How to Make a Man Fall in Love with You*. NY: Dell, 1988.

Campbell, Katie. "Feminist Press Gang." *Women's Review of Books* 2 (1984): 1.

Carpentar, Humphrey. *The Brideshead Generation*. Boston: Houghton Mifflin, 1990.

Carter, Angela. *The Passion of New Eve*. NY: Harcourt, Brace, Jovanovich, 1977.

_____. *The Sadeian Woman and the Ideology of Pornography*. NY: Pantheon, 1978.

Casey, Ellen Miller. "Edging Women Out?: Reviews of Women Novelists in the *Atheneum* 1860-1900." *Victorian Studies* 39:2 (1996): 151-71.

Cather, Willa. *Articles and Reviews, 1893-1902*. Edited by William M. Curtin. Lincoln: Nebraska UP, 1970.

_____. "Notes from the Frontline." *On Gender and Writing*. Edited by Michelene Wandor. London: Pandora, 1983.

Caughie, Pamela. "Women Reading/Reading Women: A Review of Some Recent Books on Gender and Reading," *Papers on Language and Literature* 24 (1988): 317-35.

Caulfield, Mina Davis. "Sexuality in Human Evolution: What is 'Natural' in Sex?" *Feminist Studies* 11 (1985): 343-63.

Chamberlain, Mary. Editor. *Writing Lives: Conversations Between Women Writers*. London: Virago, 1988.

Chase, Karen. *Eros and Psyche—The Representation of Personality in Charlotte Brontë, Charles Dickens, George Eliot*. NY:

Methuen, 1984.

Chaudhuri, Nupur, and Strobel, Margaret. *Western Women and Imperialism: Resistance and Complicity.* Bloomington: Indiana UP, 1992.

Chernin, Kim. *The Hungry Self: Women, Eating and Identity.* NY: Times Books, 1985.

_____. *The Obsession, Reflections on the Tyranny of Slenderness.* NY: Harper & Row, 1981.

Cherry, Deborah. "Picturing the Private Sphere." *Fan* (1983).

Chesler, Phyllis. *Women and Madness.* NY: Doubleday, 1972.

Chodorow, Nancy. *The Reproduction of Mothering, Psychoanalysis and the Sociology of Gender.* Berkeley: California UP, 1978.

_____. *Feminism & Psychoanalytic Theory.* Oxford: Blackwell, 1989.

_____. "Freud on Women," *The Cambridge Companion to Freud.* New York: Cambridge UP, 1991.

Chopin, Kate. *The Awakening.* NY: Norton, 1976.

Cixous, Hélène. "The Laugh of the Medusa" *New French Feminisms.* Edited by Elaine Marks and Isabelle de Courtivron. Amherst: Massachusetts UP, 1980.

Claridge, Laura Langland, Elizabeth. *Out of Bounds: Male Writers and Gender (ed) Criticism.* Amherst: Massachusetts UP, 1990.

Clarke, Norma. "Feminism and the Popular Novel of the 1890's," *Feminist Review* 20 (1985): 91-106.

Clément, Catherine. *The Lives and Legends of Jacques Lacan.* NY: Columbia UP, 1983.

Coffey, Irene. "Lesbian Sleuths." *SpareRib* 217 (October 1990).

Cohan, Steven. "From Subtext to Dream Text: The Brutal Egoism of Iris Murdoch's Male Narrator." *Men by Women.* Edited by Janet Todd. NY: Holmes and Meier, 1981.

Cohen, Paula Marantz. *The Daughter's Dilemma: Family Process and the Nineteenth-Century Domestic Novel* Ann Arbor: UP of Michigan, 1991.

Colmore, Gertrude. *Suffragettes: A Story of Three Women.* London: Pandora, 1984.

Coles, Claire. "Some Sexual, Personality and Demographic Characteristics of Women Readers of Erotic Romances," *Archives of Sexual Behavior* 13 (1984): 187-209.

Collins, Wendy and Friedman, Ellen. *The Directory of Social*

Change: Women. London: Wildwood House, 1978.

Cope, Wendy. *Making Cocoa for Kingsley Amis.* London: Faber & Faber, 1986.

Coward, Rosalind. "Are Women's Novels Feminist Novels?" *The New Feminist Criticism.* Edited by Elaine Showalter. NY: Pantheon, 1985.

_____. "Looking for the Real Thing." *New Statesman* (1 April 1988): 20-2.

_____. *Our Treacherous Hearts: Why Women Let Men Get Their Way.* London: Faber & Faber, 1992.

Crawford, Patricia. "Women's Published Writings, 1600-1700." *Women in English Society, 1500-1800.* Edited by Mary Prior. London: Methuen, 1985.

Creighton, Joanne V. "An Interview with Margaret Drabble." *Margaret Drabble: Golden Realms.* Edited by Dorey Schmidt. Edinburgh, TX: Pan American UP, 1982.

Crewe, Candida, "Mad Don and English Man." *The Times Saturday Review (23 May 1992): 4-6.*

Curtin, William M. *The World and the Parish: Willa Cather's Articles and Reviews, 1893-1912.* Lincoln: Nebraska UP, 1970.

Cutler, Winnifred B. *Love Cycles.* NY: Random House, 1991.

Daly, Mary. *Gyn / Ecology.* Boston: Beacon, 1978.

_____. *Pure Lust: Elemental Feminist Philosophy.* Boston: Beacon, 1984.

Davies, Stevie. *Emily Bronte: The Artist as a Free Woman.* Manchester: Carcanet Press, 1983.

de Beauvoir, Simone. *The Second Sex.* NY: Random House, 1974.

De Grazia, Victoria. *How Fascism Ruled Women.* Berkeley: California UP, 1992.

Delany, Sheila. *Writing Women: Women Writers and Women in Literature from Medieval to Modern.* NY: Schocken, 1983.

De Man, Paul. *The Resistance to Theory.* Minneapolis: Minnesota UP, 1986.

deMarneffe, Daphne. "Looking and Listening: The Construction of Clinical Knowledge in Charcot and Freud." *Signs* 17 (1991): 71-111.

Denfeld, Rene. *The New Victorians.* NY: Warner Books, 1995.

Dervin, Daniel. "Lacanian Mirrors and Literary Reflections."

Journal of Philadelphia Psychoanalytic Association 7 (1980): 129-42.

_____."Reading Freud and Returning to Lacan." *Psychoanalytic Review*, 78 (1990): 237-66.

_____. *Creativity and Culture*. Madison, NJ: Fairleigh Dickinson UP, 1990.

_____. *Enactments: American Models and Psychohistorical Modes*. Madison, NJ: Fairleigh-Dickinson UP, 1996.

_____. and Kilmartin, Christopher. "Inaccurate Representations of the Electra Complex in Psychology Textbooks." *Teaching of Psychology*, (1997).

_____. "Lacan and the Fate of Transference." *American Imago* (1997).

DeSalvo, Louise. *Virginia Woolf: The Impact of Chilodhood Abuse on Her Life and Work*. Boston: Beacon, 1989.

Diamond, Irene and Quinby, Lee. *Foucault and Feminism*. Boston: Northeastern UP, 1988.

Didion, Joan. "The Women's Movement." *The White Album*. NY: Simon & Schuster, 1979.

Dinnerstein, Dorothy. *The Mermaid and the Minotaur*. NY: Harper & Row, 1976.

Dipple, Elizabeth. *Iris Murdoch: Work for the Spirit*. Chicago: Chicago UP, 1982.

Diski, Jenny. *Nothing Natural*. London: Methuen, 1986.

Doan, Laura K. Editor. *Old Maids to Radical Spinsters: Unmarried Women in the Twentieth Century Novel*. Urbana: Illinois UP, 1991.

Dobie, Kathy. "Long Day's Journey into White." *Village Voice* (28 April 1992): 22-32.

Dollimore, Jonathan. "The Challenge of Sexuality." *Society and Literature*. Edited by Alan Sinfield. NY: Holmes & Meier, 1983.

Donovan, Josephine. Editor. *Feminist Literary Criticism: Explorations in Theory*. Lexington: Kentucky UP, 1975.

_____. "Feminist Style Criticism." *Images of Women in Fiction, Feminist Perspectives*. Edited by Susan Kippelman Cornillon. Bowling Green, Ohio: Popular Press, 1972.

Doody, Margaret Anne. *The True Story of the Novel*. New Brunswick: Rutgers UP, 1996.

Downing, Christine. *Woman's Review of Books* (8 May 1985).

Drabble, Margaret. *The Millstone*. NY: Morrow, 1966.

_____. *The Waterfall*. NY: Knopf, 1969.

_____. *The Middle Ground*. London: Weidenfeld & Nicholson, 1980.

_____. *The Oxford Companion to English Literature*. NY: Oxford UP, 1985.

D'Souza, Dinesh. *Illiberal Education*. NY: Random House, 1992.

DuBois, Ellen Carol. Editor. *Feminist Scholarship: Kindling in the Groves of Academe*. Urbana: Illinois UP, 1985.

Duchen, Claire. *Feminism in France, From May 1968 to Mitterand*. London: Routledge, 1986.

Duckworth, Alistair M. "Jane Austen and the Construction of a Progressive Author." *College English* 53 (1991): 77-90.

Duffy, Maureen. *That's How It Was*. London: Virago, 1983.

Duncker, Patricia. *Sisters and Strangers: An Introduction to Contemporary Feminist Fiction*. Oxford: Blackwell, 1992.

DuPlessis, Rachel Blau. *Writing Beyond the Ending—Narrative Strategies of Twentieth-Century Women Writers*. Bloomington: Indiana UP, 1985.

Dworkin, Andrea. *Right-Wing Women*. NY: Coward-McCann, 1983.

Eagleton, Terry. *The Rape of Clarissa*. Oxford: Blackwell, 1982.

_____. "Ideology, Fiction, Narrative." *Social Text*. 1:2 (1979).

Ebert, Teresa. "The Romance of Patriarchy: Ideology, Subjectivity, and Postmodern Feminist Cultural Theory." *Cultural Critique* 10 (1988): 19-58.

_____. "For a Red Pedagogy: Feminism, Desire, and Need." *College English* 58:7 (1996): 795-819.

Edwards, Lee. *Psyche as Hero, Female Heroism and Fictional Form*. Hanover: Wesleyan UP, 1985.

_____. "Women, Energy, and *Middlemarch*." *Middlemarch*. NY: Norton Critical Edition, 1977.

_____, and Diamond, Arlyn. Editors. *The Authority of Experience: Essays in Feminist Criticism*. Amherst: Mass. UP, 1977.

Ehrenreich, Barbara. "A Feminist's View of the New Man," *New York Times Magazine* (20 May 1984).

Eisenstein, Hester. *Contemporary Feminist Thought*. Boston: G.K. Hall, 1983.

_____. "Scholars in Women's Studies Can Help Put This Fall's Election into Perspective." *Chronicle of Higher Education* (23 September 1992).

Eisenstein, Zillah. "Specifying US Feminism: The Problem of Naming." *Socialist Review* 20 (1990): 45-56.

Ellis, Alice Thomas. *Unexplained Laughter*. London: Duckworth, 1985.

Ellis, Bruce and Symons, Donald. "Sex Differences in Sexual Fantasy: an Evolutionary Psychological approach." *Journal of Sex Research* 27 (1990): 527-55.

Erdrich, Louise. *The Blue Jay's Dance*. NY: HarperCollins, 1995.

Esman, Aaron. Letter. *New York Times Book Review* (12 June 1984).

Estes, Clarissa P. *Women Who Run with the Wolves: Myths and Stories of the Wild Woman Archetype*. NY: Ballantine, 1992.

Evans, Mary. Editor. *From The Woman Question: Readings on the Subordination of Women*. Oxford: Fontana, 1982.

Evans, Sarah. *Personal Politics: The Roots of Women's Liberation in the Civil Rights Movement and the New Left*. NY: Random House, 1979.

Eyer, Diane E. *Mother-Infant Bonding: A Scientific Fiction*. New Haven: Yale UP, 1992.

Faderman, Lillian. *Odd Girls and Twilight Lovers: A History of Lesbian Life in 20th Century America*. NY: Columbia UP, 1991.

Fairbairns, Zoe. *Benefits*. London: Virago, 1979.

_____. "I Was a Teenage Novelist." *Women's Review* 8 (June, 1986): 8-11.

_____. "It's a Feminist Fortnight!" *Everywoman* (June 1990).

_____. *SpareRib* 220 (February, 1991): 29.

Faludi, Susan. *Backlash: The Undeclared War Against Women*. NY: Crown, 1991.

Farmer, Penelope. *Eve: Her Story*. NY: Mercury, 1988.

Farwell, Marilyn. "Toward a Definition of the Lesbian Literary Imagination," *Signs* 14 (1988): 100-18.

_____. "Virginia Woolf and Androngyny." *Contemporary Literature* 16 (1975): 433-51.

Fast, Irene. *Gender Identity*. Hillsdale, NJ: Analytic Press, 1984.

Feldstein, Richard and Roof, Judith. Editors. *Feminism and*

Psychoanalysis. Ithaca: Cornell UP, 1988.

Felski, Rita. *Beyond Feminist Aesthetics: Feminist Literature and Social Change.* Cambridge: Harvard UP, 1989.

_____. "The Counterdiscourse of the Feminine in Three Texts by Wilde, Huysmans, and Sacher-Masoch." 106 *PMLA* (1991): 1094-1105.

Feltes, N.N. *Modes of Production of Victorian Novels.* Chicago: Chicago UP, 1986.

Ferguson, Mary Anne. "Feminist Theory and Practice, 1985." *College English* 48 (1986): 726-35.

Ferguson, Moira. *First Feminists: British Women Writers, 1587-1799.* Old Westbury: Feminist Press, 1985.

Ferry, Anne. *The "Inward" Language: Sonnets of Wyatt, Sidney, Shakespeare, and Donne.* Chicago: Chicago UP, 1983.

Fetterley, Judith. *The Resisting Reader: A Feminist Approach to American Fiction.* Bloomington: Indiana UP, 1978.

Figes, Eva. *The Seven Ages.* London: Hamish Hamilton, 1986.

_____. *Sex and Subterfuge: Women Writers to 1850.* NY: Dutton, 1988.

Finn, Frankie. *Out On The Plain.* London: The Women's Press, 1984.

Firestone, Shulamith. *The Dialectics of Sex.* NY: Morrow, 1970.

Fisher Seymour. *Development and Structure of the Body Image.* Hillsdale, NJ: Erlbaum, 1986.

Fisher, Helen E. *Anatomy of Love: The Natural History of Monogamy, Adultery, and Divorce.* NY: Norton, 1992.

Flax, Jane. *Thinking Fragments: Psychoanalysis, Feminism, and Postmodernism.* Berkeley: California UP, 1990.

Fleenor, Juliann. Editor. *The Female Gothic.* Montreal: Eden Press, 1983.

Fleischman, Avrom. "Two Faces of Emma," *Jane Austen, New Perspectives.* NY: Holmes & Meier, 1983.

Fliegel, Zenia Odes. "Feminine Psychosocial Development in Freudian Theory, A Historical Reconstruction." *Psychoanalytic Quarterly* 42 (1973): 385-408.

Flint, Kate. *The Woman Reader, 1837-1914.* Oxford: Clarendon Press, 1993.

Flynn, Elizabeth A. and Schweickart, Patrocinio, P., Editors. *Gender and Reading: Esssays on Readers, Texts, and Contexts.* Baltimore: Johns Hopkins UP, 1986.

Fox-Genovese, Elisabeth. *Feminism Without Illusions*. Chapel Hill: North Carolina UP, 1991.

Forster, Margaret. *Georgy Girl*. London: Secker & Warburg, 1965

Foster, Shirley. *Victorian Women's Fiction: Marriage, Freedom, and the Individual*. London: Croom Helm 1985.

Foucault, Michel. *Madness and Civilization*. NY: American Library, 1967.

_____. *The History of Sexuality*. NY: Random House, 1990.

Fraiman, Susan. *Unbecoming Women*. NY: Columbia UP, 1993.

Frank, Janrae. "Women Warriors and Earth Mothers." *Washington Post Book World* (10 October 1985).

Fraser, Antonia. *The Weaker Vessel*. NY: Knopf, 1984.

Fraser, Nancy and Bartky, Sandra Lee. *Revaluing French Feminism*. Bloomington: Indiana UP, 1992.

French, Marilyn. *Beyond Power: Women, Men and Morals*. NY: Simon & Schuster, 1985.

_____. *The War Against Women*. NY: Summit Books, 1992.

Freud, Sigmund. *Civilization and Its Discontents. Standard Edition*, 21. London: Hogarth Press, 1955.

Friedman, Susan Stanford. "Creativity and the Childbirth Metaphor: Gender Difference in Literary Discourse." *Feminist Studies* 13 (1987): 49-82.

Frymer-Kensky, Tikva. *In the Wake of the Goddesses*. NY: Macmillan, 1992.

Fuss, Diana. *Essentially Speaking: Feminism, Nature, and Difference*. NY: Routledge, 1990.

Gadpaille, W.J. "Innate Masculine/Feminine Traits: Their Contributions to Conflict." *Journal of the American Academy of Psychoanalysis* 11 (1983): 401-24.

Gallagher, Catherine. *Nobody's Story: The Vanishing Acts of Women in the Marketplace, 1620-1820*. Berkeley: California UP, 1994.

Gallop, Joan. "Reading the Mother Tongue: Psychoanalytic Feminist Criticism." *Critical Inquiry* 13 (1987): 314-29.

_____. *Thinking Through the Body*. NY: Columbia UP, 1989.

Gardiner, Judith Kegan. *Rhys, Stead, Lessing, and the Politics of Empathy*. Bloomington: Indiana UP, 1989.

Garis, Leslie. "Didion and Dunne: The Rewards of a Literary Marriage." *New York Times Magazine* (8 February

1987).

Gasiorek, Andrzej. *Post-War British Fiction: Realism and After.* NY: St. Martin's Press, 1995.

George, Margaret. *Women in the First Capitalist Society.* Urbana: Illinois UP, 1988.

Gérin, Winifred. *Emily Bronte: A Biography.* Oxford: Clarendon Press, 1977.

Gerrard, Nicci. "The Fay Weldon Academy of Laughter." *Women's Review* 9 (1986): 10-11.

_____. *Into the Mainstream—How Feminism Has Changed Women's Writing.* London: Pandora, 1989.

Giddings, Paula. *Where and When I Enter: The Impact of Black Women on Race and Sex in America.* NY: Morrow, 1984.

Gilbert, Sandra and Gubar, Susan. *The Madwoman in the Attic: The Woman Writer and the 19th Century Literary Imagination.* New Haven: Yale UP, 1979.

_____. *No Man's Land: The Place of the Woman Writer in the Twentieth Century.* New Haven: Yale UP, 1988.

Gilligan, Carol. *In A Different Voice: Psychological Theory and Women's Development.* Cambridge: Harvard UP, 1982.

_____, and Stern, Eve. "The Riddle of Femininity and the Psychology of Love." *Passionate Attachments: Thinking About Love.* Edited Willard Gaylin and Ethel Person. New York: Free Press, 1988.

Gilman, Charlotte Perkins. *Herland.* NY: Pantheon, 1979.

Glendinning, Victoria. *Elizabeth Bowen.* NY: Penquin, 1977.

Godwin, Gail. Review of *The Norton Anthology of Women. New York Times Book Review* (28 April 1985).

Goff, Barbara Munson. "Between Natural Theology and Natural Selection: Breeding the Human Animal in *Wuthering Heights.*" *Victorian Studies* 27 (1984): 477-508.

Goleman, Daniel. "Researchers Trace Empathy's Roots to Infancy." *New York Times* (28 March 1989).

_____. "New Studies Map the Mind of the Rapist." *New York Times* (10 December 1991).

Goodman, Charlotte. "The Lost Brother, the Twin: Women Novelists and the Male-Female Double *Bildungsroman.*" *Novel* 17 (1983): 28-43.

Goreau, Angeline. *The Whole Duty of Woman: Female Writers in 17th*

Century England. NY: Doubleday, 1985.

Gorsky, Susan. "The Gentle Doubters: Images of Women in
    Englishwomen's Novels, 1840-1920." *Images of Women in
    Fiction.* London: Camillon, 1973.

Gould, Stephen Jay. "Genes on the Brain." *New York Review*
    (30 June 1983).

Grant, Toni. *Being a Woman: Fulfilling Your Femininity and
    Finding Love.* NY: Random House, 1989.

Green, Katherine Sobba. *The Courtship Novel, 1740-1820: A
    Feminized Genre.* Lexington: Kentucky UP, 1991.

Green, Russell G. and Donnerstein, Edward I. Editors. *Aggression:
    Theoretical and Empirical Reviews.* NY: Academic Press,
    1983.

Greenacre, Phyllis. "Women as Artist." *Psychoanalytic Quarterly* 29
    (1960): 208-27.

Greene, Gayle. "Margaret Drabble's *The Waterfall*: New System,
    New Morality." *Writing the Woman Artist.* Edited by
    Suzanne W. Jones. Philadelphia: Pennsylvania UP, 1991.

_____. *Changing the Story: Feminist Fiction and the Tradition.*
    Bloomington: Indiana UP, 1992.

Greer, Germaine. *Daddy, We Hardly Knew You.* NY: Knopf, 1990.

Greenson, Ralph. "Dis-identifying from Mother: Its Special
    Importance for the Boy." *International Journal of
    Psychoanalysis* 49 (1968): 370-4.

Griffin, Susan. *Woman and Nature: The Roaring Inside Her.* NY:
    Harper & Row, 1978.

Grolnick, Simon. Editor. *Between Reality and Fantasy.* NY:
    Aronson, 1978.

Grotjahn, Martin. "The Primal Crime and the Unconscious."
    Searchlights on Delinquency. NY: International UP, 1949.

Grove, Robin. "From the Island: Elizabeth Taylor's Novels."
    Studies in the Literary Imagination 11 (1978).

Gunew, Sneja. Editor. "An Impasse in Psychoanalysis and
    Feminism." *A Reader in Feminist Knowledge.* London:
    Routledge, 1991.

Gupte, Pranay. *Mother India.* NY: Scribners, 1992.

Haffenden, John. *Novelists in Interview.* London: Methuen, 1985.

Hanscombe, Gillian and Smyers, Virginia L. *Writing for Their
    Lives: The Modernist Women 1910-1940.* Boston:

Northeastern UP, 1987.

Haraway, Donna. *Simians, Cyborgs, and Women: The Reinvention of Nature.* NY: Routledge, 1990.

Harding, Sandra. *The Science Question in Feminism.* Ithaca: Cornell UP, 1986.

Harmon, Claire. "Tomboy Grudge." *London Review of Books* (27 February 1992).

Hart, Nicky. "Gender and the Rise and Fall of Class Politics." *New Left Review* 175 (1989): 19-47.

Harvey, David. *The Condition of Postmodernity.* Oxford: Blackwell, 1989.

Harvey, Richard. "Early English Feminism and the Creation Myth." *The Historian* 54 (1991).

Hawkes, Ellen. *Feminism on Trial: The Ginny Foat Case and the Future of the Women's Movement.* NY: Morrow, 1986.

Hayes, Elizabeth. T. *Images of Persephone.* Gainesville: Florida UP, 1994.

Hayles, N. Katherine. "Anger in Different Voices." *Signs* 12 (1986): 23-39.

Hazleton, Lesley. "Doris Lessing on Feminism, Communism and 'Space Fiction.'" *New York Times Magazine.* (25 July 1982).

Heilbrun, Carolyn G. "Marriage Perceived: English Literature 1893-1941." *What Manner of Woman.* Edited by Marlene Springer. NY: New York UP, 1977.

_____. *Toward a Recognition of Androgyny.* NY: Harper & Row, 1973.

Held, Virginia. "Mothering versus Contract." *Beyond Self-Interest.* Edited by Jane J. Mansbridge. Chicago: Chicago UP, 1990.

Heller, Dana A. *The Feminization of Quest-Romance.* Austin: Texas UP, 1991.

Helsinger, Elizabeth K. "Ulysses to Penelope: Victorian Experiments in Autobiography." *Approaches to Victorian Autobiography.* Edited by George P. Landow. Athens: Ohio Up, 1979.

Hennegan, Allison. "A Demand That Is not Being Met." *New Statesman* (26 July 1985): 28-9.

Herik, Judith Van. *Freud on Femininity and Faith.* Berkeley: California UP, 1984.

Hess, Beth, and Ferrel, Myra Marx. Editors. *Analyzing Gender: A Handbook of Social Science Research.* Beverly Hills: Sage, 1987.

Hiatt, Mary. *The Way Women Write.* NY: Teachers College Press, 1977.

Hickok, Kathleen. *Representations of Women: Nineteenth Century Woman's Poetry.* Greenwood, CT: Greenwood Press, 1984.

Higonnet, Margaret R. "Fictions of Feminine Voice: Antiphony and Silence in Hardy's *Tess of the D'Urbervilles.*" Edited by Laura Claridge and Elizabeth Langland. Amherst: Mass. UP, 1990.

Hinz, Evelyn J. and Teunissen, John J. *Women in Love* and The Myth of Eros and Psyche," in *D.H. Lawrence: The Man Who Lived.* Edited by Robert Partlow and Harry T. Moore. Carbondale: Southern Illinois UP, 1980.

Hirsch, Marianne. *The Mother / Daughter Plot.* Bloomington: Indiana UP, 1989.

_____. and Keller, Evelyn Fox. Editors. *Conflicts in Feminism.* NY: Routledge, 1990.

Hite, Molly. *The Other Side of the Story: Structures and Strategies of Contemporary Feminist Narrative.* Ithaca: Cornell UP, 1989.

Hoffman, Martin. "Sex Differences in Empathy and Related Behaviors." *Psychological Bulletin* 84 (1977): 712-22.

Holland, Norman. *The First Modern Comedies.* Bloomington: Indiana UP, 1967.

Holt, Hazel and Hilary Pym. *A Very Private Eye, An Autobiography of Barbara Pym in Diaries and Letters.* New York: Random House, 1985.

Homans, Margaret. *Bearing the Word: Language & Female Experience in 19th Century Women's Writing.* Chicago: Chicago UP, 1986.

_____. "The Woman in the Cave: Recent Feminist Fictions and the Classical Underworld." *Contemporary Literature* 29 (1988): 369-402.

_____. "'Women of Color' and Feminist Theory." *New Literary Theory* 25 (1994): 73-94.

Honeycutt, Lois. "Female Succession and the Language of Power in the Writings of Twelfth-Century Churchmen." in

Medieval Queenship. Edited by John Carmi Parson. NY: St. Martin's Press, 1993.

Hopkins, Lisa. *Women Who Would be Kings: Female Rulers of the Sixteenth Century.* NY: St. Martin's Press, 1991.

Horney, Karen. "Genesis of the Castration Complex in Women." *Feminine Psychology.* NY: Norton, 1967.

_____. *Our Inner Conflicts.* NY: Norton, 1945.

_____. "The Flight From Womanhood." *International Journal of Psycho-Analysis* 7 (1926): 324-39.

Hosmer, Robert E., Jr. Editor. *Contemporary British Women Writers: Narrative Strategies.* NY: St. Martin's Press, 1993.

Howard, Elizabeth Jane. *After Julius.* London: Penguin, 1965.

Hughes, Ted. *Crow.* NY: Harper & Row, 1971.

Humm, Maggie. *Modern Feminisms.* NY: Columbia UP, 1992.

Hutcheon, Linda. *Narcissistic Narrative: The Metafictional Paradox.* Waterloo, Ontario: Wilfred Laurier UP, 1980.

Ikonen, P. and Rechardt, E. "On the Universal Nature of Primal Scene Fantasies." *International Journal of Psycho-Analysis* 65 (1984): 63-72.

Ingram, Angela, and Patai, Daphne. *Rediscovering Forgotten Radicals: British Women Writers, 1889-1939.* Chapel Hill: North Carolina UP, 1993.

Irwin, Raymond. *The English Library.* London: Allen & Unwin, 1966.

_____. *Women in Print.* London: Allen & Unwin, 1972.

Jackson, Guida. *Women Who Ruled.* Santa Barbara: Clio Press, 1990.

Jackson, Rosemary. *Women Who Leave: Behind the Myth of Women without Their Children.* London: Pandora, 1994.

Jacobus, Mary. *Writing Women and Writing About Women.* NY: Columbia UP, 1986.

Jaffe, Daniel S. "The Masculine Envy of Woman's Procreative Function." *Journal of the American Psychoanalytic Association* 16 (1968): 521-48.

Jagger, Allison. *Feminist Politices and Human Nature.* Brighton: Harvester Press, 1983.

James, Henry. "The Art of Fiction" in *English Literary Criticism: Romantic and Victorian.* Edited by Daniel G. Hoffman and Samuel Hynes. NY: Irvington, 1979.

Jameson, Fredric. *The Political Unconscious.* Ithaca: Cornell

UP, 1981.

Jeansonne, Glen. *Women of the Far Right: The Mother's Movement and World War II*. Chicago: Chicago UP, 1996.

Jeffreys, Sheila. *The Spinster and Her Enemies, Feminism and Sexuality, 1880-1930*. London: Pandora, 1985.

_____. *AntiClimax*. NY: New York UP, 1990.

Jin, Meiling. "Feminist Publishing from This Writer's Point of View." *SpareRib* 202 (1989).

Johnson, Deborah. *Iris Murdoch*. Bloomington: Indiana UP, 1987.

Jones, Ann Rosalind. "Julia Kristeva on Femininity: The Limits of Semiotic Politics." *Feminist Review* 18 (1984).

_____. "Writing the Body: Toward an Understanding of *L'Écriture feminine*." *The New Feminist Criticism*. Edited by Elaine Showalter. NY: Pantheon, 1985.

Jones, Gwyneth. "Imagining Things Differently." *Women's Review* 3 (1986).

Jones, Libby Falk, and Webster Goodwin, Sarah. *Feminism, Utopia, and Narrative*. Knoxville: Tennessee UP, 1990.

Jones, Suzanne W. Editor. *Writing the Woman as Artist*. Philadelphia: Pennsylvania UP, 1991.

Jong, Erica. *New York Times* (23 June 1992): B-4.

Juhasz, Susanne. *Reading from the Heart: Women, Literature, and the Search for True Love*. NY: Viking, 1994.

Kahn, Coppelia. "The Hand that Rocks the Cradle: Recent Gender Theories and Their Implications." *The (M)other Tongue—Essays in Feminist Psychoanalytic Interpretation*. Edited by Shirley Nelson Garner. Ithaca: Cornell UP, 1985.

Kaminer, Wendy. *A Fearful Freedom: Women's Flight from Equality*. NY: Addison-Wesley, 1990.

Kaplan, Donald. "The Psychoanalysis of Art: Some Ends, Some Means." *Journal of the American Psychoanalytic Association* 36 (1988): 259-93.

_____. "Three Commentaries on Gender in Freud's Thought." *Fantasy, Myth, and Reality*. Edited by Harold Blum. NY: International UP, 1988.

_____. "Some Theoretical and Technical Aspects of Gender and Social Reality in Clinical Psychoanalysis." *Psychoanalytic Study of the Child* 45 (1990): 3-24.

Kaplan, E. Ann. *Women and Film: Both Sides of the Camera*. NY:

Routledge, 1983.

Kaplan, Louise. *Adolescence: A Farewell to Childhood*. NY: Simon and Schuster, 1983.

_____. *Female Perversions*. NY: Doubleday, 1991.

Kaplan, Sydney Janet. *Feminine Conciousness in the Modern British Novel*. Urbana: Illinois UP, 1975.

_____. "Passionate Portrayal of Things to Come." *20th Century Women Writers*. Edited by Thomas F. Staley. NY: Barnes & Noble, 1982.

Kappeller, Susanne. "The White Brothel: The Literary Exoneration of the Pornographic." *Feminist Review* 16 (1984): 23-42.

Katz, Jonathan Ned. *The Invention of Heterosexuality*. NY: Dutton, 1995.

Kaufman, Linda. Editor. "The Body Writing/Writing the Body." *Gender & Theory*. New York: Oxford UP, 1989.

Kavaler-Adler, Susan. *The Compulsion to Create: A Psychoanalytic Study of Women Artists*. NY: Routledge, 1993.

Keberd, Ceclan. *Men and Feminism in Modern Literature*. NY: St. Martin's Press, 1985.

Kelly, Gary. "Jane Austen's Real Business: The Novel, Literature, and Cultural Capital." *Jane Austen's Business: Her World and Her Profession*. Edited by Juliet McMaster and Bruce Stovel. NY: St. Martin's Press, 1996.

Kenyon, Olga. Editor. *Women Writers Talk*. NY: Carroll & Graf, 1990.

Kerber, Linda K. "Anger in Different Voices." *Signs* 11 (1986): 304-333.

Kersten, Katherine. "What Do Women Want? A Conservative Feminist Manifesto." *Policy Review* 56 (1991): 4-15.

Kettle, Arnold. *An Introduction to the English Novel*, Vol. 1. NY: Hutchinson House, 1951.

Killoh, Ellen Peck. "The Woman Writer and the Element of Destruction." *College English* 34 (1972).

Kirkham, Margaret. *Jane Austen: Feminism and Fiction*. Brighton: Harvester, 1982.

Kitzinger, Sheila. *Ourselves as Mothers: The Universal Experience of Motherhood*. NY: Addison-Wesley, 1994.

Koedt, Anne. "The Myth of the Vaginal Orgasm." *Radical Feminism*. NY: Times Books, 1973.

Kolodny, Annette. "A Map for Rereading; or Gender and the
        Interpretation   of   Literary   Texts."   *The   (M)other
        Tongue—Essays in Feminist Psychoanalytic Interpretation.*
        Ithaca: Cornell UP, 1985.
Koonz, Claudia. *Mothers in the Fatherland.* NY: St. Martin's
        Press, 1987.
_____. "A Response to Eve Rosenhaft." *Radical History
        Review* 43 (1989): 81-85.
Kowaleski-Wallace, Beth. "Milton's Daughters: The Education of
        Eighteenth-Century Women Writers." *Feminist Studies* 12
        (1986): 275-93.
Krentz, Jayne Ann. Editor. *Dangerous Men and Adventurous Women.*
        Philadelphia: Pennsylvania UP, 1992.
Kristeva, Julia. *The Kristeva Reader.* Edited by Toril Moi. New
        York: Columbia UP, 1986.
_____. *The Samurai.* NY: Columbia UP, 1992.
_____. *New Maladies of the Soul.* NY: Columbia UP, 1995.
_____. *Interviews.* NY: Columbia UP, 1996.
Krontris, Tina. *Oppositional Voices: Women as Writers and
        Translators of Literature in the English Renaissance.* NY:
        Routledge, 1992.
Kuhn, Annette, and Wolpe, Ann Marie. Editors. *Feminism and
        Materialism.* London: Routledge, 1978.
Kundera, Milan. *The Art of the Novel.* NY: Grove Press, 1988.
Kushen, Betty. "Virginia Woolf and 'Dr. Freud.'" *Literature and
        Psychology* 35 (1989): 37-45.
_____. *Virginina Woolf and the Nature of Communion.* West
        Orange, NJ: Raynor Press, 1983.
Labovitz, Esther Kleinbord. *The Myth of the Heroine: The Female
        Bildungsroman in the Twentieth Century.* NY: Lang, 1986.
Lacan, Jacques. *Écrits.* NY: Norton, 1977.
LaFarge, Lucy. "The Early Determinants of Penis Envy." in *Rage,
        Power, and Aggression.* Edited by R. Glick and S. Roose.
        New Haven: Yale UP, 1992.
Lane, Ann. "Charlotte Perkins Gilman: The Personal is Political."
        Feminist Theorists—Three Centuries of Key Women Thinkers.
        Edited by Dale Spencer. NY: Pantheon, 1983.
_____. *To Herland and Beyond: The Life and Work of
        Charlotte Perkins Gilman.* NY: Pantheon, 1990.

Langland, Elizabeth. "Nobody's Angels: Domestic Ideology and Middle-Class Women in the Victorian Novel." *PMLA* 107 (1992): 290-304.

Laqueur, Thomas. *Making Sex: Body and Gender from the Greeks to Freud.* Cambridge: Harvard UP, 1990.

Lauret, Maria. "Seizing Time and Making New: Feminist Criticism, Politics, and Contemporary Feminist Fiction." *Feminist Review* 31 (1989): 94-106.

Lauter, Estelle. *Women as Mythmakers, Poetry and Visual Art by Twentieth-Century Women.* Bloomington: Indiana UP, 1984.

Lawrence, D.H. *The Plumed Serpent.* NY: Knopf, 1959.

Leavis, F.R. *The Great Tradition.* New York: Doubleday, 1954.

Lehman, David. *Signs of the Times: The Destruction and the Fall of Paul de Man.* NY: Simon & Schuster, 1991.

Lessing, Doris. *The Golden Notebook.* NY: Ballantine, 1962.

Levitt, Morton. *Modernist Survivors.* Columbus: Ohio State UP, 1987.

Lewalski, Barbara Kiefer. *Writing Women in Jacobean England.* Cambridge: Harvard UP, 1993.

Lewin, Tamar. "Feminists Wonder If It Was Progress To Become 'Victims.'" *Washington Post* (10 May 1992), C-6.

Lidz, Theodore. "Male Menstruation: A Ritual Alternative to the Oedipal Transition." *International Journal of Psycho-Analysis* 58 (1977): 17-31.

Lilienfeld, Jane. "The Dangers of Theory." *The Women's Review of Books* 4 (1986): 20-21.

Lindenbaum, Shirley. "Getting the World in a Family Way." *New York Times* (29 April 1984).

Lobel, Kerry. *Naming the Violence: Speaking Out Against Lesbian Battering.* Seattle: Seal Press, 1986.

Loeffelholz, Mary. Editor. *Explaining Lives: Women and Literature, 1900-1945.* NY: Twayne, 1992.

Lovenduski, Joni and Norris, Pippa. "Why Can't a Woman Be More Like a Man?" *New Statesman* (3 April 1992): 12-3.

Lovibond, Sabina. "Feminism and Postmodernism." *New Left Review* 178 (1989): 5-28.

Lukacher, Maryline. *Maternal Fictions.* Durham: Duke UP, 1994.

Luker, Kristin. *Abortion and the Politics of Motherhood.* Berkeley: California UP, 1984.

Lydon, Mary. "The Forgetfulness of Memory: Jacques Lacan, Marguerite Duras, and the Text." *Contemporary Literature* 29 (1988): 351-368.

Lyotard, Jean-Francois. "What is Postmodernism?" *The Postmodern Condition.* Minneapolis: Minnesota UP, 1984.

_____. "Re-Writing Modernity. *SubStance* 54 (1987): 3-9.

MacAulay, Rose. *Keeping Up Appearances.* London: Collins, 1928,

Maccoby, Eleanor and Nagy, Carol. *The Psychology of Sex Differences.* Stanford: Stanford UP, 1974.

MacKinnon, Catherine. *Toward a Feminist Theory of the State.* Cambridge: Harvard UP, 1989.

Mahler, Margaret. *The Psychological Birth of the Human Infant.* New York: Basic Books, 1975.

Mahony, Patrick. "Women's Discourse and Literature: The Question of Nature and Culture." *Contemporary Psychoanalysis* 19 (1983): 444-59.

Maitland, Sara. *Daughter of Jerusalem.* London: Blond & Briggs, 1978.

_____. "A Feminist Writer's Progress," *On Gender and Writing.* Edited by Michelene Wandor. London: Pandora, 1983, 17-23.

_____. *Virgin Territory.* London: Michael Joseph, 1984.

_____. Editor. *Very Heaven--Looking Back at the Sixties.* London: Virago, 1988.

_____. *Vesta Tilley.* London: Virago, 1986.

Malcomson, Scott. "Postmod Sex: Phallogocentrism and Its Discontents." *Village Voice Literary Supplement* (8 Dec 1987): 17-21.

Mann, Jessica. *Deadlier Than the Male: An Investigation into Feminine Crime Writing.* London: David Charles, 1981.

Mansbridge, Jane J. Editor. *Beyond Self-Interest.* Chicago: Chicago UP, 1990.

Marcus, Sharon. "The Profession of the Author: Abstraction, Advertising, and *Jane Eyre.*" *PMLA* 111:2 (1995): 206-19.

Marek, Jayne E. *Women Editing Modernism.* Lexington: Kentucky Up, 1995.

Margolis, Diane Rothbard. "Considering Women's Experience: A Reformation of Power Theory." *Theory and Society* 18 (1989): 387-416.

Marks, Elaine. "Women and Literature in France." *Signs* 3 (1978): 832-42.

Marks, Sylvia Kasey. "*Clarissa* as Conduct Book." *South Atlantic Review* 51 (1986): 3-16.

Martinez, Zulma Nelly. "From a Mimetic to a Holographic Paradigm in Fiction: Toward a Definition of Feminist Writing." *Women's Studies* 14 (1988): 225-45.

Mayer, Elizabeth Lloyd. "Everybody Must Be Just Like Me: Observations on Female Castration Anxiety." *International Journal of Psycho-Analysis* 66 (1985): 331-47.

Mayor, F.M. *The Third Miss Symons*. London: Virago, 1980.

McHale, Brian. *Postmodern Fiction*. London: Methuen, 1987.

McLeod, Karen. *Henry Handel Richardson, A Critical Study*. NY: Cambridge UP, 1985.

McLeod, Sheila. *The Art of Starvation*. London: Virago, 1981.

McMaster, Juliet. Editor. *Jane Austen's Achievement*. NY: Barnes & Noble, 1976.

McMillan, Carol. *Women, Reason, and Nature*. Princeton: Princeton UP, 1983.

Mei, Huang. *Transforming the Cinderella Dream: From Frances Burney to Charlotte Brontë*. New Brunswick: Rutgers UP, 1990.

Mendell, Dale. Editor. *Early Female Development*. Cambridge: MIT Press, 1982.

Meyers, Jon K. "The Theory of Gender Identity Disorders." *Journal of the American Psychoanalytic Association*. 30 (1982): 381-418.

Miles, Rosalind. *The Female Form*. London: Routledge, 1987.

_____. *The Fiction of Sex: Themes and Functions of Sex Differences in the Modern Novel*. London: Vision Press, 1974.

Miller, Jane. Editor. *Women Writing About Men*. NY: Pantheon, 1986.

Miller, Jill. *Happy as a Dead Cat*. London: The Women's Press, 1984.

Miller, Nancy K. "Emphasis Added: Plots and Plausibilities in Women's Fiction." *PMLA* 96 (1981): 36-48.

_____. *Getting Personal*. NY: Routledge, 1991.

_____. *The Heroine's Text, Readings in the French and English Novel, 1722-1782*. NY: Columbia UP, 1980.

_____. "Men's Reading, Women's Writing: Gender and the Rise of the Novel." *Yale French Studies* 75 (1988): 40-55.

Millot, Catherine. "The Feminine Super-Ego." *m/f* (February 1988), 23-38.

Miner, Madonna M. "Introduction and Conclusion of Insatiable Appetites: Twentieth-Century American Women's Bestsellers." *Contributions in Women's Studies*, 48. Westport, CT: Greenwood Press, 1984.

Minow-Pinkney, Makiko. *Virginia Woolf and the Problem of the Subject.* New Brunswick: Rutgers UP, 1987.

Mitchell, Juliet and Rose, Jacqueline. Editors. *Jacques Lacan & the École Freudienne: Feminine Sexuality.* London: MacMillan, 1982.

_____. *Psychoanalysis and Feminism.* NY: Pantheon, 1974.

Modleski, Tania. *Feminism Without Women.* NY: Routledge, 1991.

Moggach, Deborah. *Hot Water Man.* London: Penguin, 1983.

Moi, Toril. *Sexual/Textual Politics—Feminist Literary Theory.* London: Methuen, 1985.

Montefiore, Janet. "Feminist Identity and the Poetic Tradition." *Feminist Review* 13 (1983): 69-85.

Moore, Maureen. *The Illumination of Alice Mallory.* NY: HarperCollins, 1993.

Morgan, Robin. *Sisterhood is Global.* NY: Doubleday, 1984.

Morgan, Thais E. *Men Writing the Feminine: Literature, Theory, and the Question of Genders.* Albany: NY State UP, 1994.

Mortimer, Penelope. *The Pumpkin Eater.* NY: McGraw-Hill, 1962.

Moulton, Ruth. "Early Papers on Women: Horney to Thompson." *American Journal of Psychoanalysis* 35 (1975): 207-29.

Murdoch, Iris. *A Fairly Honourable Defeat.* London: Penguin, 1970.

_____. *The Black Prince.* London: Penguin, 1973.

_____. *The Sacred and Profane Love Machine.* London: Penguin, 1974.

_____. *Henry and Cato.* London: Penguin, 1977.

_____. Interview. *Contemporary Literature* 18 (1977): 19-40.

_____. *The Sea, the Sea.* London: Penguin, 1978.

Neu, Jerome. Editor. *The Cambridge Companion to Freud.* New York: Cambridge UP, 1991.

Nochlin, Linda. "Why Have There Been No Great Women Artists?"

Art and Sexual Politics—Women's Liberation, Women Artists, and Art History. Edited by Thomas B. Hess and Elizabeth C. Baker. NY: Collier, 1971.

Norris, Christopher. "Reading as a Woman." *London Review of Books* (4 April 1985).

Nussbaum, Martha. Review of *Mercy*, by Andrea Dworkin. *Boston Review* 17 (1992): 26-7.

_____. "Feminism and Philosophy: An Exchange." *New York Review* (6 April 1995), 48-49.

Oakley, Anne. "For Women's Equality," *New Society* (23 August 1979).

_____. *Taking It Like a Woman.* NY: Random House, 1984.

_____, and Mitchell, Juliet. Editors. *What Is Feminism?* London: Basil Blackwell, 1986.

Oates, Joyce Carol. Editor. *First Person Singular, Writers on Their Craft.* Princeton: Ontario Review Press, 1983.

_____. *NY Times Book Review* (21 Nov 1976).

_____. *The Profane Art: Essays and Reviews.* NY: Dutton, 1983.

O'Brien, Edna. Interview by Philip Roth. *NY Times* (18 Nov 1984).

_____. *The Observer Review* (14 April 1985).

_____. *Writers at Work, The Paris Review Interviews*, Seventh Series. NY: Viking, 1986.

Odent, Michael. *Birth Reborn.* NY: Pantheon, 1984.

Offen, Karen. "Defining Feminism: A Comparative Historical Approach." *Signs* 14 (1988): 119-57.

Olesker, Wendy. "Female Genital Anxieties: Views from the Nursery and the Couch." Paper at the Fall (1996) Meeting of the American Psychoanalytic Association.

Olsen, Tillie. *Silences.* NY: Delacorte Press, 1965.

Ortner, Sherry. "Is Female to Male as Nature is to Culture?" *Woman, Culture, and Society.* Edited by Rosaldo and Lamphere. Stanford: Stanford UP, 1974.

Ozick, Cynthia. "Sexuality is Condition, Not Tradition." *NY Times Book Review* (6 Jan 1984).

_____. "Women and Creativity." *Woman and Sexist Society.* Edited by Vivian Gornick. NY: Basic Books, 1971.

Palmer, Paulina. *Contemporary Lesbian Writing: Dreams, Desire, Difference.* Philadelphia: Open UP, 1993.

Panken, Shirley. *Virginia Woolf and the "Lust of Creation."*
Albany: New York State UP, 1987.

Patai, Daphne. "The Struggle for Feminist Purity Threatens the
Goals of Feminism." *Chronicle of Higher Education*
(5 February 1992), B-1-2.

Pearson, Carol and Pope, Katherine. *The Female Hero in American
and British Literature.* NY: Bowker, 1981.

Peel, Ellen. "Subject, Object, and the Alteration of First- and
Third-Person Narration in Novels by Alther, Atwood, and
Drabble: Toward a Theory of Feminist Aesthetics." *Critique*
30 (1989): 107-22.

Perriam, Wendy. *After Purple.* London: Penguin, 1982.

Perry, Richard J. "Why Do Multiculturalists Ignore
Anthropologists?" *Chronicle of Higher Education* (4 March
1992), A-52.

Peterson, Carla L. *The Determined Reader: Gender and Culture in
the Novel from Napoleaon to Victoria.* New Brunswick:
Rutgers UP, 1983.

Peterson, Linda H. "Martineau's Autobiography: The Feminine
Debate Over Self-Interpretation." *Victorian Autobiography:
The Tradition of Self-Interpretation.* New Haven: Yale UP,
1986.

Phelan, Peggy. "Growing Up Absurd." *Women's Review of Books* 7
(1990): 16.

Phillips, Kathryn. "Why Can't a Man Be More Like a Woman...and
Vice Versa." *Omni* (October, 1990): 42-48, 68.

Polan, Brenda. "Myth Perfect." *The Guardian* (27 May 1987).

Pollitt, Katha. *Reasonable Creatures: Essays on Women and
Feminism.* NY: Knopf, 1994.

Pratt, Annis V. *Archetypal Patterns in Women's Fiction.*
Bloomington: Indiana UP, 1981.

_____. "The New Feminist Criticisms: Exploring the History
of New Space." *Beyond Intellectual Sexism: A New Woman,
A New Reality.* Edited by Joan L. Roberts. NY: David
McKay, 1976.

Prior, Mary. *Women in English Society, 1500-1800.* London:
Methuen, 1984.

Pykett, Lyn. *Emily Bronte.* NY: Barnes & Noble, 1989.

Pym, Barbara. *Jane and Prudence.* London: Granada, 1981.

Quinn, Susan. *A Mind of Her Own: The Life of Karen Horney.*
    NY: Summit Books, 1987.
Rabinowitz, Paula. "Maternity as History: Gender and the
    Transformantion of Genre in Meridel Le Suer's *The Girl.*"
    Contemporary Literature 29 (1988): 538-48.
Radecki, Susanna. "Agreeing to Differ." *SpareRib* 170 (1986):
    36-41.
Radway, Janice. *Reading the Romance.* Chapel Hill: North
    Carolina UP, 1984.
Redinger, Ruby. *George Eliot: The Emergent Self.* NY: Knopf,
    1975.
Restuccia, Frances. *Joyce and the Law of the Father.* New Haven:
    Yale UP, 1989.
Reynolds, Margaret. Editor. *Erotica: An Anthology of Women's
    Writing.* London: Pandora, 1990.
Rich, Adrienne. *Of Woman Born.* NY: Bantam, 1977.
_____. "When We Dead Awaken: Writing as Re-Vision." *On
    Lies, Secrets, and Silences: Selected Prose, 1966-1978.* NY:
    Norton, 1979.
Riley, Denise. *Am I That Name?: Feminism and the Category of
    "Women" in History.* Minneapolis: Minnesota UP, 1988.
Roazen, Paul. *Helene Deutsch: A Psychoanalyst's Life.* NY:
    Doubleday, 1985.
Roberts, Michele. "First Person." *Guardian* (27 May 1987), 10.
_____. *The Visitation.* London. The Women's Press. 1983.
_____. *A Piece of the Night.* London: The Women's Press,
    1978.
Robinson, Sally. "The 'Anti-Logos Weapon': Multiplicity in
    Women's Texts." *Contemporary Literature* 29 (1988): 105-124.
_____. "Misappropriations of the 'Feminine.'" *SubStance* 59
    (1989): 48-70.
_____. *Engendering the Subject.* Albany: NY State UP, 1990.
Rochefort, Christiane. "The Privilege of Consciousness." *The
    New Feminist Criticisms.* Edited by Elaine Showalter. NY:
    Pantheon, 1984.
Rogers, Katherine M. *Feminism in Eighteenth-Century England.*
    Urbana: Illinois UP, 1982.
_____. "Richardson's Empathy with Women." The *Authority
    of Experience.* Edited by Arlyn Diamond and Lee R.

Edwards. Amherst: Massachusetts UP, 1977.

Roiphe, Herman and Galenson, Eleanor. *Infantile Origins of Sexual Identity*. New York: International UP, 1981.

Roller, Judi M. *The Politics of the Feminist Novel*. Westport, CT: Greenwood Press, 1986.

Rose, Ellen Cronan. *The Novels of Margaret Drabble: Equivocal Figures*. NY: Barnes & Noble, 1980.

Rosenvelt, Deborah Silverton. "Feminism, 'Postfeminism,' and Contemporary Women's Fiction." *Tradition and the Talents of Women*. Edited by Florence Howe. Urbana: Illinois UP, 1991.

Rosinsky, Natalie M. *Feminist Futures--Contemporary Women's Speculative Fiction*. Ann Arbor: UMI Research Press, 1984.

Ross, Andrew. Editor. *Universal Abandon?* Minneapolis: Minnesota UP, 1988.

Roth, Philip. *The Breast*. NY: Holt, Rinehart, & Winston, 1972.

Roudinesco, Elisabeth. *Jacques Lacan & Co.: A History of Psychoanalysis in France*. Chicago: Chicago UP, 1990.

Rovner, Sandy. "Debunking the 'Empty Nest' Syndrome," *Washington Post* Health Section (18 December 90), 14.

_____. *NY Times Book Review* (18 Nov 1984).

Rubin, Lilian. "On Men and Friendship." *Psychoanalytic Review* 73 (1986): 165-81.

Rubin, Nancy. *The Mother Mirror*. Boston: Putnam, 1984.

Russ, Joanna. *How to Suppress Women's Writing*. Austin: Texas UP, 1983.

_____. "What Can a Heroine Do? Or Why Women Can't Write." *Images of Women in Fiction: Feminist Perspectives*. Susan Koppelman Cornillon. Editor. Bowling Green: Popular Press, 1972.

Ruthven, K.K. *Feminist Literary Studies: An Introduction*. NY: Cambridge UP, 1984.

Sanday, Peggy Reeves. *Female Power and Male Dominance, On the Origins of Sexual Equality*. NY: Cambridge UP, 1981.

Scarr, Sandra. *Mother Care / Other Care*. NY: Basic Books, 1984.

Schafer, Roy. "Problems in Freud's Psychology of Women." *Journal of the American Psychoanalytical Association* 22 (1974): 459-85.

Schenck, Celeste M. "Songs (From) the Bride: Feminism

Psychoanalysis, Genre." *Literature and Psychology* 32 (1986): 109-118.

Scheper-Hughes, Nancy. *Death Without Weeping: The Violence of Everyday Life in Brazil.* Berkeley: California UP, 1992.

Scheuermann, Mona. *Her Bread to Earn: Women, Money, and Society from Defoe to Austen.* Lexington: Kentucky UP, 1993.

Schmidt, Dorey. Editor. Margaret Drabble: Golden Realms. Edinburg, Texas: Pan American UP, 1982.

Schofield, Mary Anne. "Exploring the Woman Question: A Reading of Fielding's 'Amelia.'" *Ariel* 16 (1985): 45-57.

Schorer, Mark. "Pride Unprejudiced." *Kenyon Review* 18 (1956).

Schwenger, Peter. *Phallic Critiques—Masculinity and Twentieth-Century Literature.* London: Routledge, 1984.

Sederer, Lloyd and Seidenberg, Robert. "Heiress to an Empty Throne: Ego-Ideal Problems of Contemporary Women." *Contemporary Psychoanalysis* 12 (1976): 240-51.

Sedgewick, Eve Kosofsky. *Between Men: English Literature and Male Homosocial Desire.* NY: Columbia UP, 1985.

_____. "Jane Austen and the Masturbating Girl." *Critical Inquiry* 17 (1991): 818-37.

Sheets-Johnstone, Maxine. "An Empirical-Phenomenological Critique of the Social Construction of Infancy." *Human Studies.* 19 (1996): 1-16.

Sherfey, Mary Jane. *The Nature and Evolution of Female Sexuality.* NY: Random House, 1972.

Sherkow, Susan. "The Role of Vaginal Awareness in Female Development." Paper given at the Fall (1996) Meeting of the American Psychoanalytic Association.

Showalter, Elaine. *A Literature of Their Own.* Princeton: Princeton UP, 1977.

_____. "Towards a Feminist Aesthetics." *Women Writing and Writing About Women.* Edited by Mary Jacobus. NY: B&N Imports, 1979.

_____. Letter to *NY Times Book Review* (6 Jan 1984).

_____. "Women Who Write Are Women." *NY Times Book Review* (16 Dec 1984).

_____. *The New Feminist Criticism.* NY: Pantheon, 1985.

_____. *The Female Malady.* NY: Pantheon, 1986.

Shuttle, Penelope. *The Wise Wound.* NY: Bantam, 1990.

Singer, Peter and Wells, Deane. *Making Babies.* NY: Scribners, 1985.

Smith, Catherine. "The Invention of Sex in Myth and Literature." *The Binding of Proteus—Perspectives on Myth and Literary Process.* Edited by Marjorie McCune. Lewisburg: Bucknell UP, 1980.

Smith, Philip M. *Language, The Sexes and Society.* Oxford: Basil Blackwell, 1985.

Snitow, Ann. *Powers of Desire: The Politics of Sexuality.* NY: Monthly Review Press, 1983.

Snitow, Ann and Stansell, Christine. *Powers of Desire: The Politics of Sexuality.* NY: Monthly Review Press, 1983.

_____. Review of *Am I That Name?: Feminism and the Category of "Women" in History* by Denise Riley. *Village Voice Literary Supplement* (Jan-Feb, 1989), 36-7.

_____. "Pages from a Gender Diary." *Dissent* (Spring, 1989), 205-24.

Solomon, Jon. "The Wandering Womb of Delos." *Woman's Power, Man's Game.* Edited by Mary DeForest. Waucond, IL: Bolchazy-Carducci, 1993.

Sommers, Christina Hoff. *Who Stole Feminism?* NY: Simon & Schuster, 1994.

Soper, Kate. "Feminism, Humanism, and Postmodernism." *Radical Philosophy* 55 (Summer, 1990): 11-17.

Southam, B. C. *Critical Essays on Jane Austen.* NY: Barnes & Noble, 1968.

Spacks, Patricia Meyer. "Oscillations of Sensibility." *New Literary History* 25 (1994): 505-20.

Spark, Muriel. *Curriculum Vitae.* Boston: Houghton Mifflin, 1993.

Spelman, Elisabeth. *Inessential Woman: Problems of Exclusion in Feminist Thought.* Boston: Beacon, 1988.

Spellmeyer, Kurt. "After Theory: from Textuality to Attunement with the World." *College English.* 58:8 (1996): 893-913.

Spencer, Jane. *The Rise of the Woman Novelist: from Aphra Behn to Jane Austen.* London: Blackwell, 1986.

Spender, Dale. *Mothers of the Novel.* London: Pandora, 1986.

_____. *The Writing or the Sex.* London: Pergamon, 1989.

_____. *Living By the Pen.* NY: Teachers College Press, 1992.

Sperling, Susan. "Baboons with Briefcases: Feminism,

Functionalism, Sociobiology in the Evolution of Primate Gender." *Signs* 17 (1991): 1-27.

Springer, Marlene. *What Manner of Woman: Essays on English and American Life and Literature.* NY: New York UP, 1977.

Steinem, Gloria. "A Basic Human Right." *Ms.* (Aug, 1989), 38-42.

_____. *Revolution From Within.* Boston: Little, Brown, 1992.

Sternburg, Janet. Editor. *The Writer on Her Work.* NY: Norton, 1980.

Sternhell, Carol. "Sic Transit Gloria." *Women's Review of Books* 9 (1992): 5-6.

Stetz, Margaret Diane. "Anita Brookner: Woman Writer as Reluctant Feminist." *Writing the Woman Artist.* Edited by Suzanne W. Jones. Philadelphia: Pennsylvania UP, 1991.

_____. "Planting Corpses in Our Mother's Gardens: Feminist Criticism and WWI," *IRIS* (1985).

Stewart, Grace. *A New Mythos, The Novel of the Artist as Heroine, 1877-1977.* St. Alban's, VT: Eden Press, 1979.

Stoller, Robert. *Sex and Gender.* NY: Aronson, 1975.

_____, and Herdt, Gilbert. "The Development of Masculinity: A Cross Cultural Contribution." *Journal of the American Psychoanalytic Association* 30 (1982): 29-59.

Stone, Lawrence. *The Family, Sex, and Marriage in England 1500-1800.* NY: Harper & Row, 1980.

Straub, Kristina. *Sexual Suspects: Eighteenth-Century Players and Sexual Ideology.* Princeton: Princeton UP, 1992.

Streitfield, David. "Doris Lessing and the Madness of Our Times." *Washington Post Book World* (25 Dec 1988).

Stubbs, Patricia. *Women and Fiction, Feminism and the Novel, 1880-1920.* Brighton: Harvester, 1979.

Sulloway, Allison G. *Jane Austen and the Province of Womanhood.* Philadelphia: Pennsylvania UP, 1989.

Sutherland, John. *Mrs. Humphry Ward.* New York: Oxford UP, 1990.

_____. *Victorian Fiction: Writers, Publishers, Readers.* NY: St. Martin's Press, 1995.

Symons, Donald. *The Evolution of Human Sexuality.* New York: Oxford UP, 1979.

_____, and Ellis, Bruce. "Sex Differences in Sexual Fantasy: An Evolutionary Psychological Approach." *Journal of Sex*

Research 27 (1990): 527-55.

Tannen, Deborah. *You Just Don't Understand.* NY: Morrow, 1990.

Tatum, James. *The Search for the Ancient Novel.* Baltimore: Johns Hopkins UP, 1994.

Tavris, Carol. *The Mismeasure of Woman.* NY: Simon & Schuster, 1992.

Taylor, Ina. *A Woman of Contradictions: The Life of George Eliot.* NY: Morrow, 1990.

Taylor, Irene and Luria, Gina. "Gender and Genre: Women in British Romantic Literature." *What Manner of Woman: Essays on English and American Life and Literature.* Marlene Springer. Editor. NY: New York UP, 1977.

Templeton, Alice. "*Miss Julie* as a 'Naturalistic Tragedy.'" *Theatre Journal* 42 (1990): 468-80.

Tennant, Emma. See Kenyon, Olga. *Women Writers Talk.*

Thomson, Patricia. *The Victorian Heroine: A Changing Ideal, 1837-73.* London: Oxford UP, 1956.

Thurer, Shari L. *The Myths of Motherhood: How Culture Reinvents the Good Mother.* Boston: Houghton Mifflin, 1994.

Thurman, Judith. *Isak Dinesen: The Life of a Story Teller.* NY: St. Martin's Press, 1988.

Thurston, Carol. *The Romance Revolution.* Urbana: Illinois UP, 1987.

Todd, Janet. Editor. *A Dictionary of British and American Women Writers, 1660-1800.* Totowa, NJ: Rowman & Allanheld, 1985.

_____. *The Sign of Angellica: Women, Writing, and Fiction, 1660-1800.* NY: Columbia UP, 1990.

_____. *British Women Authors: A Critical Reference Guide.* NY: Continuum, 1989.

Tong, Rosemary. *Feminist Thought.* Boulder: Westview, 1989.

Trebilcot, Joyce. Editor. *Mothering: Essays in Feminist Thought.* Toronto: Rowman & Allanheld, 1984.

Tuchman, Gayle, and Fortin, Nina E. *Edging Women Out: Victorian Novelists: Victorian Novelists, Publishers, and Social Change.* New Haven: Yale UP, 1989.

Turkle, Sherry. "Dynasty." *London Review of Books* (12 June 1990). 22

_____. *Psychoanalytic Politics.* NY: Guilford, 1992.

Turner, Cheryl. *The Growth of Published and Professional Fiction*

Written by Women Before Jane Austen. Ph.D. dissertation,
   University of Nottingham, 1985.
Tyrrell, William Blake. *Amazons, A Study in Athenian Mythmaking.*
   Baltimore: Johns Hopkins UP, 1984.
Tyson, Phyllis and Robert. *Psychoanalytic Theories of Development.*
   New Haven: Yale UP, 1990.
Uglow, Jennifer. "'George Eliot' and the Woman Question in the
   1850s." *George Eliot.* London: Virago, 1987.
Vagas, Melinda. Letter. *Women's Review of Books* 7 (February
   1990):5: 5-6.
Veeder, William. "Fictions of Feminine Voice: Antiphony and
   Silence in Hardy's T*ess of the D'Urbervilles.*" *The Sense of
   Sex: Feminist Perspectives on Hardy.* Margaret R. Higonnet.
   Editor. Urbana: Illinois UP, 1993.
Walbank, F. Alan. *Queens of the Circulating Library.* London:
   Evans Brothers, 1950.
Wandor, Michelene. *Gardens of Eden--Poems for Eve & Lilith.*
   London: Journeyman, 1984.
_____. Editor. *On Gender and Writing.* London: Pandora, 1983.
_____. "The Real Jane." *Spectator* (19 January 1985).
Ware, Vron. *Beyond the Pale: White Women, Racism and History.*
   London: Verso, 1992.
Waugh, Patricia. *Feminine Fictions: Revisiting the Postmodern.*
   NY: Routledge, 1989.
_____. *Practicing Postmodernism / Reading Modernism.* NY:
   Hodder & Stoughton, 1992.
Weisser, Susan Ostrove and Fleischner, Jennifer. Editors. *Feminist
   Nightmares: Women at Odds.* NY: New York UP, 1994.
Weldon, Fay. *Letters to Alice.* NY: Penguin, 1984.
_____. *Praxis.* NY: Summit Books, 1978.
_____. *Puffball.* NY: summit, 1980.
Wharton, Edith. *Summer.* NY: Berkley, 1981.
Willett, Cynthia. *Maternal Ethics and Other Slave Moralities.* NY:
   Routledge, 1995.
Williams, Marjorie. "Fay Weldon, Fancifully." *Washington Post*
   (24 April 1988).
Wilson, A.N. *Scandal.* London: Hamish Hamilton, 1983.
Wilson, Elizabeth. *Only Halfway to Paradise, Women in Postwar
   Britain, 1945-1968.* London: Tavistock, 1980.

Winnicott, D. W. *Collected Papers*. London: Tavistock, 1958.

Winterson, Jeanette. *Oranges Are not the Only Fruit*. NY: Atlantic Monthly Press, 1985.

_____. *Sexing the Cherry*. London: Vintage, 1990.

Wolfe, Naomi. *The Beauty Myth*. NY: Morrow, 1991.

Woodress, James. *Willa Cather: A Literary Life*. Lincoln: Nebraska UP, 1987.

Woolf, Peter. "'Malformed Treatise' and Prizewinner: Iris Murdoch's *The Black Prince*." *Studies in the Literary Imagination* 11 (1978): 97-114.

Woolf, Virginia. *Moments of Being*. Sussex: The UP, 1976.

_____. *Orlando, A Biography*. NY: Harcourt, 1928.

_____. *A Room of One's Own*. NY: Harcourt, 1929.

Yeager, Patricia. "Violence in the Sitting Room: *Wuthering Heights* and the Woman's Novel." *Genre* 21 (1988): 203-229.

Yorburg, Betty. "Psychoanalysis and Women's Liberation." *Psychoanalytic Review* 61 (1974): 71-7.

Young, Cathy. "Women in the Nineties." *Washington Post* (20 May 1990).

_____. "Women, Sex, and Rape." *Washington Post* (31 May 1992).

_____. "Female Trouble." *Washington Post* (4 Oct 1992).

Young-Bruehl, Elizabeth. *Anna Freud: A Biography*. NY: Simon & Schuster, 1988.

Young, Iris Marion. "Is Male Gender Identity the Cause of Male Domination?" *Mothering: Essays in Feminist Theory*. Totowa, NJ: Rowman & Allanheld, 1983.

Author's Name and Subject Index

WOMEN'S STUDIES